Could it be Forever?

David CASSIDY

Could it be Forever?

My Story

headline

First published in 2007 by
HEADLINE PUBLISHING GROUP

2

Cataloguing in Publication Data is available from the British Library

Hardback ISBN 978 0 7553 1579 6
Trade paperback ISBN 978 0 7553 1675 5

Typeset in Goudy Old Style by Palimpsest Book Production Limited,
Grangemouth, Stirlingshire

Printed and bound in Great Britain by
Mackays of Chatham plc, Chatham, Kent

HEADLINE PUBLISHING GROUP
A division of Hachette Livre UK Ltd
338 Euston Road
London NW1 3BH

www.headline.co.uk
www.hodderheadline.com

Contents

Acknowledgements

As human beings, what have we got other than the relationships that we make in our lives? As you're lying on your deathbed, do you think, *God, I wish I had spent more time at the office?* I think not. You thank God you were able to stop, look into somebody's eyes and say, 'You know what? I love you. Thank you. You mean something to me. Thank you for what you've given me. Thank you for allowing me to be a part of your life. Thank you for being a part of mine. Thank you for every breath that I've been able to take. Thank you for all of the support and the love that you've given me. Thank you for making a difference in my life.'

This book could not have been written without the help and support of so many people who have touched my life along the way. My friends, colleagues and, most of all, my closest family:

I wish to thank you *all* from the bottom of my heart. And, alas, special thanks to Jo-Ann, who has toiled through the long nights.

Happy trails,
David,
2007

Introduction

Henry Diltz (photographer): David is a really interesting guy. He is witty. And he's intelligent. He's an Aries, which is kind of a go-for-it sign. One time David told me, 'You know what it's like to be an Aries?' He said, 'It's like, if there's a brick wall in front of me, I put my head down and just go for it.' I mean, just full speed ahead, and that's the way he is on stage and that's the way he is in his life.

I will now attempt, at the tender age of 56, to give you the unadulterated truth about my life and experiences. Although, as a celebrity, I'm certainly not curing cancer or doing anything else earth shattering, hopefully there is something of significance to be learned, insofar as the human experience is concerned. What is unique about my own experience is that the fame happened to me at a truly remarkable time on this planet, a time that we'll never see again. A time of innocence, of lost innocence, of helter skelter, of purple Osley, of Nixon, of Hendrix, of the Beatles, and, yes, of *The Partridge Family*. A time of madness and psychedelia, of euphoria, and the silent moral majority. A time of indulgence and of over-indulgence.

As children of the 60s, we went into the 70s with insatiable appetites for change. We were witnesses to social revolution as we boogied ourselves through that decade with reckless, careless abandon. ''Cause that's the way, uh-huh, uh-huh, we liked it.' Actually, we *loved* it.

And now, with that time long behind us, I have written this from a new perspective, as I am no longer the same person. My life has gone through a tremendous metamorphosis. No apologies; no, 'Sorry folks, I did it, but I really didn't mean it.' With all this in mind, you're probably now thinking, *Oh, it's a Hollywood kiss-and-tell book!* Rather, this is my way of setting the record straight, of providing a measuring stick of true growth to pass along to my children. I am still amazed by it, awed by it, and often proud of it. I have been questioned endlessly for over thirty years about my life and career. However, I simply wish to live in the now. Fortunately for me, I have a great now. Now is where my happiness lives. But, man, did it take me a long time to get over that hump.

When people say to me, 'Don't you get sick of being asked the same questions over and over again about what happened when you were on *The Partridge Family*, and what it was like to be a teen idol?' I've tried answering them this way. It would be like every person who met you, who was introduced to you, only ever asking you about the great touchdown you made in the closing seconds of that one college game on a Saturday in October half your life ago. Of course it was great, of course you'll never forget it, of course at that moment it seemed like the world was focused on you and you alone. It was your moment. But for you, it's over. You aren't in college any more.

And as much as they'd like to see you in the cleats, pads and helmet again, it's just not gonna happen.

In addition to revealing my innermost thoughts and life experiences, I have found photographs never before seen by anyone outside my family and friends – until now. I spent many hours going through boxes of memories and searching through tens of thousands of shots from my friend Henry Diltz's photo collection, taken over the years when he was my official photographer and travelled the world with me. Some of the photos were sent in by fans; I had never seen them before! I hope you enjoy them as much as I do.

There has been catharsis in the process of writing this book and, yes, even nostalgia, too – sometimes pleasant, sometimes very difficult. What you need to know is that I really do love you all for being there with me then, and for still being here with me now.

1 The Early Years

You want to know my most vivid childhood memory?

It's early 1956. I'm five, nearly six, and I'm playing with a couple of my friends out in the street in front of our house at 23 Elm Street in West Orange, New Jersey. They begin to taunt me with that casual cruelty kids can have.

'Hey, Wartie, your parents are divorced.'

They called me Wartie because my grandfather's last name was Ward. And at this time in my life, my mom and I lived with my grandparents, in the same house they had lived in since 1918. We moved back there so she could work on the road, performing her nightclub act with the Blockburn Twins. She did national theatre tours and things, and would be gone for weeks and months at a time.

'No, they aren't,' I respond, unnerved.

I have never heard the word 'divorce' before, but somehow I know what it means.

'Maybe in a play they are, but not in real life.'

My parents, Jack Cassidy and Evelyn Ward, were actors – not very successful ones, but they'd appeared in plays and musicals, sometimes together, mostly apart.

'They're divorced,' one of my friends assures me, like it's a well-known fact. But nobody I know has parents who are divorced. That just doesn't exist in my world. I suddenly feel very uneasy. I think that was the first time I can remember feeling naked. I ran into the house for assurance.

Even though I'm sure my mom will say, 'Don't be silly,' I ask her hesitantly if she and my dad are divorced. She takes a long breath and says, 'Why don't you ask your father that? You're going to see him next weekend.' That was enough for me to feel whole again, at least until I saw my dad.

I don't see a lot of my father lately. He's usually on the road, doing plays, as my mother often explains to me. The plays keep him very busy – so busy, in fact, that even when he promises he's going to come visit me, he isn't always able to keep his promise. I'm used to that. After all, this is Jack Cassidy we're talking about, folks.

Our neighbourhood is purely middle class, very white Anglo-Saxon Protestant. Very church oriented. Elm Street is made up of unpretentious, closely spaced, single-family homes, with clothes lines in clear view. There are people across the street from us who keep chickens in their backyard. The 'rag man' comes down the street collecting people's old rags and bottles. My friends' parents are carpenters, plumbers, policemen. I'm the youngest kid on the block and the only one who has begun school at Eagle Rock Elementary School. This is the local public school located about four hundred yards from the Indian reservation near where I grew up. My friends have all been going to Our Lady of Lourdes, the Catholic elementary school across the street. It's a small, solid kind of place.

My mom never worried about me walking to Eagle Rock

or running off to play at Eagle Rock Reservation. As I think back on those years now, it's almost as if that was another person's life. For Hollywood . . . gasp . . . distorted who I really am.

I didn't hate West Orange, because my mother's family was there. My grandfather was really fantastic. He was more of a father to me than my own dad. Born in 1889, he worked in public service all his adult life, reading meters. My grandmother, Ethel, was like a second mother to me. She and my aunt Marion, along with some other relatives, had factory jobs. My grandmother never missed a Sunday at Holy Trinity Church, which she and her sisters had been attending for decades. My grandmother was the head of the senior choir. They had me singing in the choir as soon as I was old enough.

I'd watch the Yankees with my grandfather. He took me to Yankee Stadium for the first time when I was seven. He didn't drive, so we had to take a bus and a train. And he was getting on in years. It was one of the biggest thrills of my life. I saw all the greats – Mickey Mantle, Yogi Berra, Bobby Richardson, Gil McDougald. He took me one more time, in 1960, when we saw Roger Maris. I'm still a sports enthusiast, particularly baseball, and have a good collection of 1961 Yankees memorabilia.

I remember waiting for my father to visit the weekend that I was to ask him the important question. He drove up to the house in grand style in a shiny new Cadillac. So Jack. Even when he didn't have much money, he always looked the part. My mother used to say, 'If he had fifty dollars, he'd spend forty on a suit for himself and leave ten for us to live on.'

When he arrived, I remember him bundling me into a bulky overcoat – it was winter – and saying exuberantly, with a wave of his hand, 'We're going to New York!' He could make it sound as if he had just invented New York and was about to make a present of it to you. He had so much charm you couldn't help but love him.

Before I started school, I'd spend almost every day in Manhattan with him and my mom and we would go to all the matinees. The first time I went to New York City was when my father was starring in the Broadway show *Wish You Were Here*. I was only three and a half, yet I remember him in the back seat of a taxi saying, 'You have to be quiet during the show.' But when I saw my dad come out on to the stage I got excited and shouted, 'That's my daddy!'

I can remember his presence so vividly. I knew when I saw him standing on the stage, with his arms spread out, singing, and everybody clapping for him, that I wanted to be a performer, just like him. And as I grew older, maybe a part of me even believed that if I became a performer like he was, it would bring us the closeness we never had.

My first impressions of show business are wonderful and inextricably linked in my memory with him – bright and gay and buoyant. My primary childhood memories of West Orange – coloured by my dad's absence so much of the time – are that it was grey and drab. Even when I was as young as six, I secretly felt that I belonged much more in the bright-lights world of my father in New York than in West Orange. My mother felt that way, too. That's why she left home as soon as she could and headed for Broadway.

We lived less than 20 miles from New York City. On this particular trip, as my dad and I drove there on Route 3, passing the marshlands of Secaucus, New Jersey, I finally asked him the big question.

'Are you and Mom divorced?'

I knew he would say 'No' and then everything would be exactly the way it was before my friends had started taunting me. But, instead, he paused, drew his breath, and said, 'Yes.'

Whatever problems I have today with trusting people, whatever problems I have with dealing with rejection, with loss – and I'm hypersensitive about abandonment, about needing people around me to be consistent and loving – have their origins in that moment.

When I heard him say that, and learned that they had been divorced for over two years, I could hardly keep myself together. It felt like every part of my body came unglued at once and I began to shake and convulse out of pain, fear and rejection.

I was stunned that he had decided to leave me and my mother – and hadn't even bothered telling me. And with that first lie comes the first time you know that you can't trust people. When I found out that I'd been deceived by my own parents, I was so devastated that I've never completely recovered.

It couldn't have taken much time to drive the rest of the way into Manhattan, but in my memory it took hours. Dad said he would still come and see me. But throughout my growing-up years, he never did come around very much. I felt shunned, like I'd done something wrong. I was a very sensitive kid.

I've largely gotten over the pain of it. But I recognise that it still lives inside me. It's just like when you cut yourself. At first it's really sore. Eventually it heals over, but you're left with a scar. Now, years and years and years later, the scar is still there, but after 15 years (on and off) in psychoanalysis – three and a half of them intensely, three times a week – trying to heal myself, to rid myself of some of the darkness and heartache I've felt through the years as a result of my father's selfishness, the pain has subsided. I now understand that those years in therapy weren't about me being a miserable sod. I really had an interest in being a detective and discovering who I was and why, and finding out what makes me tick.

I'm basically a very positive person, and want to believe people are of good intent. But trusting love has always been a difficult thing for me. This is true of almost anyone who has come from a broken home and has not had much contact with a parent who left. There's a certain naïvety in unconditional trust because, for the most part, as we all learn, people disappoint you. To paraphrase Carole King, you can expect to have pieces of your heart torn out along the way, and people *will* desert you.

When I became famous, I never had a doubt about whether people liked me for me. There is a certain amount of intuitiveness that I've always had about whether people are good or bad. Most of the time, I have surrounded myself with people who know me and were friends of mine before I was successful. People used to say, 'Boy, you can't tell who your friends are.' I said, 'Oh, yeah, I can.' Consequently, those closest to me now are my brothers, my wife, my son, and a few close friends.

My father got married again in August 1956 to actress Shirley Jones, whose career was going much better than his. She had starring roles in the film versions of *Oklahoma!* (1955) and *Carousel* (1956). She and my father had met in a stage production of *Oklahoma!* They made their home in New York until 1957 then moved to California, which meant I saw even less of my dad. There he began getting some guest shots on television.

My dad and Shirley lived quite comfortably. They were even considered rich, thanks largely to Shirley's earnings. She went on to appear in movies like *April Love* (1957), *Never Steal Anything Small* (1959), *Elmer Gantry* (1960), for which she won an Academy Award for Best Supporting Actress, *Two Rode Together* (1961) and *The Music Man* (1962). After she won the Oscar, they moved into a 40-room mansion on five acres in Bel Air that had belonged to Merle Oberon that must be worth

$20 million today. I remember visiting my father once in the early 60s and counting the shoes in his closet. He had 104 pairs! Even at the peak of my success, I don't think I ever had more than five pairs. I'm happy with two. But he was so self-indulgent. A self-absorbed man, I came to understand as I got older, who expected everyone in his life – his children, his wife, the people he worked with – to deal with him on his terms. His reality. The world according to Jack.

Although my childhood was marred by my sense of abandonment, I was inspired by my father's phenomenal sense of the theatrical. He was the epitome of grandeur and had a certain charisma and a genuine connection with all people – he treated every human being on the face of the earth the same way, no matter how high or low they were on the social or financial scale. I guess this was because he needed everyone to love him. He didn't ever discriminate. Treating everyone equally, and truly feeling no prejudice against anyone is all I knew from my upbringing.

His grandiose persona as a human being had an enormous influence on me and my brothers. We each inherited a lot from him. Shirley has said I'm like him in so many ways – I walk like him, I talk like him, I move like him, my gestures are like his. My mother had also told me that a lot. He taught me the work ethic I live by, in addition to the responsibilities of being a good role model, knowing how to deal with people, how to connect with them. He had all those qualities. I always had ambition, but he raised the bar for achievement.

My mother, Evelyn, was born in 1923 in West Orange, New Jersey. Prior to her birth, her mother and father, Ethel and Fred Ward, had five other children die as infants. When my mother was ten she got very, very ill with strep throat. They thought they were going to lose her but her life was saved by penicillin, which had just come on the market. As a result, my mother was pampered, babied, protected, doted on; she became their life. She was treated like a little princess, which is a dangerous thing for a child. When the real world smacks you in the face, it's a very difficult pill to swallow. My mother has suffered the pains of accepting her beauty, accepting her talent, but not accepting her lack of real success. She did accomplish quite a bit as an actress and a singer–dancer in the theatre but, much like my father, her frustration was that she was never a movie star.

My mother was a genuine innocent. She believed in right and wrong and in doing good. She had to accept her parents' very staunch religious beliefs and was a black sheep in that environment because she went to New York and became a showgirl and worked at the Roxy as a Roxy-ette (she was too small to be a Rockette at Radio City Music Hall). But she was magnificently beautiful, sang wonderfully and danced very well. She aspired to be a Broadway musical comedy star, much like Ethel Merman, Gwen Verdon and Mary Martin, only more beautiful.

My mother was always aware that I was different from most of the other kids we knew. She also knew that my father was different. And that she was different. After all, it was a small town and people looked at show-business people as being a separate breed.

My father, unfortunately, was not kind to her and was not willing to support us financially after the divorce. My mother had to take him to court a couple of times because he refused to pay child support, claiming he couldn't afford it, even though when he and my mom were first married, he had thought nothing of sponging off my mom's parents, living with them rent-free. He had washed his hands of us emotionally as well as financially. My mother loved me and cared for me as much as she was capable of, bearing in mind that she, too, was extraordinarily narcissistic. She wanted me to have a relationship with my father but was stunned and hurt by his leaving her.

My father was raised in Jamaica, Queens. As a child, he was an Irish tenor and performed all over Queens with the church. Later on, he was hugely influenced by the movies of the early 30s. When he saw John Barrymore, he realised that's who he wanted to be. Barrymore was the prototype of the Jack Cassidy we all knew. My dad wanted to get out of a very tough environment. He used to tell me that he had to either give the local kids a dime so they wouldn't beat him up when he went to school or he had to fight them.

He came from working-class Irish Catholic stock. According to family lore, his mother, Lotte, was a really hard nut. Everyone said she had ice water running through her veins. She bore my father exceptionally late in life, in 1928, when she was 48. She was unhappy to have this unwanted change-of-life child; she seemed embarrassed by him, as if she believed a woman her age shouldn't be having sex any more, much less children. And she rejected him, handing him over to a woman a few houses away, who nursed him and looked after him. He once told me he couldn't remember his mother ever kissing him.

My father, I'm sure, was damaged goods from the moment his mother rejected him. The various psychological problems he had, including that insatiable need of his for attention, no doubt had their origins right there. As did the fully fledged mental illness he would develop later in life.

His father, Willie Cassidy, a railroad engineer, was by all accounts a wonderful man. When I was a lad of about eight or nine, he always made me laugh. A big drinker, but lovable. He had a remarkable sense of humour. And he was a notorious rogue. He was quite the womaniser, according to my aunt Gertrude, my dad's sister. She claimed that he had a woman at every stop. Eventually, I began to hear talk from various people that my own father also did his share of philandering. Nothing people told me about my father has ever really surprised me. He was a larger-than-life kind of guy.

He invented himself early on, that dashing, debonair, devil-may-care guy, but the transformation wasn't complete until he appeared in the starring role as the womaniser, Kodaly, in the Broadway show *She Loves Me* in 1963. He took on that persona in real life, but there was a significant part of him that was still the blue-collar working guy. He could sit in bars and entertain the boys for hours, and yet he could dine with kings and queens. You never knew who you were going to get with my dad.

Patrick Cassidy: I think David has the ups and downs my father had. My father's highs were incredibly high and his lows were unbelievable. My father was diagnosed a manic-depressive. He was a complete puzzle of narcissism and I think David suffers from that too. I think we all suffer from it. My father's narcissism was so huge that you couldn't help but get wrapped up in it and have it affect your life. I think David is constantly battling with that.

My father was tormented his whole life by not being recognised as a genius, except by the people who really knew him and worked with him. He was driven to be famous because of his work, not simply for fame's sake like so many people today. What's so fascinating about the culture we live in now is that it's celebrity-obsessed, fame-obsessed. It's no longer about what you do to become successful. The craft mattered enormously to my father and he passed that along to me and all of my brothers.

My father was eventually revered as one of the finest American theatrical actors. But he wanted to be a movie star and he never accomplished that. He wanted to be a leading man. He wanted to be Barrymore. Ironically, he got to play Barrymore, in *W. C.*

Fields and Me, during the last two years of his life, when he was very, very unstable. He was taking pills to keep him up and then sleeping pills to come down – with alcohol added to the mix. He was diagnosed later on in his life as bipolar (manic-depressive), and he would often go into a deep depression. If he had lived 20 years longer, there would have been medication for him. He was magnificently gifted and kind and good and wicked and cruel – all this in one human being.

Yet, for all his flaws, I worshipped him. He could be an incredibly affectionate man. Being around him was an intense experience – in both the good times and the bad. As a child, I always wanted to be like him.

A lot of people I've met over the years assume that Shirley Jones and Jack Cassidy raised me. This is far from the truth. When Shirley and I appeared in *The Partridge Family*, the network got a lot of publicity mileage out of the fact that Shirley played my mother on the show and is my stepmother in real life. Even today, I'll meet fans who assume I had this fabulous showbiz upbringing, raised by movie stars Shirley Jones and Jack Cassidy. They don't picture me back in West Orange.

I was sort of scrawny and looked young for my age. I played in Little League and all that stuff but I had severe eye problems as a kid. I had to wear corrective lenses for a while due to a wandering eye caused by two deformed eye muscles and I was also extremely far-sighted. I used to go twice a week after school with my mom or my grandmother on the bus down to South Orange to the eye doctor. They would do different treatments and exercises with me to try to strengthen my eye. Kids would laugh at me and call me cross-eyed. Eventually, when I was eleven, I had an operation to fix the problem. But until then, the older kids were very physically abusive to me.

I also had a certain learning disability that was never

diagnosed when I was younger, which is why I was unable to do well in school academically. If I was interested in a subject, I excelled in it, otherwise I couldn't concentrate at all. As a teenager, I found myself lost. I had to fit in to the public-school system and I couldn't do it. School wasn't made for people like me, who already knew what they wanted to do when they grew up.

I never developed great reading skills. I wasn't a good student. I clowned around a lot in school. I found ways to make myself the centre of attention. By being a screw-up. I always felt somehow 'different' from my classmates. It wasn't just because I was the only kid in school whose parents were in show business (although that was weird enough to my friends), or the only kid I knew whose parents were divorced (which carried a stigma in the 50s). I had two very, very different parents from anyone else. My parents were 'artists' and my father was half crazy. I never felt like I fitted in. And I knew I was different not because of the clothes I wore or my haircut, but because I thought differently.

Shirley Jones: David had a lot of difficulty as a child. He was a very sensitive little boy. He was not very open to me because he felt I'd really taken his father away. So my meetings with him were a week or two in the summer and maybe a few days over the Christmas holidays when he would come and stay with us. He was always very polite, very sweet – almost to a fault – because he was trying to be on his best behaviour. His father was a big disciplinarian. Jack was really from the old school of spare the rod and spoil the child.

I think when my father periodically decided to play disciplinarian in my life, he was trying to make up for the fact that he was so rarely in my life at all. He was guilt-ridden his entire life because of his behaviour, his lifestyle, his treatment of his children, his treatment of his wives and the distance he put between himself and his brother and sister. Despite being brought up Catholic, he was not a guy who could go to church; he wouldn't go to confession.

I remember he came and visited me when I was about seven or eight and he brought me a black-and-white television set. For a kid to have his own television set when he was eight years old was so unusual. Not every home had a television at all, and I had my own 18-inch TV. It looked like a rocket ship; it was really cool. I watched a lot of sports, and in the afternoons and in the evenings I'd watch the popular TV shows *The Three Stooges*, *The Lone Ranger*, *Mighty Mouse* and *Sky King*.

I started visiting my dad in California when I was nine. I'd spend a week or two with him during my Christmas vacation. Christmas was always a big deal to my dad. He loved it. I guess it was the happiest time in his childhood. He dressed a tree, there was always music playing and he loved to buy gifts. This was his way of compensating for not being there the rest of the year. Generally, Christmas was one of the saddest times in my childhood because, from the time my parents split up until I started seeing my dad in California, both my mother and father were gone. My father was rarely around for the holidays.

What other early memories of my father do I have? Well, I remember him taking me to a restaurant and downing 17 Scotch and sodas. He seemed to handle it back in those days; he just seemed to be in very good cheer. His mood would become even more expansive. I felt good being around him at those times. As I got older though, I realised he was an alcoholic (even if he never acknowledged it), as was one of his brothers, as was their father, William Cassidy.

My father wasn't the type to say, 'I'm proud of you,' or to give me much confidence. He wasn't good with stuff like that.

But I really adored him. So, I might add, did my younger brothers, Shaun, Patrick and Ryan – the three sons he had by Shirley – although we all suffered the consequences of his habitually putting his own desires first. Even though my dad's marriage to Shirley Jones eventually ended in divorce in 1975, I don't think Shirley ever really got over him any more than my mother did. Or my brothers. Or me.

The reason I now spend time every day with my own son is that I was cheated out of that time with my father. Everything he did with me, I now do the opposite with Beau. I couldn't live with myself any other way.

2 My Dads

In 1961, four years after my father moved out to California, my mom and I followed. I was 11. I'd spent summers and Christmases with my dad since 1958, so California wasn't really new to me. I loved the idea of living there.

My mom did it partly because she figured it would be good for her acting career. She had had some success in New York – the high point was when she succeeded Gwen Verdon in George Abbott's production of *New Girl in Town* on Broadway – and it was reasonable for her to want to try Hollywood. That's where the money was. The big show.

But, mostly, she moved for my sake. She knew I needed more contact with my father. My grandfather, for all his virtues, couldn't really take the place of my dad. I was growing up wild and undisciplined. My mom was great, but she was a lax disciplinarian. If she was tied up with a play in New York or on tour, she couldn't always be there for me. I was getting into a fair amount of mischief. A psychologist might say I was 'acting out' my anger at my dad. My mom was worried I might be on the road to becoming a juvenile delinquent.

We moved to a little street called Crestview Court in West Los Angeles, right off Beverly Glen. It was a small Spanish-style house – maybe 1,200 square feet. I began fifth grade at Fairburn, near where we lived. My mom was getting some acting jobs – in plays and occasionally TV shows like *Ben Casey* or *Dr Kildare* – to pay the rent. Barely. Then, in 1962, she married director Elliot Silverstein. She'd been seeing him for about five years in New York. He was then working primarily in television, on such classic 60s television shows as *Playhouse 90*, *Omnibus* and *Naked City*. He would later make his mark directing such feature films as *Cat Ballou* (1965), *The Happening* (1967) and *A Man Called Horse* (1970). My mom pretty much gave up her acting career after she married him, and tried to spend more time being my mother and his wife. Her life became invested first in Elliot's career, and then in mine.

The first couple of years, Elliot tried very hard to fill the void my dad had left. I know it can't have been easy for him. Elliot graduated from Yale as a theatre major. He was an intellectual and an artist with the highest integrity. He was incredibly good to me. He challenged me intellectually. He challenged me morally. When he began to date my mother, my initial reaction as a young boy was that he was going to take my mother away. As I got to know him, I began to feel really comfortable with him. I found him to be a good role model and a true parent, a loving, caring, giving disciplinarian.

Elliot Silverstein: David was a normal, generally very good, kid who occasionally got into a little bit of trouble. He was a very curious kid. I remember that there was a hose coiled up on the lawn and David turned on the water and the hose whipped around. He wanted to know why it did that. We sat on the lawn and I explained to him about Newton's law. Newton's law is every action has an equal and opposite reaction and that applies not only to physical things but also to social behaviour. I was very surprised at the way he listened. He listened very hard to things like that. He was really absorbing it.

I remember one night in our house in West Hollywood and David was sitting on a sofa and was being very quiet. I was sitting in another chair reading something. He said, 'El?' I said, 'Yeah?' And he said, 'Who am I?' And I said, 'What do you mean, David?' He said, 'Am I David Cassidy or am I David Silverstein?' So I said, 'Of course, you're David Cassidy and you always will be David Cassidy.' He let out a sigh of relief. He was relieved that he knew who he was.

The biggest problem David had back then was the same kind of problem any kid has, staying in school and not playing hooky. I remember one time I got a call saying he hadn't shown up for school. I confronted him and it turned out that he'd played hooky. He denied it at first. I gave him a lesson and said, 'You're grounded for a month, but not because you played hooky. It's because you lied about it.' I think that stuck with him for a long time. That was one of the more important moments in his moral maturity.

There was a conflicted relationship between David and his father. I remember one time in particular, early in my marriage, when David, his mother and I were planning a little trip. His father called and wanted David to be with him that weekend. I told him that we'd already made plans. Jack got very emotional and didn't care about that. He made some threats that he was gonna come over and take possession of his son. When he arrived, I told Evelyn and David to get in the back room. When I opened the door, Jack was standing there screaming, 'I want my son!' I told him we had plans but he could see David any other time he and David wanted to be together. There was no restriction on that. Jack was very upset by that. That was the kind of terrible situation that this poor kid had to deal with. His mother told me that when Jack used to wrestle with David he'd never let David win. He was very competitive with David. So I tried hard when we were together to let David win at least part of the time.

I'd just finished a television show with Sal Mineo and he took a liking to my wife and me and to David. David set up the drums that Sal gave him in his room and that began a nightmare. David couldn't stop playing those drums. I couldn't work, I couldn't do anything. Finally I had to arrange with his mother that David could play his drums only at a certain time of day. Then he formed his own garage band. Playing drums and being in that garage band were the first signs of his interest in music. Of course, his mother had great musical talent and his father was a prominent actor and singer, so David had all the right genes and his talent was beginning to flower.

When his mother and I got divorced, David was kind of caught between us. He did the right thing and sided with his mother and I lost contact with him for a while.

I was moving from one location to another and had found some eight millimetre home movies from the time before I married his mother. There was some footage of him when I let him get behind the wheel of the car we had and back it up five feet. I wanted to instil a sense of power in him. I think he felt powerless from his relationship with his father. I also had a boat and put him in charge of the helm and let him steer. When I found all these movies, I didn't know where he was. I called everyone and finally found [his] manager and she passed on my phone message. He called me a few weeks later and I gave him copies of the footage. David and I arranged to meet and it was very emotional. I was stunned and shaken by the number of emotional memories he had. He even remembered a saddle he got when he first became interested in horses. He explained how conflicted he had been back then, between me and his mother, and I understood.

I have no children and I feel he's a part of my family. My relationship with David has been an enormously emotional one. We're very, very close today. David is knockout of a performer, but I'm more interested in him as a decent, honourable, caring person with very high values, which involve a great sense of social integrity.

As recently as four or five years ago, I reached out to Elliot and basically poured my soul out to him. I told him how much I missed him and how much his influence, love and care meant to me, and how much I had appreciated all that he did for me as a stepfather. We bonded again and he is someone whom I have the utmost respect for. He doesn't have a family of his own; I'm his family, and my family is his family.

It's hard even now to compare my father with other dads. I know he wasn't great in a lot of ways; he was terrible. He wasn't there for any of my Little League games. He promised he would be, but only showed up once – for half an hour. I can still hear his voice, telling me over the phone, 'Honey, I'm not going to be able to come to this one, but, remember, I'll be there in spirit.' Gradually Shirley and I became a little closer. I came to see that she was really a warm, giving and consistent person and that she recognised how unreliable my father was and didn't want me to get hurt. She knew who he was; he was the same with her kids.

Around Christmas 1962, when I was 12, my father went on an overnight father–son camping trip with me. My mom and Shirley nagged him until he had to make the decision to go with me. It was a camping trip in the snow, at a Boy Scout camp up in the San Bernardino Mountains. Now, my dad was used to staying in digs like the Plaza and the Sherry Netherland hotels when he was in New York. He lived in a huge mansion with a pool, guesthouse, servants' quarters, the works, in Bel Air, California.

He showed up for the trip dressed like David Niven. He was

wearing a brand-new outfit – sheepskin gloves, boots, silk scarf. He must have bought them at the most expensive store in Beverly Hills. His hair, as always, was absolutely perfect. Everybody else's dad is just, ya know, dad. Flannel shirt and jeans. But not Jack. We drove up to the mountains, to the forest, and we built our tents, and then sat around the campfire listening to the Scoutmaster tell stories. About nine o'clock we said goodnight. It was freezing. All the fathers went into the cabin together. I just couldn't imagine my father in that funky cabin.

At about six a.m. we all got up. The other dads start coming out of the cabin. The first thing they do is look at me, smile, pat me on the back and say, 'Your dad. What a guy! He kept us up all night telling jokes and stories. What a father! It must be great growing up with him. I've never met anyone like him! Your dad's in there holding court.'

And I'm thinking, *Yeah, that's really great. I've seen him like four times this year and he can't even spend this time with me!* Somebody said, 'Oh, by the way, don't get concerned when you see his hand. He picked up a hot poker in the middle of the night. He was building a fire for us.' Pure romance, my dad.

Apparently he'd brought some booze with him. He was passing the Scotch around while the kids slept. My dad sat by the fire telling show-business stories. Just being one of the guys. He could do that for days! He had such a cunning wit. He knew, seemingly, everybody in the business, from Cole Porter to Stephen Sondheim. I was proud of him, but our one big weekend wound up becoming *his* big weekend. I don't remember the 'us' part. He had a need I couldn't quite understand: always to be the centre of attention, an insatiable need always to be 'on'.

My father began taking me with him on summer stock tours for maybe a week at a time, when he could, which sure beat hanging around Los Angeles over the summer vacation. I not only got to see more of my dad, I saw different parts of America and different aspects of show business. I became a savvy, sophisticated kid.

Looking back, I'm sure it bothered my dad that his career was then so greatly overshadowed by Shirley's, although he wouldn't have admitted it. She was in demand for films; he wasn't. In Hollywood he was still, in effect, 'Mr Shirley Jones'. That began to change when he starred in the Broadway musical *She Loves Me* in 1963–4 and won a Tony Award; after that, his career began to take off. But in 1962 Jack Cassidy was not considered a star. However, he expressed great pride to me in being what he termed a 'working actor'. It was an honourable profession, he stressed, just not an easy one. He always said that I could expect a similarly long, slow struggle to master my craft and gain respect and recognition from my peers. I accepted that reality.

He was doing enough guest roles on TV shows by then that people were beginning to know his face. In 1961 and 1962 alone he appeared in episodes of the popular TV series *Alfred Hitchcock Presents*, *Wagon Train*, *Hawaiian Eye*, *Bronco*, *Hennessey*, *Maverick*, *The Real* McCoys, *Cheyenne*, *Surfside* 6 and *77 Sunset Strip*, and also lent his distinctive and cultured voice to the soundtrack of a cartoon special, *Mr Magoo's Christmas*. That's a lot of work.

My dad didn't have to tell me that he had become a credible actor; he was always acting – and quite grandly. The Jack Cassidy persona the world saw was probably his finest performance of all. If you remember any of his talk-show appearances with Johnny Carson, Mike Douglas or Merv Griffin, I'm sure you saw him as this ultra suave, charming, refined man. But in reality, as I've said, he came from a tough, working-class background and simply invented the man you've seen.

As I spent more time with him, I came to realise there was

one person whose opinion he valued, whose esteem he sought even more than Shirley's. And that was Ruth Aarons'. He worshipped her. And she him.

Ruth was my dad's manager, and Shirley's manager too. It's as if she was almost always part of our family. And she always took an interest in me. I found her entertaining and engaging with a great sense of humour. She was attractive, but looked kind of tomboyish. She was almost always by herself. People presumed she was gay; only at the very end of her life was I aware there was a man in her life. When I was a kid, she could talk to me easily about things that really interested me – music, sports, and so on – in a way that other adults couldn't.

And there didn't seem to be anything about show business she didn't know, which shouldn't have been surprising, since both her father, Alex Aarons, and her grandfather, Alfred Aarons, had been famed theatrical producers. Her father, in partnership with Vinton Freedley, had produced such smash Broadway hits as *Lady, Be Good!*, *Oh, Kay!*, *Funny Face*, *Hold Everything* and *Girl Crazy* and had built and owned New York's Alvin Theatre, though he lost his fortune in the stock market crash of 1929. As a little girl, Ruth sat under the piano at parties at which the likes of George Gershwin and Cole Porter entertained. When she was in her teens, she had become a table tennis world champion. By the late 40s she had become a theatrical manager and I believe she may have been the first female to accomplish that. She had very few clients, but didn't need many. They were all successful. She was so personally involved in the development and maintenance of her clients' careers that most stayed with her forever. They knew her touch was golden. And she would do anything for them. By the early 60s, she was working with Celeste Holm, George Chakiris, who later found huge fame in *West Side Story*, Janis Paige, Shirley, and my father.

She was vibrant, wise and sophisticated. Class, real class. Someday she would be my manager and, consequently, one of the most important people in my life. But that was still a half dozen years or so in the future. Back then, she was still just Auntie Ruth.

3 Those Swingin' 60s

Maybe I should have been in school that day, but I used to cut class pretty often. Bored, mostly. I was walking through Westwood Village in Los Angeles, when I heard the news that President Kennedy had been shot. I was 13 years old on 22 November 1963. That day still carries a certain weight for me. It's the sense of loss again. I couldn't believe we didn't have our President any more.

As people heard the news, the streets emptied. People who'd been out shopping quietly went home. I'd never seen Westwood totally deserted like that.

That date marks the beginning of what we think of as the 60s – those turbulent years when everything in our society seemed to be changing. Up until then, it had been damned near inconceivable that anyone would kill a president. And then Martin Luther King, Bobby Kennedy and Malcolm X were all assassinated.

Did the shooting of JFK make it easier for the others to carry out cold-blooded murders? Did it somehow make it easier for many of us – in ways large or small – to consider breaking laws or codes of conduct? Did it contribute to the unravelling of the social fabric? Back in the 50s it was as if nobody except real criminals broke the law. We all stayed in line. Butch haircuts, pressed shirts. And now, in the 60s, all laws, all rules, all codes of conduct seemed suddenly open to question. Restraints were loosening throughout society. A lot of the changes in those years were excessive. There was an element of madness loose in our culture – think of the killings, the lives lost to drug overdoses. Tune in, turn on, drop out.

But to me, the 60s were about freedom. There was the Free Speech Movement and, of course, the struggle for civil rights. The 60s also saw the birth of the modern feminist and gay rights movements. Everyone was seeking freedom and justice. Drugs were perceived as something that would help liberate us, expand our consciousness.

Did I feel a part of that growing movement, the counterculture? Was I anti-war? You better believe it! I, like many others, didn't understand what America was doing in Vietnam. My mother and I were both strongly opposed to the war; she said if I was drafted, we'd move to Canada. I couldn't imagine myself going to Vietnam; I wasn't exactly the military type. There was a draft lottery to select those who would be called to go to Vietnam. Fortunately, at 19, I lucked out. I was not selected, so I was not called to serve. The peace symbol really meant something to me, to all my friends. I was, at the time, considered totally unpatriotic. To me, a child of the 60s, a patriot was somebody who blindly supported the government's increasingly militaristic policies.

The establishment was trying to keep the younger generation in line, to keep the lid on all of the growing pressures for change. Back then, wearing your hair long – and I was the first in my school to start doing so – symbolised some degree of allegiance to the counterculture, which seemed to make adults feel threatened. Adults wanted to control how kids wore their hair, as if, by doing that, they could control the kids' thinking. If everyone's hair was cut short and matted down with Brylcreem, then rebellious impulses would be similarly under control.

My stepfather didn't approve of me letting my hair grow longer. He got even more upset when I later dyed it blond. The gap between us grew wider and wider as the 60s wore on.

When I started University High School in 1965, I was ordered to the vice principal's office because the length of my hair was questionable. He made me shake my head in front of him, saying that if a single hair on my head moved, I wouldn't be allowed to enrol. And it wasn't even that long then. But that's how seriously they were cracking down. They were drawing a line.

I was already someone who was anti-establishment. So was my good friend Kevin Hunter. We'd hang out in Westwood Village every day after school with some other guys – Ross Nogen, David Greene. We were wild. We were the rebels. We started wearing bell-bottoms because everyone in the older generation wore straight pants. It was all about freedom, about self-expression.

We didn't like that we had to dress the way they dictated if we wanted to get an education. So when we first heard about 'love-ins' – celebrations for hippies and people who aligned themselves with the philosophy that any behaviour or form of dress (or undress) was acceptable – you can bet they sounded more attractive to us than school.

As far as I was concerned, California was *the* place to be in the 60s. It was really the hub in terms of the whole social/sexual revolution. What people in the Midwest were reading about in magazines or following via radio and TV, we were witnessing and experiencing. My appetite to be a part of the culture, the new social culture, the new musical culture, was really keen.

I tuned in to watch the Beatles on *The Ed Sullivan Show* and the next day I said, 'Please, Mom, let me get an electric guitar.' At that time, I was playing drums and had just begun to play the guitar. I'd play in garage bands and little combos. We'd get together and play Beatles songs. But I didn't want to be a professional musician, I just loved to play. What the Beatles did for me when I saw them on *Ed Sullivan* was make me want to be in a band with three other guys and do what I eventually ended up doing with *The Partridge Family* – influence millions of people. I'm not comparing the two in any way. It's just that the Beatles inspired people.

My musical heroes through the 60s also included the Beach Boys, Eric Clapton, John Mayall and the Bluesbreakers, B. B. King, Albert King, Albert Collins, Marvin Gaye, Otis Redding. And, of course, Jimi Hendrix. He was the greatest performer of the era. I went to see him with my friends Kevin Hunter and Sam Hyman when I was in high school. He played the Hollywood Bowl, opening for The Monkees. We watched him from up in the trees to get the best view. He was electric and angry. He was not enjoying the fact that he was playing to a bunch of teenyboppers.

Sam Hyman: The Hollywood Bowl was a gorgeous place to see a concert. The night lights would be reflecting in this huge pond in front of the stage and it was just beautiful. Hendrix had such a magnetism and appeal that people starting rushing to the front and jumped in the pond and the water started to get on stage. All of a sudden he had to stop and he said, 'Hey, whoa, cool it, we're going to get electrocuted.' Because of that, they cemented the pond up shortly thereafter.

Jimi had soul. He was so charismatic as a performer, and had a sexual presence that no one else had at that time. He had broken through in England with *Hey Joe* and somehow I got a copy of it. And then I saw him at the L.A. Forum twice and I saw him at Devonshire Downs. You know how he inspired me? Not so much as a guitar player, but as an individual. It was at the time when individuality was heralded and it confirmed to me that you could be an individual and be willing to reveal yourself as a unique songwriter, singer, performer. That's why, decades later, he's seen as the great innovator.

Jimi blurred all the lines. Was he R&B? Yeah, he was an R&B guitar player. Was he a rock guitar player? Yeah. Was he a soul guitar player? Yeah. Was he pop? Yeah. He was all of that. Most of his audience was white but that didn't matter. Back then, there was very little musical prejudice in terms of defining culture by colour, race or theme. We were exposed to so many different musical influences. You could hear Petula Clark, Otis Redding, Cream, the Beach Boys, Frank Sinatra, Dean Martin, Louis Armstrong and Marvin Gaye on the same radio station, and often even on the same stage, because they were great artists and they made great records. Unfortunately, if you turn on the radio today, you're going to get hip hop here, jazz there, R&B somewhere else. Music and art are much more segregated today even though it all comes from the same place.

Steve Ross, a friend who played guitar in the first garage band I was in (and would be an important friend for many years to come), turned me on to guitar. We could jam on basic blues or a Hendrix number for an hour and a half at a time. I'm sure it stunk, but to us it was the stuff.

When I was in bands, we started off playing Beatles' songs. But I progressed from being a real pop music fan, like any average kid, to listening to rhythm and blues, which was deeper, more authentic. I then moved on to hardcore acid rock –

Hendrix, Clapton, Jeff Beck, Peter Green, John Mayall, Paul Butterfield, Mike Bloomfield. The music of the era reflected all the social changes that were happening, the whole social revolution.

Because of *The Partridge Family* I became publicly identified with a kind of sweet, lightweight, mainstream pop music. I was the antithesis of that. I wanted to be on the cutting edge of pop culture.

Drugs, of course, became a big part of the youth movement. We came to think of drugs as recreational, fun, something that could expand your mind, make you more loving and enhance sex. And drugs were new, something my generation did that, generally speaking, the previous generations didn't do. In the 60s my friends and I went to rock concerts and saw Cream, with people selling – and some even giving away – acid. I went to a party up in Laurel Canyon one night in late '66 or early '67 and Janis Joplin was there. She was a big deal at that time, but she was there getting high like everybody else. Sunset Strip in Hollywood was a gathering place for people who shared that philosophy and were really committed to change. Hendrix and Joplin were role models for teenagers in the revolution that I identified with.

When I was 15 a friend of mine who was a few years older offered me and Sam Hyman our first joints. I already knew how to smoke, of course – I'd been smoking regular cigarettes since I was 13 and would continue to do so until I was 20 – but this was something different. Pot was just coming on to the scene as far as kids my age were concerned. None of my friends had yet seen pot or even talked about it. Don't forget, this was 1965 – we're talking about the period just slightly pre-psychedelia, pre-Haight-Ashbury, before *Life* magazine reported that people were experimenting with LSD, which was how, as a curious ninth-grader, I first learned that LSD existed. Drugs would really explode on to the scene in 1966 and 1967. In 1965 I didn't know much about marijuana at all, except that there were some jazz musicians like Gene Krupa who'd messed with it.

The first time I smoked a joint, I felt like a real derelict. Sam and I had gone to visit this unbalanced guy down by the railroad tracks around Sepulveda, a pretty funky neighbourhood. The guy had an alcoholic mother; Sam and I bought her a bottle of Cutty Sark, as our friend had suggested, so she wouldn't care what any of us were doing. We went around to the back of the house and he showed us these two wilted, hand-rolled cigarettes. I thought they looked bizarre, really sleazy. But I was a curious, adventurous lad. I rarely had anything to do except go to school. And this older guy showed us how to smoke pot – inhaling real deeply and holding it in. And I was profoundly affected by it. I got hammered.

Eventually, I told my mom I smoked dope. She surprised me when she told me that she and my dad had actually tried it back in their early theatre days and so she knew it wasn't hell, although she hadn't cared for it. I was impressed that mom thought so 'young'. Because she'd been brought up in and around the theatre, I guess, nothing really shocked her. She was open-minded compared to most adults. So she was really my friend, I felt then. My pals from school all used to tell me how cool my mom was. She was really good looking, too, which probably impressed them. She looked like Elizabeth Taylor. She was a knockout.

Over the next few years, I was to discover I was deeply sensitive to almost any kind of drug. As a teenager in high school, I found myself experimenting with all sorts, as opportunities arose. It became an important part of my life, part of my zest for living. I was reckless, wild. We were young kids experimenting with pot, hash, psychedelics, mescaline, THC, speed, Tuinal and more. In 1966–7, when I was 16 and 17, I'd take speed maybe once a month, or once every couple of weeks, and sometimes go on a binge for two or three days. Maybe some diet pills or something. My body always reacted violently to amphetamines, though; I was never able to handle them well. Everybody I knew in school experimented with drugs Now that I have my own kids I shudder to think about it.

In 1967 I hitchhiked up to Haight-Ashbury in San Francisco with Kevin Hunter because we'd seen it on the news. We spent a couple of days and nights there smoking weed and taking acid. We'd heard it was the place to be and we considered ourselves to be tuned-in guys. I had just finished eleventh grade, although I guess I looked about 12 years old. But I had pretty long hair and I felt a part of the whole hippie movement. Kevin and I figured we were just like those older guys, except that we were still living at home.

We stayed at this place right off the Haight. The door was open to us. Hippies everywhere. It was a crash pad – a small room with people sleeping on the floor. There was one really weird-looking guy wearing a white robe. He was probably 98 pounds; he looked like a skeleton. He was clutching this bottle that must have held a hundred pills, like a miser with a purse. Every so often, he'd flip the top open, take a couple of pills, then flip it closed. His mind was obviously lost already.

We crashed in this room on the floor that night. In the morning, the guy was gone but his shoes were there along with the bottle that had two little pills left in it. I wondered what had happened to him from taking so many pills, I wondered if he had died. Nobody knew.

Later that day we went to Golden Gate Park. As we walked in, someone handed us some purple Osley acid. Free. It was the summer of love and we were at a love-in. I think either Jefferson Airplane or Iron Butterfly was playing. We were too ripped to know. We hitched back home. Kevin and I had hardly slept the whole weekend, maybe two or three hours a night, and we were blown away from the acid and the hitching. I went up to my room and slept for twenty-one hours. My mom just assumed that this was all normal teenage behaviour.

LSD wasn't even illegal when I first heard about it. We tried it because it was part of the cutting-edge culture of the time. I also experimented with peyote buttons, which come from cactus and are hallucinogenic. I can remember holding a friend's hand during a bad trip. I watched people who were not terribly secure really lose it.

I think my psychedelic experiences, by and large, were with the wrong people or in the wrong environments. If you're not in good shape to begin with, believe me, LSD's not going to make it any better for you. Some people have told me that they enjoyed blissful, beautiful, magical psychedelic trips. But I didn't. I think I often took it with guys who were lost – the most insecure, sad, lonely, desperate guys I could have picked – kids from school or people I'd met hanging around a pool hall I used to go to. One druggie friend I knew had tried to commit suicide a few times.

I had an appetite for living on the edge from the time I was 13 or so. I'd take a bike on my way home from school, paint it or fix it up a little, use it for a month or so, and then guilt would take over and I'd return it. A while later, I'd swipe another one and do the same. I'd always return them or I couldn't have lived with myself.

Stealing wasn't really a part of my life. It was more that if I saw a rule of any sort, I'd think, *Let's see, how can I break this? Or bend this?* Being told not to do something was an enticement for me.

My mom had me go to a psychologist for a period of time when I was using drugs. In the 60s, that was considered a very sophisticated, intellectual way of dealing with children. I basically manipulated the psychologist, so my mother would be told I needed more love, trust and understanding. As far as I was concerned, the only problems I had were how I was going to get through the school year without doing any homework and how could I pull the wool over my parents' eyes so I could continue having the lifestyle I wanted?

I was very good at being a teenager. I was good at getting away with anything – staying out all night, messing around, lying to my parents, all the while trying desperately to act older than I was – until the arrival of Judgment Day, the day report cards came. I wound up having to go to summer school between tenth and eleventh grades, and then again between eleventh and twelfth grades, and then again right after twelfth. I got kicked out of two high schools for cutting classes. My parents didn't know what to do with me.

I wound up getting sent to what they called continuation school, which is what they had in Los Angeles for incorrigibles who were too young to drop out of school legally. There were students with a lot of emotional problems. There were a lot of losers. I saw guys who brought guns and knives to school, guys whose future was clearly a stretch in San Quentin.

Everybody is a jerk to some degree in their teenage years. Everyone I've ever met, who has been honest, has told me of their irrational or outrageous behaviour during that period of their lives. Rebelliousness was the norm. OK, so I didn't want to go to school. I wanted to play music. I'd much rather stand out on the street and get an education there than sit in a classroom and learn things I was never going to use. I've never once found a use for the algebra I learned.

I scratch my head when I hear what courses my son has to take in school so he can go to college. And I think, *When he's 25, is he going to need geometry or chemistry? Is he going to learn the things that we use as tools in our lives?* What we should learn is how to be parents, how to be married, how to coexist with each other and other cultures, or we're not going to have a planet any more.

I couldn't take the continuation school any longer, so I begged my mom.

'There is a private school called Rexford where they let you grow your hair, where they let you be who you are. They encourage individuality. Let me try it there and I promise I will work hard.'

I went to Rexford for my last year and a half and I actually flourished a little bit. There were only five to twelve kids in a class. I began drama classes, too, which I loved. The teachers related to me. It sparked my interest.

Kevin was already going there when I enrolled midway through my junior year. He was wild, but he had a lot of gifts. He had a great mind, was an artist, a very good writer, and he was a great pal. He'd make up all these great characters with names like Jackson Snipe. I mean, who could forget a name like Jackson Snipe? Kevin had a tape recorder. We'd get high and write and act and tape 'radio shows' together. A lot of our creativity, we believed, came out of beer and drugs. We played two homosexuals in some really silly one-act plays. We wrote plays together, which we performed in drama class and for our graduation. We were headed, or so we presumed, in pretty much the same direction: acting.

By our senior year in high school, 1967–8, Kevin was occasionally getting high on heroin. And I, foolishly, tried it with him. Once. I was into experiencing as much as I could back then. So we went out and bought a dime bag of heroin and shared it. I never used a needle. I just snorted it. I became very dark and slow. I could see how you could become a human wasteland very quickly, and I wanted no part of it. Way too bleak.

Kevin and I also liked doing poppers – amyl nitrate – the fumes of which produce an intense, short-lived rush. I remember when we were in a school play, right before we were supposed to go on, performing for all our parents and teachers, we popped an 'amy'. We walked out on stage in our costumes and blew it completely. I mean, we were in hysterics, just bent over, knocking things over, bumping into people. It was more like a slapstick routine. Embarrassing now, looking back. The adults may not have been too impressed, but we were having a good time. I have good memories of that period. And of Kevin, who would be dead in two years.

My stepfather had fantasies of me going to college, but I knew I wasn't headed in that direction. My academic interest was next to nil. My grades weren't much better. Sex, drugs and rock and roll came first. OK, kids, let's talk a little about the sex.

I reached puberty pretty early. By 11 or 12, I had matured sexually and had an incredible appetite for it – driven by it, in fact. It's all I could think about. I'd walk around with a hard-on all day long. At 13, all I did was play with myself and think about getting laid, getting blown. Sex, glorious sex.

Sex was available and I was very sexually precocious. Like most teenagers, I had raging hormones. Most of my friends and I were interested in sex. At the time, there was no sex on television so it was more of a taboo than it is today. My Christian upbringing repressed me and that's also probably why I felt so inclined to experiment sexually. Try telling a 13-year-old boy with a strong sexual appetite that he can't do anything about it. As I've learned through having a teenage son, views are very different today.

I wanted to touch every girl I saw. I was always curious about sex. My earliest experiences – going back to when I was as young as nine – were feeling up a friend's older sister. By the time I was 12 or 13 I'd be making out with 15-year-olds, who were thrilled that I was thrilled by them because they had big breasts. I was like their toy. I came close but I didn't actually have sexual intercourse until I was 13.

There was a girl who lived down the street from a pal of mine, Gary, in Bel Air. One night, when my friends and I were staying at Gary's house, we all went down the street to see this girl, who was a year or two older. There were six of us. We snuck up to a loft above her garage and asked her to take her clothes off, and she did. I was in awe. For 13-year-old boys, seeing this girl's tits was the biggest deal in the world. You know, we must have spent hours feeling them. I didn't want to do anything more in front of everybody else. In fact, I was already a little self-conscious. I called her up one weekend night and asked to see her by myself. And that was the first time I ever had sex. Once I started, I pretty much lost whatever interest I'd had in playing basketball and baseball.

I fell for a junior high-school girl named Laurie. I still in some way carry a torch for her. She eventually went for an older guy and broke my heart. So I thought, *Well, parents – adults – don't stay together. Why should we?* I spent my life going through these short, failed relationships. I'd fall in love with one girl for a spell, then, a little while later, I'd just lose interest. I stayed like that until I met my first wife, Kay Lenz.

When I was 16, I dated an African-American girl. I used to go to South Central L.A. and hang out with her and her friends, and I was the only white guy there. It mattered to them more than it mattered to me. She was a fantastic girl and I felt completely at home with her and her circle, but her black friends thought it was unacceptable. *A white boy is taking out my girlfriend.* It was difficult for both of us. We went to see Marvin Gaye together. We saw Wilson Pickett. We saw Hendrix. She loved music and I loved her. But we found ourselves questioning our commitment to one another every day and wondered why we had to be under this kind of constant scrutiny.

In high school I had a new girlfriend every month or two. I can't imagine what it must be like for teens today, because we didn't even have the fear of getting a venereal disease back then, much less AIDS. No one worried. There was no fear of death. Only fear of pregnancy. No one thought about it. Everyone just went out and did it. Sex was the best thing in the world.

This was our code: we smoked pot, got high and went to drive-in movies, because it was the place you could get away from your parents and have sex. God, I loved having sex in a car. To this day, I think it's one of the hottest things. I'd dream about it all week at school. It got really interesting when it was a double date, when you and your buddy and your girlfriends would all be in the same car. Back in 1966–7, drive-in theatres were like brothels. Everybody was screwing everywhere. You'd drive in, put the audio box in the car, eat popcorn for five minutes, and then *bang*, you'd be doin' the pop 'n' gobble.

Eventually I told my mom, 'Look, I'd like to bring a girl over. Would you mind? I'd like to take her up to my room.'

My mom kind of turned a blind eye and said, 'OK, you can bring girls to your room, but I don't want you having intercourse.'

'Oh, we would never do that,' I assured Mom.

Well, of course, the girl and I would be going at it within five minutes of closing the door. I'm sure my mom knew what was going on. I'm sure she was just glad I wasn't out on the street getting into some kind of serious trouble. After all, this was the 60s.

Perhaps because of my physical appearance – my build was slight, my features were sort of on the delicate side, my hair was long – there were some people who assumed I was homosexual. I clearly wasn't into any macho trip. My manner was kind of gentle, soft-spoken. At least at that time it was. And I did have some gay friends. When I was 15 and 16, that kind of talk hurt me a lot. I remember overhearing a couple of friends of mine – or guys I had thought were friends of mine – snickering and saying, 'Ah, David's a fag,' and so on. I'd wonder, *God, why do people say that about me?* It disturbed me because I didn't really know whether I was or I wasn't.

This is sort of hard to explain, because I honestly wasn't attracted to men. I hadn't slept with any men. And I was incredibly active with girls. But I guess we're all insecure when we're young. I had some thoughts about homosexuality – I'm sure we all have some thoughts about it as we're growing up, finding ourselves. I knew gay guys who found me attractive. And there were these other jerks snickering that they could 'tell' I must be homosexual. So I was, at times, unsure. It was only when I was actually confronted with the situation – when I had a real opportunity to get into a sexual relationship with a friend of mine who was homosexual and I declined his invitations and felt comfortable about that – that I realised, *Hey, I'm not sitting on the fence. I'm really just not into it.* And I became very secure with my own sexual identity.

When I became famous, through *The Partridge Family* and concert appearances and all of that, I found I had a pretty strong gay following. I kind of liked it. Gay publications ran pictures of me; one named me gay pin-up of the year. I'd get fan letters from gay guys saying things like, 'I can tell by the look in your eyes that you're one of us.' A gay liberation organisation in London wrote to ask me for my support. I never did anything to encourage or discourage anyone's interest. If there were guys who found me attractive and perhaps fantasised about me, I was flattered. I found it mostly amusing how much people were discussing my sexuality, like it really mattered if I slept with men, women, snakes or sheep!

There were some people who assumed that because Sam Hyman and I shared a home and travelled together we were lovers. There's always going to be some talk about guys who are roommates. You can't control what people are going to imagine. It's not worth the effort to try.

Through my parents, I had been exposed to a culture and environment that was very open. My parents were very tolerant of homosexuality and I was taught to be tolerant, too. Both my parents had many homosexual friends whom I knew to be really wonderful people. And I've always felt very protective of my friends who are gay. I defend them and their right to be who they are. I believe that people should make their own choices about how they live their lives, providing they are not hurting anyone, and I don't believe the government, the church or anybody else should be able to interfere in those choices.

In my teens I was fortunate to become good friends with the actor Sal Mineo, who had done some television work with my stepfather. Then in his late 20s, this one-time teen star who'd specialised in playing troubled youths was being ill-treated by Hollywood as a has-been. A swarthy, handsome, black-haired guy, Sal had found fame in Hollywood quite early on, after having been kicked out of school. I could relate to that. He'd been just 16 when he got his first Oscar nomination, for his supporting role in *Rebel Without a Cause* starring James Dean and Natalie Wood. He appeared again with Dean in *Giant* and in other films such as *Crime in the Streets*, *Somebody Up There Likes Me*, *Rock*, *Pretty Baby*, *The Gene Krupa Story* and *Exodus*, for which he earned a second Oscar nomination. And then the work suddenly dried up. Sal Mineo – one of the kindest, most honourable people I've ever known – was rejected by most of Hollywood as old news by the time he reached his mid 20s (and, believe me, I can now relate to that as well).

Hollywood has a way of chewing people up and then spitting them back out. In the later years of his career, Sal appeared in mostly minor films. He also directed plays, some with gay-related themes, like *Fortune and Men's Eyes* and *P.S., Your Cat Is Dead.*

I knew Sal had some girlfriends. And I knew that from time to time Sal also had guys staying at his house. I didn't care about that. Sal was just a great friend. He was one of the most incredibly warm, gentle, sensitive, funny and hip people I'd ever met. He had magnetism. There always seemed to be a lot of young people around him.

Over at Sal's, we would talk about things like concerts that were coming up. Sal had a drum set, guitars and amps and I remember playing guitar and drums, jamming with other guys. It was cool because we were all mostly around the same age – 17, 18 years old. We loved having a place where we could go to hang out, where no one was going to hassle us.

Sal took a genuine interest in me. Would you believe he actually gave me the set of drums that he used when he starred in *The Gene Krupa Story*? That was some special gift to give a kid. Years later, when I was moving around a lot, I passed on that drum set to my brother Patrick who had told me he loved it.

It was at Sal's that I first met Don Johnson and Elliot Mintz. Elliot and Sal shared a place for a while in the late 60s. Elliot, a radio personality on KPFP, a public radio station in Los Angeles, was really into the political movement. He was very much the voice of change and political thrust in the 60s and into the 70s. He was very tuned in and was part of the whole 60s hippie generation, part of the 'revolution', and I learned quite a bit from him. Elliot and I were good friends for several years – we travelled together, got drunk together, the whole bit.

I also became pretty friendly with Don Johnson through Sal. Back then he was just another young, good-looking, struggling actor from the Midwest, desperate for a break. He wouldn't become a household name until he appeared on the TV series *Miami Vice*, which ran in the mid 80s. When I first met him I was still in high school and he had just gotten out. He was very charming and self-centred. I liked him because he had a sense of humour and was interesting. We were contemporaries with the same goal: to make it as actors. Don was always gushingly friendly towards me, although I sometimes sensed a certain degree of competitiveness under that friendliness.

I'm sure Don believed Sal could help his career. I felt pretty confident that Don was going to survive in Hollywood – which can be pretty rough, especially for a newcomer – no matter what it took. I've seen that a lot in Hollywood over the years. You'd be surprised at the lengths that people will go to to be successful in show business.

Don was already a very talented actor when I first met him. Around 1969, I remember going to see him in Sal's production of *Fortune and Men's Eyes*, and he was very good in it. I had every confidence he'd make it.

As my mother and stepfather's marriage finally ground to a halt, I aligned myself fervently with my mother. At one point in their break-up, I threatened to kill my stepfather if he hurt her. As I grew up, I could clearly see the pain my dad had caused my mom and I hated seeing her go through that again.

My stepfather was respected in the industry. After he and my mom got divorced, he continued directing films, including *A Man Called Horse*, a Richard Harris film and *The Car*, a popular film about an obsessed car that chases people. He eventually went on to spearhead the drive against colourising black-and-white movies. But by the time I was 18, he was essentially out of my life. He was gone. I actually felt relieved that there was no longer the tension between them in the house, but I missed him.

I lived with my mom in my final year of high school. My mom wasn't happy with the way her life had worked out. She had two failed marriages behind her. And she had given up a promising show-business career to give more attention to a son who appeared to be pretty much going nowhere.

But I always knew I wanted to be an actor and I wanted to perform. I sang mostly theatre stuff as a young kid, music from some of my dad's shows, like *Wish You Were Here*, and I learned *The Music Man* when I was around seven. Years later I taught my own son *The Music Man*. Because I could sing, I was always singled out in chorus and music and glee club. I was a soloist in the choir.

I started listening to the radio when I was nine or ten and I was a really quick student. It was easy. I could pick out harmony parts. I loved to sing all the background parts. When I was 17, I joined the Los Angeles Theater Company (LATC). I was the only non-professional that they allowed in and I worked in two productions during my senior year. I also wrote a play and directed it. It was pretty avant garde, an unstructured piece that didn't have a title. It was part improv, and it was politically driven in a humorous way. Myself, Kevin Hunter and an actress performed it in the closing ceremony of the theatre company's season.

During my last year of school, my mom did some plays with the same company. I auditioned for and got a couple of parts in the production myself. It gave me a chance to work, for the first time, with some professional actors, including my mom. I liked the experience.

My grades weren't quite good enough for me to graduate with my high-school class in June of 1968. So I went to one last session of summer school to get the credits I needed. It was important to me to get a diploma. I didn't want my mom to feel she'd raised a failure. Two weeks later, I moved back to New York with my dad and Shirley to become . . . an actor!

4 Time for a Haircut

My father was back in my life. Once he accepted the fact that I was determined to follow in his footsteps and make acting my profession, he tried to help me as best he knew how. He paid for my first professional photographs. He got me connected with agents who could help find me parts to audition for. And – most significantly over the long haul – he asked his manager, Ruth Aarons, who knew as much about the business as anyone, to give me whatever help she could.

Initially, Ruth advised me more as a friend than a manager; for the first couple of years of my career she took no payment from me. She saw no need to take from me a few hundred dollars that I could really use. Ruth became almost like another parent to me. In fact, I got along better with her than with my father, since I didn't have any emotional baggage with her.

My father decided that the best way for me to get my start would be to do exactly as he had done – learn my craft in the

New York theatre and gradually become a respected 'working actor'. In this instance, I agreed wholeheartedly with my dad. He was, after all, *the* authority.

My dad had a real flair for comedy, often playing vain, shallow buffoons. He'd most recently been featured on Broadway in the 1964–5 success *Fade Out Fade In,* starring Carol Burnett and staged by George Abbott. Now, in the summer of 1968, he was preparing to co-star with Shirley in a forthcoming Broadway musical, *Maggie Flynn.*

My father had rented a veritable castle, high on a hill overlooking the Hudson River in Irvington, New York, about 45 minutes north of Manhattan. It was a stone-crafted mansion, complete with turrets, stained-glass windows, swords and armour. There was plenty of room for him and Shirley and my brothers Shaun, Patrick and Ryan. I could live with them rent free. In fact, there was a pool house I could use so I could have privacy if I wanted to entertain any young ladies.

This would be the first time I'd ever lived with my father, stepmother and my three brothers. I didn't even meet Shaun until he was about four months old and I was visiting for Christmas. It only made me feel more abandoned and isolated. Later, as my brothers got older, I felt blessed to have them, as I do today. We don't consider ourselves half-brothers, we're brothers.

Patrick Cassidy: My memories of David as a kid are of seeing him on the set of *The Partridge Family*, seeing him in concert, or when he was visiting our house. It was always an event when he came over. He was always very jovial and really supportive. We'd have pillow fights and we'd wrestle. When David would come over, Shaun would torture me that much more to get David's attention. I would then scream for David to help me out of situations where Shaun was completely abusing me. That was David's role at that time.

Shaun looked up to David and would constantly try to get his attention.

My father said he would help me find a part-time job and I could take acting classes and audition for roles in New York until I established myself as a working actor. It sounded almost too good to be true.

And it was.

For starters, the part-time job my father found for me was in the mailroom of a textile firm in the city. At the time, $1.85 an hour was the minimum wage. The boss said, 'I tell you what, we're going to give you $2 an hour.' I earned $50 a week. After deductions, I took home $38.80, which didn't do much more than cover the cost of commuting from Irvington to New York City.

The youngest person I worked with was 48. The others working there were 55 and 74. And I was 18. I had to don a light-blue smock and sort mail. I had no friends there and was lonely. I lived in a fantasy world. I just couldn't identify with those people.

I'd get up early in the morning to catch a commuter train filled with serious-looking people in business suits from affluent Westchester County, whose only goal was to move up the corporate ladder. My whole life I'd somehow felt different from most people. And those feelings were never more intense than while riding on that train and working in that mailroom. I'd tell myself, *I don't look like these people or think like these people.* I had dreams that were different from theirs. I really wasn't money-oriented (although I didn't like being broke all the time, either). I longed to achieve artistic success by being a working actor.

I was starting to have doubts as to whether I'd ever achieve that. In my first few months in New York, I went to nearly 200 auditions for parts on Broadway, off Broadway and even tried out for off-off-Broadway as a last resort, as well as TV commercials and anything else I could interview for. I didn't get one job offer. Not one. Not even for the smallest part. There'd be 50 guys competing for every part, even if the job paid no money.

I'd be so depressed, so despondent after auditioning. Each new rejection would bring back old feelings from when my dad walked out on me and my mom. I made a much bigger deal out of being rejected than did the other aspiring actors I knew. I was plagued with self-doubt.

I'd think about the fact that I'd never had much success in school. I'd wonder whether I was ever going to have any success in my career or in my personal life. I couldn't dull those feelings with drugs or drink; I didn't have much money for any non-essentials. My dad, unlike my mom, wasn't the sort of person you could hit up for spending money. And even if I had the money for pot and knew where to get some, I didn't have anyone to smoke with.

I'd wonder sometimes what the guys back in California were doing – Kevin Hunter, Sam Hyman, Steve Ross, Sal Mineo, Don Johnson and others. All of them, I was sure, had to be leading happier, more rewarding lives than I was. Kevin was the only one I really wrote to. His letters were always a treat; he was such a good writer.

I did nothing but work: half the day in the mailroom, the rest of the time going to auditions or acting classes. I had to cut my hair off for my stupid part-time job. I felt totally alone. Isolated. I lost my identity as a part of the hip, young, 60s generation.

And my father didn't seem satisfied with anything I did. He criticised everything about me, beginning with my wardrobe. If I wanted to attend high school dressed as a hippie that was one thing. But he was not going to have Jack Cassidy's son going around New York looking like a bum.

My total wardrobe, when I arrived in Irvington-on-Hudson from Los Angeles, consisted of one pair of regular shoes, one pair of tennis shoes, three pairs of jeans, six shirts and a jacket. Standard teenage gear.

'How can I present you to my friends, the way you're dressed?' he'd ask. 'And what are you going to wear to work and auditions?'

I had to admit that had been the last thing on my mind. My dad said it was essential I bought a good suit. One day I told him, 'Look, Dad, I've been going through the newspaper for suits and I found some really good buys. I was wondering if I could go into Manhattan with you?'

He looked at the ads I'd found and declared curtly, 'Look, you don't want to shop in those places. I'll take you into New York and get you some nice clothes.'

I thought, *I'm 18 years old and my dad is going to buy me some clothes. Great! It's about time.*

After all, he knew I was only clearing $38.80 salary a week.

My dad took me to his tailor at Roland Meledandri, which must have been the most expensive clothing store in New York. He picked out a couple of suits for himself and then put me in a terrific suit. He also picked out an overcoat, a great sports jacket and slacks. The bill was running up to $800 – a fortune in those days – and I was thinking, *This doesn't feel like me at all.* But I knew my dad was happy.

My dad put his arm around me affectionately as we left the store – at times like that, I could really feel his love for me – and simply asked, 'Well?'

I mean, what could I say except, 'Gee, thanks. Thanks a lot, Dad.'

'Oh, you don't have to thank me,' he responded, 'because you are going to pay for it.'

What?!

'You're going to pay me $15 a week until you've paid it all back.'

Bastard.

That was a significant day for me. I felt like I was finally seeing my father the way my mother had long seen him. That was a dirty trick to play on a son.

How much can I get my son in debt to me? I'll take him to the most expensive shop in town and make him owe it to me!

My dad said that no one had given him money when he was young, and he expected me to do exactly as he had done. And you know what? I eventually paid him back every cent.

My relationship with my father was very strange, but I developed a good relationship with Shirley. Anyone who knows her knows it would be hard not to like her. She is a wonderful human being.

But when I was 18, my dad – who hadn't really been a part of my life at all up to that point – suddenly decided he was going to be my father. In Irvington-on-Hudson he laid down all sorts of ground rules for me that I'd never had when I lived with my mom.

There was always a lot of friction between us. And heaven help me if I told him I'd done something like arrive at an audition 15 minutes late. He'd rage, 'You don't show up for an eight o'clock call at eight-fifteen! That's unprofessional!'

And I'd be like, 'Give me a break, Dad. I'm *not* a professional yet. I'm 18 years old.'

But he was stubborn. And I was stubborn.

Shaun Cassidy: The trait David and our father shared is the acknowledged self-destructive streak. That's the negative. He also has our father's great humour and great charm and great charisma when he wants to. I think David has very specific aspects of our

> father but I think all of us have some. I see as much of my father in Patrick and Ryan as I do in David. The parts of our dad that David has might be the more theatrical parts and the more obvious ones. I would say I have the least amount of similarities on the surface but I think I'm a writer because of my father. He always wanted to be a writer and actually wrote a script. He was a sponge for knowledge. He educated himself and surrounded himself with smart people. And I have followed the same course. I don't think I do it consciously, but that's obviously a gift I got from him.

Dad and Shirley went on the road for previews of *Maggie Flynn* prior to its scheduled October 1968 opening at the ANTA Theater in New York. They were out of town when I got hired for my first real professional job in a new Broadway musical comedy, *The Fig Leaves Are Falling* with Barry Nelson, Dorothy Loudon and Jenny O'Hara. It was being staged by George Abbott, the legendary octogenarian director/writer/producer, who had worked in past years with both my parents. I was in four scenes and got to sing two songs with Dorothy Loudon.

My dad and Shirley were thrilled when I telephoned them with the news. Then I telephoned my employers and declared I'd never be going back to that hated job. 'Send my final cheque to my home. No, better yet, keep my cheque!' I told them. What did I need with a cheque for $38.80? I was being offered $175 a week – a veritable fortune – to appear in a show staged by George Abbott. In a career spanning five decades, Abbott had worked on more Broadway hits – *Pal Joey*, *On the Town*, *Pajama Game*, *Damn Yankees*, *A Funny Thing Happened on the Way to the Forum* and countless others – than probably anyone else in the business. I could imagine *The Fig Leaves Are Falling* running for many years to come, and me collecting those huge $175 cheques week after endless week. At 18, I had a good imagination.

The Fig Leaves Are Falling opened at Broadway's Broadhurst Theater on 2 January 1969. It closed on 4 January 1969.

My dad and Shirley's show, *Maggie Flynn,* didn't fare all that much better. Shirley's popularity as a film star helped generate some ticket sales, but not enough. By mid-January we were all out of work. My dad and Shirley decided to return to California.

Fortunately for me, while we were doing previews in Philadelphia for *Fig Leaves* . . . a casting director from CBS films had seen me and wanted me to screen-test for a movie he was casting. So two days after we closed on Broadway I was on a plane back to Hollywood.

5 California Dreamin'

Ruth began managing my career for real. She really cared about me, my dad, and my stepmom. She was an extremely loyal person. If my dad wanted her to look after me, she would, even though there wasn't any guarantee there'd be much in it for her. She helped me find a good agent to send me out to audition for appropriate parts. Then it was Ruth's job to help me decide the right career moves.

For those who imagine that show business is all fun and parties and everyone is guaranteed to make a huge fortune immediately, you should consider this: if you hadn't seen me in any of the three performances of *The Fig Leaves Are Falling* before its untimely close on Broadway, you would have had no other chance to see me perform professionally in 1969 until the year was almost over. I didn't get the film role I screen-tested for, nor did I get a number of other parts I auditioned for. In the final two months of the year, I was seen on episodes of two television series, *The Survivors* on ABC and *Ironside* on NBC (my first major role on television). And that was it for the year.

My total earnings for 1968 were well below the poverty level. And they weren't much better for 1969. Even so, Ruth mirrored my great hopes for the future.

I was back living with my mom in Los Angeles and feeling a little too old for that. She covered most of my costs while I saved money, but she made it clear, however, that I'd have to become self-sufficient as soon as possible, because she had decided she wanted to move back to West Orange. She had never really bought into the Hollywood lifestyle. And now, after two painful divorces, she wanted to return to her roots. She felt that spending more time with my grandfather, who was 81 and in declining health, would be good for both him and her.

I caught up with some of my old friends, like Kevin Hunter, who wasn't having any luck at all finding acting work, and Sam Hyman, who had found steady, if far from high-paying, employment as an apprentice film editor. I wasn't sure how serious Kevin was about making it as an actor. I thought that creatively he would have been better suited to being a writer.

One night Kevin and I got on his lightweight, girls' model Honda 50 motorcycle and drove up to the Los Angeles V.A. hospital. We scaled an 11-foot fence and stole a big metal tank of nitrous oxide – laughing gas. We rode back to his place with me carrying the tank. We got high on that for a week, then one night we went back to the hospital, returned the empty tank from the room we'd taken it from and liberated another tank for us to party with. Had we been caught, I later learned, we could have been sent to a federal penitentiary. But we never thought about the consequences of our actions. We didn't actually steal them. We just borrowed them for a week. We did return them, albeit empty.

I started seeing Don Johnson again from time to time once

I was back in Los Angeles (Sal Mineo was in London for a spell, directing a play). Don and I would often wind up seeking the same parts. Sometimes we'd both get shot down. But a couple of times, it came down to a choice between Don and me, and I was chosen. He was always really nice to me about it, but I have to believe he must have resented me at least a little. I certainly would have felt that way, but he was always decent about it. Don and I saw each other for the next few years around Hollywood; he was having a hard time getting work back then.

I saw Elliot Mintz a little, too. For a while we even wound up living right across the street from each other in Laurel Canyon. He was more interested in the struggle for political change than I was. I'd sort of become disillusioned with politics when Richard Nixon was elected president in 1968. I couldn't believe people couldn't see through Nixon's act. (I felt the same way when Reagan was elected in 1981.) I was more concerned with building a career and a life for myself.

When things start to happen in television, they can happen very quickly. The casting directors hear about you and the next thing you know you are working a lot. That began happening to me. In 1970, I appeared on episodes of a half dozen network series. You could've seen me acting on *The FBI* (the episode called 'The Fatal Imposter' which aired on 4 January 1970 on ABC); *Marcus Welby, MD* ('Fun and Games and Michael Ambrose', 13 January 1970, ABC); *Adam 12* ('A Rare Occasion', 14 February 1970, NBC); *Bonanza* ('The Law and Billy Burgees', 15 February 1970, NBC); *Medical Center* ('His Brother's Keeper', 1 April 1970, CBS) and *Mod Squad* ('The Loser', 7 April 1970, ABC).

I was gaining experience quickly. My acting was lame on my first couple of shows, but I was really pleased with the job I did on *Marcus Welby*. I played a diabetic youth who, as a way to punish his father, wouldn't take his insulin. I had to do some highly emotional stuff. Ruth said it was a great piece of work and she would help me get more. That sounded good to me. So long as I could make enough money to live simply, I'd be happy.

Sam Hyman and I used to enjoy driving up to Laurel Canyon, so we decided to buy a house there. Because of his apprentice film-editing job and my assorted TV acting jobs, we had enough money to make a down payment. My income was not steady, but we knew we could carry the house for at least the next three months. We just crossed our fingers that I'd keep getting enough guest shots on television to cover our bills beyond that point. Because I was making more money than Sam, I offered to pay about two-thirds of the mortgage. Our monthly payments were $315; I paid around $200 and he paid the rest. Sam and I were good friends. We're still friends. When I became famous, he went all around the world with me; he went through the whole experience with me. Although we rarely see each other now, he's still one of the only people I really can talk to and trust.

Back in that first home in Laurel Canyon, we lived like hippies. No furniture to speak of. I found an old mattress someone had discarded behind a supermarket and carted it home. We had no money in our pockets, but we were in great spirits nonetheless. We were the most successful guys from our high-school years, the only ones who had made it and were living independently.

Sam Hyman: At 19 years old, we got a house together in Laurel Canyon so we could have freedom and act grown-up, a place to bring your girls. Our first house consisted of a mattress on the floor in each bedroom. In those days they used to deliver fruit in flimsy wooden crates and so we went to the supermarket and picked up orange crates that became our nightstands. It was a real funky bachelor pad and neither of us was accustomed to doing housework.

We considered Laurel Canyon the hippiest place in town. Bohemian Rhapsody. It was just very cool there, still very much in the spirit of the 60s. Hippies next door, acid rock everywhere you went. I used to think, *This is the life. Freedom in Laurel Canyon.*

In mid 1970, with only eight network TV appearances to my credit, I was hardly someone the average American would have known. I was just one of a thousand faces on the tube. But I could take pride – and figured my dad could also take pride – in the fact that I was becoming, like him, a reliable working actor. My career seemed to be on the upswing. And, at least as important, I was totally satisfied with my life outside of work. What more could I possibly ask for?

If anyone had told me that by year's end I'd be a household name, a best-selling recording artist, the number one 'teen idol' with my picture on the back of Rice Krispies boxes, I would have asked him if the acid had kicked in yet.

6 Get in the Partridge Family Bus

'Listen, David, don't start.'

I can hear Ruth Aarons' voice now, silencing me when I tried to say I wasn't too interested in auditioning for a situation comedy that was being developed over at Screen Gems, the television subsidiary of Columbia Pictures. It was something about a widow and her five kids who had a rock band. It sounded contrived.

She said, 'By next year you'll be asking me if I think two swimming pools in the backyard is a little much.'

Everyone Ruth represented became very successful – they won Oscar and Tony awards, they made lots of money. Many other aspiring young actors in Hollywood would have died to have someone as savvy as Ruth Aarons take an interest in them. And I certainly respected her judgment. Yet I could not quite understand why she seemed to be pushing me toward this fluffy-sounding sitcom. My instincts told me I should be doing more sophisticated work. My television appearances to date had all been on dramatic shows. No comedy. No music. I was building up a reputation with casting directors as a serious young actor. Ruth wanted me to try out for this show and I was deadly opposed to it. She saw this as an opportunity for me to become a superstar and felt I was uniquely right for this role because I could sing and I could play. She went so far as to get my father to sit me down and tell me to do it. She never mentioned to me who else might be trying out for a role in it.

I read for the part a couple of times. I went into Screen Gems and met Renée Valente, who headed casting, Paul Witt, one of the show's producers, who was just beginning his career but would go on to produce the Emmy-winning TV series *Golden Girls* and the Robin Williams film *Dead Poets' Society*, and Bernard Slade, the writer of the pilot, who'd created a lot of the studio's half-hour TV shows like *The Flying Nun* and *Love on a Rooftop*. He would later write the hit Broadway plays, *Same Time, Next Year* and *Tribute*.

Renée Valente (casting executive): We auditioned kids of all ages. We auditioned Jodie Foster for one of the parts when she was six years old. Somebody had called to tell me about David Cassidy. I'd always had an open door to talent and that's how I found so many wonderful actors. What made David the right choice was he had the look. I have always said that the eyes are the mirror of the soul. It's very difficult to hide yourself, especially when you have the eyes David Cassidy did. When I looked into David's eyes I saw a young kid who would look great on camera, who could act pretty good for his age and could be Shirley Jones' son. I didn't know Shirley was David's stepmother until just before the screen test. I thought David was so right for the part that I did something that I'd never done before. I said to David, 'We can't mention your relationship to anybody at the company.' In my contract there was a clause that said nepotism was not allowed and I could have been fired for allowing it. I told David that if anybody knew about it at the company they wouldn't hire him and I didn't know what they would do to me.

Paul Junger Witt (producer/director): He read for us and knocked us out; we chose him before we knew that his stepmother was Shirley Jones. In casting the part of Keith Partridge, we were looking for someone who could act and could at least show potential for learning how to do comedy. It takes an actor a long time to become adept at comedy. Ideally we were also looking for someone who could sing. This was a couple of years post-Monkees. It was the *Tiger Beat* [teenage magazine] world. If we could get a heartthrob, if we could get *that kid,* he could serve as the centrepiece for that audience. The whole package walked in and read for us. David was the guy. He could do it all. His comedy chops were sufficient so we knew he would get it very quickly. It was very important that Keith would be a relatable kid. You can destroy that kind of character with a young male audience by having someone who's too perfect. Because of his looks and being so multi-talented, he had to be able to play that character realistically, otherwise we wouldn't have gotten the mixed audience we wanted so desperately.

Bernard Slade (creator/writer): When I was working in Canada I wrote a drama with music called *The Big Coin Sound*, which was about a vocal group. I came down to Los Angeles and one night I was watching the Johnny Carson show and saw a family group called The Cowsills. I thought it would be a good idea for a television show, having a situation comedy centred on a family with music. *The Sound of Music* was very popular around that time. So I came up with the idea of a travelling family group.

The show was originally called *The Family Business* and later changed to *The Partridge Family*. I went to school in England and played on the soccer team. The centre-half was a guy named Partridge, which, as it turned out, was not that uncommon a name. But at the time I thought it was unusual and it seemed fitting.

We got very lucky with the casting. You had David who was the teenage idol, Danny who was the comic, and you had Susan who was the pretty girl. Then you had Shirley who was the glue. And to cut the saccharine we got Dave Madden who was the cynical manager. Keith was the name of a boyfriend of my daughter's. Laurie was my daughter's name. Chris was my son's name. I just named the characters after people I knew.

They felt this could become a popular, family-oriented show. They said it was about a rock group. Screen Gems, they noted, had had considerable success in this field with The Monkees. When they mentioned rock, I started telling them about Jimi Hendrix and Eric Clapton, as if that really mattered to them. The scenes they had me read seemed awfully thin. I had lines like 'Gee, Mom . . .' and 'Can I borrow the keys to the bus?'

I said, 'This doesn't really seem like any kind of part for me.'

Their position was, 'Well, you're not a star, what do you want?'

I said, 'I want to be an actor, eventually in the movies. I want to be deep and real and serious. I've already done some weighty roles on TV. On *Bonanza* I played a killer.'

I told Ruth I wasn't interested in the show. I knew from my father that turning down the wrong roles is very important for an actor's career. My father had turned down plenty of roles he didn't feel were quite right, and rarely regretted his decisions. In fact, he'd just turned down a role that was actually written with him in mind – a vain, shallow, buffoon-like newsman on a proposed sitcom starring Mary Tyler Moore. Ruth said that, as a newcomer in Hollywood, I was not in a position to turn down any potential opportunities for work. And there was that dark cloud hanging over my head called the rent.

She convinced me to do a screen test the following Monday morning. And who was the first person I saw? Shirley Jones. Genuinely puzzled, I looked at her and asked, 'What are you doing here?'

'I'm playing your mother!' she told me. And I nearly fell over.

She explained that she'd been talking to them about the lead in the proposed sitcom for weeks and the night before she'd been told that the producers had in fact chosen her for it. Ruth, who was, of course, Shirley's manager as well as mine, had told Shirley that I was auditioning for the role of Shirley's son, but hadn't told me anything at all about Shirley's involvement. I was happy to find Shirley there; I really liked her and had always respected her acting ability.

That same morning I also met Susan Dey, who would be playing my sister Laurie on the show. She was 15, a teenage model who'd appeared in *Seventeen* magazine. Her skin was almost translucent. Very beautiful. Very skinny. Very naïve. And she seemed somehow very alive. She'd never been to California before. She lived in a little town in upstate New York, Mount Kisco. I remember the first time we did a scene, when they said they were going to do a close-up, she came over to me and said, 'What's a close-up?' I would remind her about that many times, which irked her no end.

Because we were so close in age (she was almost 16 and I was 19), we instantly got along. But because of her sweetness and her naïvety and her age, I just couldn't take advantage of her. She also had her agent as a constant chaperone. We went on a couple of dinner dates, but it was always the three of us, her agent watching me like a hawk.

Susan and I hung out a lot and became friends. She confided in me about her life, I confided in her about mine. I met her family. She had depth and was a kind soul. There had been a cool song out by The Buckinghams in 1966 that had the line, 'Susan, looks like I'm losin', I'm losin' my mind.' So every time I called her, for many years, I'd start by singing that line.

We filmed *The Partridge Family* pilot in Los Angeles and Las Vegas. I remember when they showed us the outfits they had designed for us – these ridiculous velvet suits. I was a guy who lived like a hippie in Laurel Canyon. How could I possibly wear these costumes? But I put them on like they asked me to and told myself the pilot would probably never lead to anything anyway. In Hollywood they shoot countless pilots that never actually become TV series.

In the pilot, Shirley, playing a widow, hears a racket in the garage one day. It's her five wholesome but high-spirited kids, who are forming a band. The kids decide to get her to join their band. In reality The Cowsills, consisting of a mother and her six children, had, in 1967 and 1968, recorded such hits as *Indian Lake*, *Poor Baby*, and *The Rain, the Park and the Other Things*. In the proposed show, the family records a number. The smart-aleck middle son (played by Danny Bonaduce) forces a hapless agent (Dave Madden) to listen to their music by shoving a tape recorder under his bathroom stall. Bernard Slade, the creator of the show, thought that scene was so funny that it helped to make the pilot a success.

The agent then books the family for a show in Las Vegas. They drive there in a bus that they've painted in psychedelic colours, don their stunning velvet suits, and, after uplifting words from Mom to get them over their stage fright, proceed to wow the crowd. Everyone loves their music. They're a hit.

The proposed series was expected to track the family's adventures in show business as well as the kids' antics offstage. For me, the biggest thrill of making the pilot was seeing Las Vegas for the first time in my life, although I was bummed out that they wouldn't let me in the casinos because I was under 21.

At the time, I felt that even if the series did become a reality, I didn't see how it could do much for me. After all, I wasn't the star of it. Shirley had top billing; I was just one of the kids. And in scenes with six of us around a dinner table, I figured we'd each get a line or two. After the various dramatic guest shots I'd done, the part seemed like a real comedown. I mean, how much could an actor do with a line like, 'Hi, Mom, I'm home from school' or 'Please pass the milk'?

But we soon got word that ABC had decided to buy the show. It would air Friday nights at 8.30 p.m. Screen Gems didn't offer me a great deal of money for doing it – just $600 a week – but I accepted that. I had heard they didn't pay anyone much money. Three years earlier they had hired The Monkees for $400 a week apiece. I figured at least I'd have steady work for a while. Even if the series just lasted 13 weeks, it would mean I'd be able to hold on to the house I had just bought.

If *The Partridge Family* show clicked, I'd be contractually obliged to do it for seven years, but I'd had too many disappointments to dare assume the show was going to be a hit. This contract also had something in there about the studio owning the rights to my name, voice, likeness and blah, blah, blah. I couldn't really imagine why they'd want those rights. I was just some struggling, unknown actor.

In the summer of 1970, things felt really fine. I had a job. I was making a good living. I had a nice house. My career was just about to break. It was kind of all set up for me. ABC was beginning to crank up the publicity machine. Although I hadn't yet filtered into the consciousness of mainstream America, my face was starting to appear in teen magazines.

Sam Hyman and Steve Ross, another old friend from garage-band days, planned a day for us to all hang out and get back to nature up at Tuna Canyon in Malibu. Steve arrived at the house around 5 a.m. with a couple of girls he knew. They brought peyote buttons. We drank them in blended shakes that tasted awful, really nauseating. In fact, I threw up in Venice before we got to Tuna Canyon.

We drove out there in my 1968 Mustang. There was nothing around the canyon – maybe four homes. The area was a wilderness. We parked on Tuna Canyon Road and hiked up into the mountains. We stripped down to our underwear. Actually, I was in a little loin cloth I made specifically for the occasion. I kept referring to myself as 'Soaring Eagle', saying things like, 'Soaring Eagle see such and such' and 'Soaring Eagle want to fly.' I called Sam 'Running Deer'. Steve was 'Bircher Boots' because he was wearing these black military boots that made me think of the right-wing John Birch Society.

We were there for six hours, from about 8 a.m. to 2 p.m. My nervous system was tumbling but it made me feel really good. It was a magnificent day: blue sky, 75 degrees, perfect. We'd brought a joint with us and enjoyed that. We were just all hanging together. It was simply an experience of being in tune with nature, feeling like a wild animal. We barely noticed it when the girls left, saying that their throats were parched and they had to go find some water.

Sam, Steve and I were sunning ourselves, with our clothes lying nearby on some rocks, when suddenly we heard this whirling and this loud – really loud – amplified voice from above us.

'Dave, Sam and Steve. Go back to the road. We are the sheriffs.'

We looked up and there was a whirlybird. Since the cops were always hassling young people in those days, instinctively we started running, but how do you escape from a helicopter? We were stoned and confused. Our mouths felt like they were filled with camel dung. We hadn't had any water in God knows how many hours. We couldn't find the girls. One minute we were in paradise, the next it was like *Apocalypse Now*.

We got our clothes together.

'Can you handle it?' Sam asked me. His eyes were like saucers.

'I can handle it,' I said, but I could barely get the words out.

Our hearts were pounding. We hiked maybe a mile and a half back to the road and we heard: 'This is one Adam-12. I have three Caucasian males . . .' Cops were tearing my car apart. They had already questioned the girls, who had by this point wandered back to the car. They looked scared and were worried that they'd blown it by giving the cops our names.

Those cops were classic – butch haircuts, military swagger. And to them we were just some freaky hippie scum. They pulled everything out of my car: the seats, the floor mats, the spare tyre, my guitar. They spent hours looking for some sign of drugs saying, 'We know you've been smoking pot. We can see it in your eyes.' I was shaking. All I could think of was my manager. How would I be able to explain being busted for drugs to Ruth? My whole career would fall apart because there was a morals clause in my contract. I got really scared. All I could think was, *I could easily lose my job. Screen Gems will hire someone else to play Keith Partridge in a second.* This was a lot more serious than getting kicked out of some high school.

The cops found no drugs in the car, nothing stronger than my bottles of aspirin and vitamins. They let us go with just a ticket for illegal parking. I was still shaking. I was in no shape to drive home. And once I got there, I was too wired to sleep for almost two days.

7 Back in the USSR . . .

The good folks at Screen Gems anticipated making money not just from the TV show but from recordings, which would be released on Bell Records, an offshoot of Columbia Pictures and Screen Gems, and whatever other *Partridge Family*-related items teenagers could be persuaded to buy. The producers hoped *The Partridge Family* might prove as popular with TV viewers as *The Monkees* had, and thus generate comparable sales of albums and other merchandise. In reality, *The Partridge Family*, in terms of audience appeal and merchandising success, far surpassed *The Monkees*.

Needless to say, I didn't see any of this coming. I never dreamed how it might impact on me. And, of course, I had no aspirations – much less expectations – of becoming a recording artist. I just thought of myself as an actor when I signed to do the show. In fact, when we filmed *The Partridge Family* pilot, which included a couple of musical numbers, I didn't actually sing. Like the other cast members, I simply lip-synched to tracks that had been pre-recorded by a group of highly respected studio musicians and singers. As it turned out, however, those would be the only Partridge Family recordings on which I didn't sing.

> **Bob Claver (executive producer):** We never planned to have any of the cast sing. The singing was all going to be done by the Bahler brothers (John and Tom) and Jackie Ward.

Ruth was eager to have Shirley and me participate in the making of all Partridge Family recordings and get a share of whatever profits they might generate. She telephoned Wes Farrell, who had been selected by the record company and the studio to produce The Partridge Family records. Ruth insisted, 'You guys don't know this, but David is actually a very good singer. He sang on Broadway, he played in rock and roll bands in high school. He can give you just what you need.'

The head of Bell Records, Larry Utall, could hardly have cared whether I sang or not. His attitude was always, 'We don't need artists. We just need good producers. *They're* the ones who create hit records.' To him a singer was just someone to be used. I always felt as if he treated me with a certain contempt, and he's one of the few people from those days I still loathe. But the decision to use me or not was Wes Farrell's.

> **Wes Farrell:** The project was offered to me because we had had success that paralleled *The Partridge Family* in several ways with The Cowsills and Every Mother's Son. We knew how to put Top 40 projects together. The image matching the music was the name of the game. Larry Utall showed me the pilot and the rest is history. You had a young guy named David Cassidy who had star image written all over him.
>
> When I entered into the agreement to produce, I was told that the only person who would be singing was Shirley Jones. At my

> request, the producers of the show called David Cassidy and asked him if he knew how to sing. He came down and sang to a couple of records, Crosby, Stills & Nash and Chicago. Then I wrote the songs for The Partridge Family in David's vocal range. Everything was written with him in mind. David was a one hundred-percenter. He never backed away from his commitment one iota.

Screen Gems had turned over the recordings part of the deal to Bell Records. Unbeknownst to me, Bell in turn had signed a contract with Farrell giving him long-term control of The Partridge Family recordings, including the rights to produce records featuring any or all members of *The Partridge Family* cast. Farrell already 'owned' me before I even met with him. I was naïve about the business.

It was Farrell who created The Partridge Family's sound. He selected the songwriters, the songs (some of which he wrote himself) and put the studio musicians and singers together. He had had such 60s successes as *Come a Little Bit Closer*, a 1964 hit for Jay and the Americans, *Hang on Sloopy*, a 1965 hit for the McCoys, *Let's Lock the Door (and Throw Away the Key)*, a 1965 hit for Jay and the Americans and *Come on Down to My Boat*, a 1967 hit for Every Mother's Son. He'd also written *Boys*, which was recorded by the Beatles as well as The Shirelles. He'd produced records for Johnny Maestro and the Brooklyn Bridge and The Cowsills, which is, I'm sure, why Larry Utall hired him. A no-brainer, right?

Farrell said I sounded great, adding, 'We'll be doing a recording session in two weeks. I'll give you the lyrics beforehand so you can learn them.'

We recorded most of The Partridge Family songs at Western Studio Two, where all those hits by the Beach Boys, Sonny & Cher and The Mamas & the Papas were cut.

The Partridge Family songs were chosen by Wes and Uttal

and presented to me in batches. In the very beginning I would be given lyric sheets and a cassette, a piano player would come and play the tunes, then I would go away for a couple of hours and learn them. Then it became clear that I didn't need that much time. I could learn the songs in a second. We'd record three or four songs at each session, depending upon their complexity. Every one was a live vocal in the vocal booth at Western Two. At 7.10 p.m. we'd wrap shooting *The Partridge Family* and I'd hop in my car, drive over the hill and they'd have a sandwich and water or a Coke or 7 Up waiting for me. Then I would go in the studio, where Wes was already working with the band, putting the first arrangement together.

I worked all night, every night. I would sing live on every track. The first step was to record the rhythm section and then the song with a lead vocal. Then the background singers would come in after the tracks were done and then the sweetening, the strings and horns. The background singers, John Bahler, his brother Tom and Jackie Ward, were some of the most successful commercial singers in the business. John Bahler did all of the vocal arranging. He was amazing.

I can't say I didn't like any of the finished songs, but I preferred the rawness of just the rhythm section and myself singing the song. But I understand that they were more commercial records with the great horns and strings and the background vocals.

Among the few songs we recorded at the very first session was *I Think I Love You*. When they played that back in the studio, it was the first time I'd ever heard a vocal of mine on tape. I was happy that Farrell was using me as the group's lead singer. He had come up with songs that were real pop showcases for me.

Contractually, Shirley had to be on every track, so she recorded but rarely did we mix her in. She'd overdub her parts for a whole album in a single session and they'd put in a little blip of her going, 'do do do do do do, I think I love you'. She is on the records, but you never actually hear her. It was all background singer Jackie Ward. Shirley didn't care at the time, though I think she cares now, when people think that's her voice.

I was nervous. I didn't want to screw up or cause problems for all these pros who had no idea who I was. We'd be chatting and I'd hear some voice on the loudspeaker saying, 'Could you please ask the singer, whatever his name is, to shut up?' Or we'd start to do a take and some voice would request, 'Can you ask the singer not to slow down?', or 'Can you ask the singer not to rush?' I was totally overwhelmed by the experience.

In a three-hour period we'd cut three or four sides. That's without strings or horns or background vocals, which would be added later. I didn't really play the guitar on the early sessions. On TV it would look like I was playing, but the audience would actually be hearing some pop session player like Larry Carlton, Louie Shelton or Dean Parks. As time went on, I did get to play on a few Partridge Family tracks, but basically Farrell wanted to leave it to better, quicker players. I really only got to play on a regular basis later, on my own records.

To give The Partridge Family a distinctive, readily recognisable instrumental sound, Farrell decided to feature the harpsichord, rather than the usual acoustic or electric piano, on our recordings. Playing the harpsichord for us on *I Think I Love You* was Larry Knechtel, who had played piano on *Bridge Over Troubled Water* by Simon & Garfunkel and had worked with Duane Eddy, The Byrds and Phil Spector, and who would soon become part of the successful band, Bread. I remember him breaking up laughing during the harpsichord solo when we recorded *I Think I Love You*. I have no idea what was so funny, but they managed to filter or edit it out somehow.

The bright horn leading the ensemble on *The Partridge Family* theme song, *C'mon, Get Happy*, belonged to none other than jazz great Shorty Rogers, who periodically contributed music to the show, as did such seasoned pros as Hugo Montenegro and George Duning. The producers finessed the issue of whether The Partridge Family actually played and sang on their recordings by running a line in the show's closing credits claiming that The Partridge Family's performances had been 'augmented' by other musicians.

During the four years I was recording The Partridge Family albums, I was never allowed to become the songwriter I should have been because of the control that Wes Farrell had. I did write a few songs on those albums, but I'd usually have to write with Wes; rarely would I be allowed to write or record anything of my own. Part of the reason was money and at times I blamed Wes's ego, although he was good at what he did and I was young and inexperienced.

Although most people didn't appreciate the merit of the songs back then, I think that the fact that they've held up to time proves they were good. Although it wasn't my personal taste in music when I was 19 and 20, I've always been proud of the work I did. I was fortunate that I was working with the greatest musicians, the greatest writers. I learned how to write from being around amazing songwriters like Tony Romeo, Wes Farrell, Gerry Goffin, Barry Mann and Cynthia Weil. I had an education that no college or music academy could have ever given me. I learned fast. I was like a sponge.

Tony Romeo, who wrote *I Think I Love You*, had previously written some of The Cowsills' most memorable songs, including *Indian Lake* and *Poor Baby*. He was one of the great lyrical and musical forces of the era – unique and very special. Through Wes, Tony and I became friends. Wes didn't have the depth that Tony had. Years later I had to remind Tony about *Point Me in the Direction of Albuquerque*. He'd forgotten about it. I told him it was a brilliant song. Tony was a romantic and he painted pictures with every line.

Tony Romeo: The story in the song *Point Me in the Direction of Albuquerque* actually occurred one summer night in New York City. I was browsing at a newspaper kiosk when I first laid eyes on the little waif. Wherever you are darlin', I hope you made it to Albuquerque.

Another song of Tony's, *Summer Days*, is very evocative and provocative. I also really liked *You Are Always on My Mind*. I loved the first line. 'Wake up in the morning feeling all right, 'til I recall you're gone from my life, and I stare like a dummy against the wall.' That was such a great hook. I loved that song and I've never done it live.

Russell Brown and Irwin Levine, who wrote *I Woke Up in Love This Morning*, one of the biggest Partridge Family hits, also wrote such chart-toppers as *Tie a Yellow Ribbon*, *Knock Three Times* and *Candida*, which Tony Orlando and Dawn recorded for Bell in the early 70s. Farrell got Gerry Goffin, who'd co-written pop hits like *The Loco-Motion*, *Up on the Roof*, *Pleasant Valley Sunday*, *I'm into Something Good*, *One Fine Day* and *Will You Love Me Tomorrow*, to write material for The Partridge Family, too. Even Paul Anka was persuaded to do a little writing for us, contributing songs like *One Night Stand*.

Everything we did was about happiness, joy, light; the songs are positive, inspirational. Love them or hate them, you need to look at them objectively for what they are. *Sound Magazine*, the third album, is the best Partridge Family album we ever did. It had the best songs and, to me, it all came together during those sessions.

Not to say that *I Can Feel Your Heartbeat* and *It's One of*

Those Nights aren't great songs and records; I love them. But the first album and the third album were the best, in my opinion. There were two or three great songs on the first album: *Point Me in the Direction of Albuquerque*, *I Think I Love You* and *Heartbeat*. And the third album had songs like *Summer Days*, *Echo Valley 2-6809*, *One Night Stand* and *You Are Always on My Mind*.

The studio drummer, Hal Blaine, has played on more hits than anybody on the face of the earth, I think. He made classic records from *Good Vibrations* to *The Beat Goes On* to *California Dreamin'*. He played with Elvis. He played with everybody. And he played on almost all of my Partridge Family and solo records.

Jim Gordon, who was also a drummer and played on *Rock Me Baby*, was in Derek and the Dominoes. Their song *Layla* was on the car radio as I drove to the studio. I said to Jim, 'Hey, I heard your new single. *Layla*'s great.' And he said, 'Yeah, I wrote it.' And I went, 'You did not.' He went, 'Yeah. I wrote it.'

Mike Melvoin was at the piano and Jim said, 'Mike, get up.' Jim got out from behind the drums, walked over to the piano and played the whole song, all seven minutes of it. My jaw dropped. I went, 'Jim, where did you learn how to play like that?'

A very tragic story about him. I got to know him fairly well, but he was getting burned. I think Eric Clapton, Duane Allman and those guys were heavily into drugs and it was tough hanging around them without indulging. I think Eric's talked quite a bit about it, you know, the amount of drug-induced creativity and what happens to you when they stop the tape. And poor Jim, he started hearing voices in his head and he just couldn't cope. It was very, very tragic, very sad. Jim has been in an institution since he was convicted of a felony and lost his mind. I think that very few people now think of him or acknowledge him, but he was one of the greats.

Mike Melvoin was a big influence on The Partridge Family sessions. He played on 90 per cent of the material that we recorded. He created and played the piano lick on *I'll Meet You Halfway*. He arranged the rhythm sections with Wes. Wes was valuable, but Mike was the real arranger and the players would sometimes give their input. Each player would listen to the demo and a key was chosen based on everything they knew about my voice.

Mike Melvoin: Bubble gum music for kids was often quite dumb and very unsophisticated. The Partridge Family music was crafted to be very smart. I'm very proud of the music we made. We knew we were in the presence of the absolute 'A' band. This is as high as it gets on the studio-musicians' food chain. As a result, we had a standard to maintain. It was a matter of personal pride. Our names were on these records as the people who played this music and we had a reputation to uphold and we were bound and determined to do it.

We really loved David. David was a joy in the studio. We had a lot of fun together. He knew what it meant to be a pro and he was a *mensch*. We all became friends with him and we wanted to make David sound great. David was stage-ready when he was a kid. There was no hint of the amateur about him. He was a young tenor. A young guy with a higher voice is capable of singing love lyrics and sounding innocent. That was part of the sociological formula of David's appeal to young girls. He was not a threat. Putting the same lyrics in the hands of a baritone singer would have been ominous.

Wes had some problems with the way I naturally sounded. In his opinion my voice had too much power. He wanted my voice to sound light and young and airy. He didn't want any character in it. But what was so flawed about that idea is that you lose any sense of individuality. He had me double-track vocals (the way Neil Sedaka had so often done) to give my voice added pop-ness and, by altering the tape speed, he was able to raise the pitch of my voice a half-tone above what it actually was. I didn't catch on to that trick until we'd made a couple of albums. When we made *Sound Magazine* I insisted he stopped doing that.

John Bahler: David was unbelievable. When he started he was 19 years old. David had a lot of confidence, but I don't think he knew how good he was. He was a monster talent and a neat guy. He was an entertainer as well as a singer and that came across on tape. He had personality to his voice and that's why he was so huge, because that is very rare.

Right before *The Partridge Family* aired in the summer of 1970, I was on the set making episode three or four. When I was on a break somebody walked me out of the gate and into a studio. Wes Farrell was there and said, 'Here's the theme for the television series. It's called *C'mon, Get Happy*.'

They played me the track and Wes sort of sang me the song once. I read through the lyrics, did one take and that was it. I was in the studio maybe 11 minutes. I walked back on to the set and never thought another moment about it. I re-recorded one verse the next year, because they'd changed some of the lyrics. And I never heard it again. Never. I never saw the show. I was working every Friday night. There were no videotape recorders then, so if you missed the show, you missed it. Which also explained a lot of the hysteria. You didn't see performers on MTV or VH1 in those days. People saw their favourite stars in live performances and on filmed television shows that could only be seen when they were broadcast.

For the last 30 years, people have walked up to me singing, 'Hello, world, here's a song that we're singing, c'mon get happy.'

For a long time, I'd go, 'Huh?' It was never on an album until Arista put the song on a *Partridge Family Greatest Hits* CD. People still play *C'mon, Get Happy* or *I Think I Love You* every time I visit a radio station to do an interview. It's a great little theme song and is really representative of the show and the era.

All the recordings we made were intended for eventual use on the TV show and for release as singles and/or on albums, which the show would be promoting. Remember, this was the same company that had brought America *The Monkees*. So, of course, they knew exactly what was going on from day one. But even when we began recording, I still didn't get it. My attitude was, *Gee, I'm going to be a rock and roll singer!* I wasn't really even listening to the songs. I was just so caught up in being among such great musicians. I was naïve.

They made me some test pressings of the unfinished recordings. I took these lacquer pressings over to my friend Don Johnson. We spent an evening together. I played a few songs, all excited that the producers of *The Partridge Family* were now permitting me to make records, not just act. Don was an aspiring singer himself, not just an actor (he got his first film work that year in the low-budget *The Magic Garden of Stanley Sweetheart;* he was still really struggling as an actor). Don seemed really happy for me, just blown away that I'd somehow parlayed my interest in music into what could be an actual recording career. Neither of us could anticipate what was in store for me as a singer. Over the next couple of years, I continued to see Don from time to time. He and Sal Mineo went in separate directions. Don hooked up with one of Sal's ex-girlfriends, as I recall.

Meanwhile, on *The Partridge Family* set at The Burbank studios, where we were filming, an optimistic spirit developed well before the first episode aired in the fall.

Shirley Jones: I had a very strong feeling about the show. One never knows with television, of course; it's a roll of the dice at best. But everybody felt good about it. It was new and had a lot of things going for it: the humour, the music, the possibility of hit records, the possibility of David becoming a young teen idol. We were aware of all of those possibilities and they all came to be. The music was not my cup of tea, but I figured it was aimed at a younger generation. I was used to singing Broadway and other 'legit' music.

As we got closer to the first broadcast, I started realising that people from coast to coast would see me singing these songs and think that's the kind of music I was into. The more I thought about it, the more uncomfortable and out of control I felt.

I realised Screen Gems had every intention of trying to market me as a teen idol. When they started talking about all of the merchandise and music they planned to sell, I got really scared. I panicked. I thought: *I don't want to be a teen idol. I want to be thought of as a serious actor.*

I saw the first teen magazines bearing pictures of me, playing guitar in the Keith Partridge clothes Screen Gems had had custom made. The studio was beginning to craft an image of me as this innocent young singer/guitarist/songwriter. I lost it. That just wasn't me.

I called Ruth and said I wanted out. I was only 20 and highly concerned with what other people thought about me. You know, you're just becoming a man, you're feeling like, *I want to be cool, I want to be accepted, I don't want to do cute records for young kids, because that's not cool.* I didn't want my friends to think less of me. I got into a lengthy argument with Ruth.

I tried to tell her, 'This isn't me. I'm into Hendrix and B.B. King. And I want to be thought of as a credible artist, perceived, like my father, as a respected, working actor.'

And she said, 'You'll be perceived as a respected, working superstar.'

I had moved out on my own, done what I wanted to do rather than going to college like everyone else. I'd forged my own way as a struggling actor. And suddenly there's my dad, stepmother and manager standing before me saying, 'You've got to do it. If you don't, you'll be sued. You won't have an agent. You won't get jobs. You can forget about keeping that house on Laurel Canyon. Bye-bye, baby!'

It was at that point that I gave up and said, 'OK, I'll do what I've got to do.'

I certainly wasn't given much, if any, chance to express myself artistically, either on The Partridge Family records or on the solo albums (yes, albums!) I began making under my own name the following year. They were produced by the same producer, also for Bell Records. Contractually, I had to do as I was told. I felt they were using me, and I resented that. As I became more popular, I certainly would have liked to have had some say over what and how I recorded, and what image I projected to the public.

That said, I've also got to acknowledge – as an adult looking back over three decades later – that I have great respect for Farrell and the others who created that music. Farrell didn't get a lot of recognition for his accomplishments because bubble gum music was not taken seriously. But, I have to say, it was quality bubble gum music. It was innocent but well-crafted. In retrospect, I realise Farrell had a great understanding of the genre. He understood commercial viability and how to translate that into a pop song.

And Wes had a real instinct for spotting talent. The songwriters he brought to The Partridge Family were gifted pros. As Keith, I was supposed to write all of the Partridge Family songs and I'm sure there were some young fans who believed that. In fact, we used the best songwriters in the field.

By the time the air date for the first episode of *The Partridge Family* approached – 25 September 1970 – we all felt confident the show would catch on. I was a little skeptical of how my friends would react to it. I'd been so busy working of late I hadn't had a chance to hang out much with Kevin Hunter or any of my other pals. I looked forward to us all getting together some time. Maybe we could celebrate what I hoped would be the show's success. I hoped they wouldn't think what I was doing was too lame.

At the 'suggestion' of the studio, I watched the first episode at my Laurel Canyon house with the editor of *Tiger Beat*, Sharon Lee. I even cooked (if you want to call it that) macaroni and cheese.

Even though the music (and the show, I have to admit) was a little lightweight for my taste, I thought the basic fantasy we were offering on the show was one any teen would want to buy into. Here we were, a family who all got along well enough to form a band. And this band, organised in our garage, was soon turning out hit records and playing on the road. What kid wouldn't want to believe in that fantasy? In fact, as soon as the show went on the air, we began getting letters from kids saying they'd been inspired to take up an instrument or form a band. Many of them went out and bought Partridge Family sheet music so that they could play our songs, which I'm sure pleased the Columbia corporate bigwigs, since Screen Gems also owned the publishing rights to all the songs The Partridge Family performed.

Our confidence was shaken somewhat by the first reviews the show received. Upon viewing the initial episode of *The Partridge Family*, in which the family formed the band and achieved its first hit record, *The Christian Science Monitor*'s Diana Loercher sniped (28 September 1970): 'The show stacks implausibility upon implausibility from the hit record to the psychedelic bus they tool around in . . . It's all so predictable that the viewer is left with a sense of wasted time and effort . . .'

And two days later, *Variety*, the showbiz bible, itemised a slew of shortcomings. Their critic complained that Dave Madden 'overplays unmercifully, only Miss Jones and David Cassidy look like they're singing their own roles, the songs (by Shorty Rogers and Kelly Gordon) were nondescript bubble gum tunes with no believable hit potential, and there are just too many loopholes. Even the teenage girls who now buy records will see through the flimsy premise that the "Partridge" kids could make it in today's record market. Show's chances look slim.'

We wondered if The Partridge Family records were going to be accepted. After all, the first release, *I Think I Love You*, didn't seem to be moving the first few days it was out. I'm sure a lot of people believe that if a record company spends enough money on publicity and promotion and payola, it can make any record a hit. But that's not quite true. The public has to want the record. And some disc jockeys were reluctant to play *I Think I Love You* because they knew The Partridge Family was a manufactured-for-television group. I actually saw one programme director turn down a hundred dollars that was offered to him by a record promoter to play *I Think I Love You*. Not for any amount of money was he willing to give it air play.

Sam Hyman: I remember when it was just starting to take off and I was sitting in David's bedroom and he was strumming the guitar. *I Think I Love You* was already out but we had no idea how big he was going to be. He was trying to practise *Voodoo Child (Revisited)* by Jimi Hendrix. He said something to me like, 'I'm going to be big. I'm going to be bigger than Elvis.' I remember he brought up Elvis because Elvis was the king at that point and we had gone to an Elvis concert at The Forum with Wes Farrell. David watched it and said, 'I could do that better.' He wasn't too impressed with the show. He liked Elvis but he was watching with a critical eye even then.

It's interesting that he had that much confidence in himself. I guess that's part of what made him who he is. There was a level of confidence, which might have been construed by some as cockiness.

There's an old saying in sales. 'A woman won't buy from a hungry salesman.' And the young girls wouldn't have been attracted to a young guy who was somewhat desperate, not confident about himself.

I saw Elvis for the first time at The Forum in Los Angeles. That night he wasn't electric. I wanted to see him and the boys playing like they did on the 1968 TV special, but the show was very slick and kind of Vegas-y. They made the announcement, 'Ladies and gentlemen, Elvis has left the building,' and I remember Wes Farrell turned to me and said, 'Who cares?'

Sam Hyman: The first time we heard *I Think I Love You* on the radio, we were driving on Pacific Coast Highway and all of a sudden it came on, and it was like time stood still for that second. We both kind of looked at each other, eyes getting real wide and we were so stoked. And then it started climbing the charts. David was hearing from the record company every day and they'd say, 'We sold another 12,000 units. It's going to go up another six spots in *Billboard*.' Then it was, 'We got a shot for number one.'

When it reached number one we were all excited, 'Oh my God! You've got the number one song! It went gold!'

The record broke first in the smallest markets, not the sophisticated big cities. But before long, public demand ensured that every rock station was playing it. It made its first appearance on the *Cash Box* pop chart on 26 September 1970 and on the *Billboard* chart 14 days later. It enjoyed a 19-week run (with several weeks in the number one position) on both publications' charts. It turned out to be the biggest-selling record of 1970, with total sales of over three million units in the U.S. and close to five million worldwide.

I Think I Love You is one of the greatest pop songs ever. It was Tony Romeo's third gold record in two years and ensured his staying power. I'll never forget how good I felt when Tony acknowledged that I wasn't just a teen idol and that my talent was much bigger than my fame. And that was the thing that I always believed would carry me through. I had the goods, and I just needed the opportunity to show it.

Lyrically, *I Think I Love You* deals with that moment in our lives when we're faced with the fear of commitment, the obsession with love, the obsession with not being alone, not being lonely, not being abandoned, having a partner, having a romantic endeavour. It's saying, *I'm so afraid of the commitment. I'm afraid to say I don't know what it's all about. I don't know what I'm up against, I have so much to think about, but hey, I think I love you.*

It makes me love it all the more knowing that, generations later, people still carry it with them. As Tony puts it, *I Think I Love You* has been loved, loathed, covered by artists, clobbered by the press, satirised, camped, tramped, muzaked, be-bopped and hip-hopped. To this day, everywhere I go in the world, people come up to me and sing it. A three-year-old kid once left a message on my phone, singing, 'I'm sleeping, and right in the middle of a sweet dream . . . I think I love you.' It was so beautiful. You know, great songs stand the test of time.

I occasionally play it in concert as a ballad on guitar. The song has twelve chords and I don't play all of them correctly because I'm not a sophisticated enough guitarist. My dream would be to play like Eric Clapton, but I don't have the commitment or talent. I could be better than I am, but I'm good enough to satisfy myself and competent enough to do what I want to do. Sometimes, though, I sure wish I could make the instrument sing and speak like very few people can. Jeff Beck makes it speak. Hendrix made it speak. And every time Clapton plays, you just know it's Eric. Even on George Harrison's *While My Guitar Gently Weeps*, you know which guitar licks are Eric's.

The Partridge Family TV show was a hit with the public soon enough, too. It became the most popular show Screen Gems had on the air. And I became the focus of a lot of attention. I began getting constant requests for press interviews, which meant my already meagre amount of free time was being further reduced. When was I supposed to be able to see my friends?

Just one week after *I Think I Love You* hit number one, an old friend I hadn't spoken with in quite a while calls. He starts telling me something about Kevin Hunter having gone down to Westwood Village that day. And I'm remembering how, back when I was younger and had an unlimited supply of free time, Kevin and I used to hang out there almost every day. And this friend is telling me something about Kevin buying some Tuinal from a guy he met down there. Tuinal is a barbiturate. A sleeping pill. And this friend is saying how you never know when you buy drugs on the street what they've been cut with, that maybe this Tuinal had been cut with strychnine or something. But whatever it was, Kevin had overdosed. And he was dead.

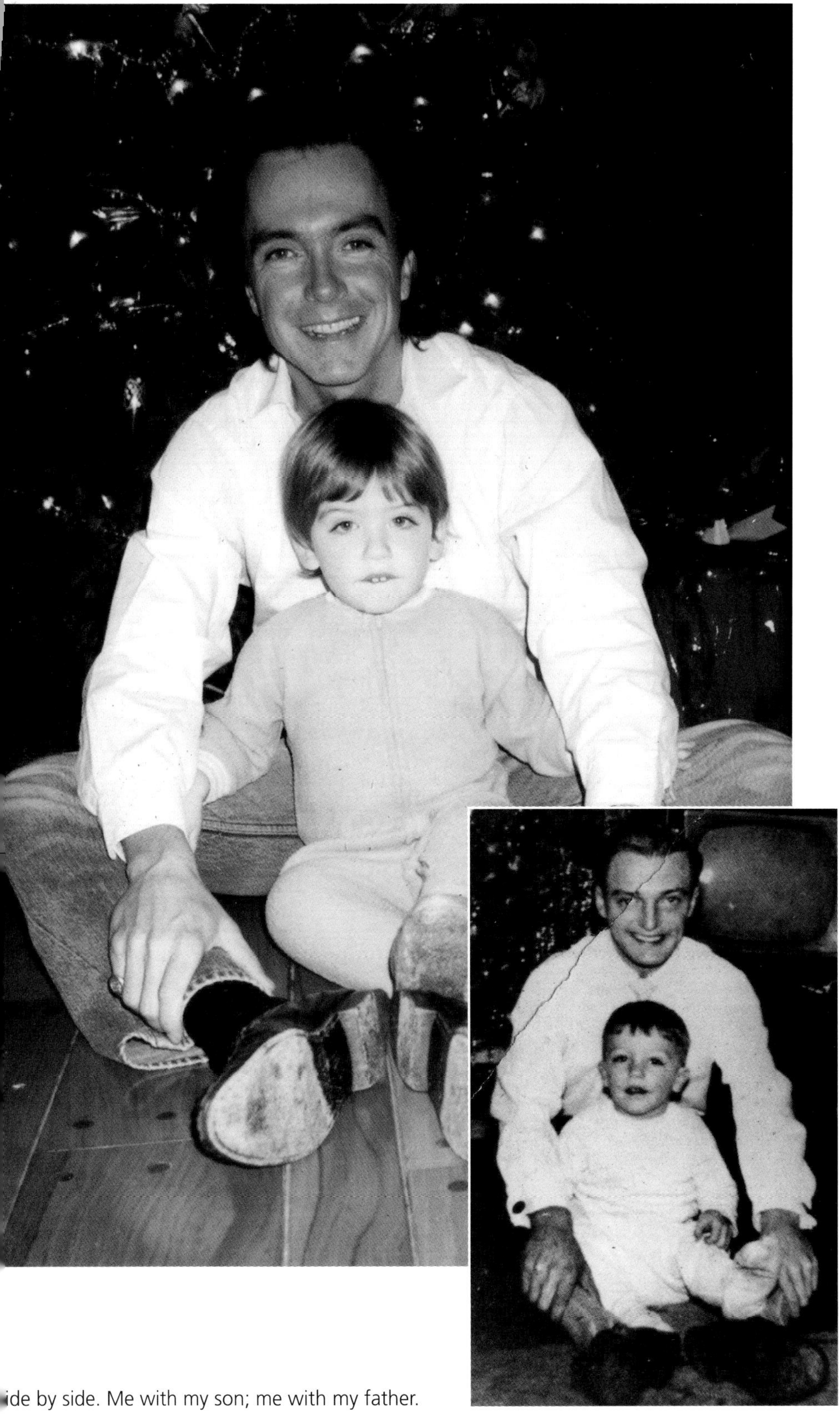

ide by side. Me with my son; me with my father.

The Happy Days
with my 'T.V. sis'.

Shirley and m
on se

THE P.F... WOW!
That was fun...
I miss them now.

PHOTOGRAPHS BY HENRY DILTZ

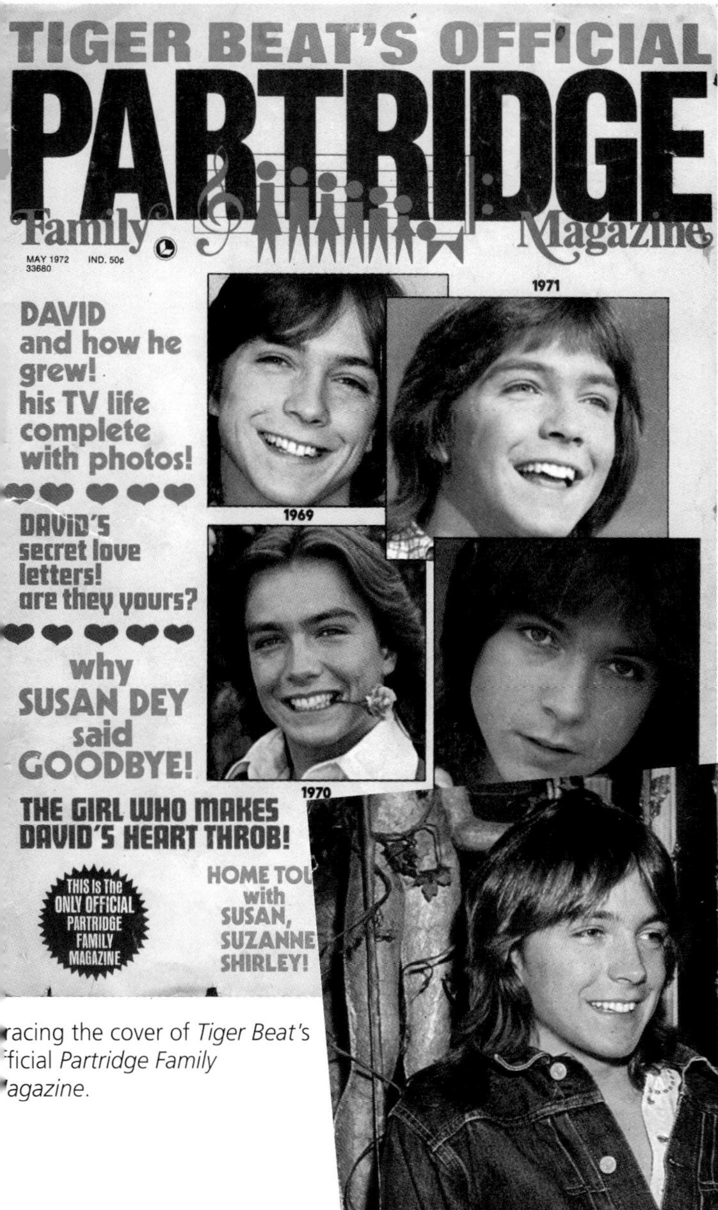

racing the cover of *Tiger Beat*'s
ficial *Partridge Family*
agazine.

TIGER BEAT'S OFFICIAL
PARTRIDGE
Family
Magazine
MAY 1972 IND. 50¢
33680
DAVID
and how he grew!
his TV life complete with photos!
DAVID'S secret love letters! are they yours?
why SUSAN DEY said GOODBYE!
THE GIRL WHO MAKES DAVID'S HEART THROB!
THIS Is The ONLY OFFICIAL PARTRIDGE FAMILY MAGAZINE
HOME TOU
with
SUSAN,
SUZANNE
SHIRLEY!
1969
1970
1971

PHOTOGRAPHS BY PETERSEN PUBLISHING

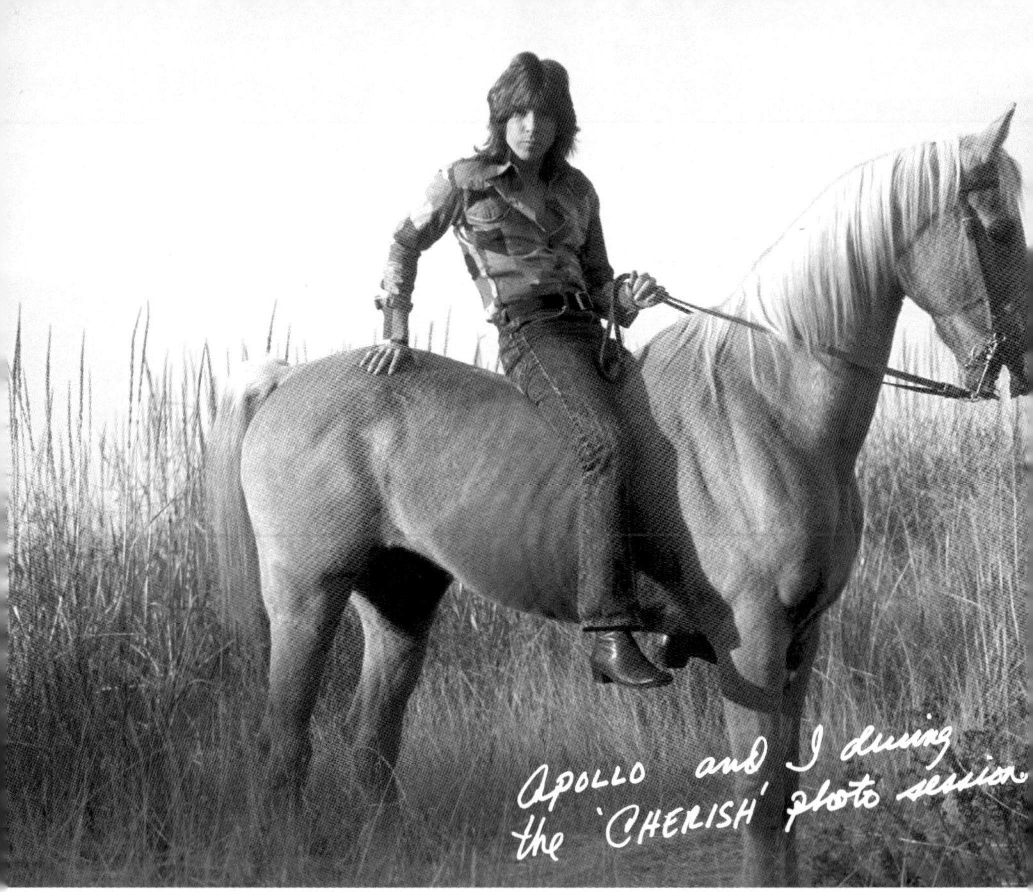
Apollo and I during
the 'CHERISH' photo session

Above: Making album covers in 1972.

Below: Bob Hope and me in 197

The ODD COUPLE.

PHOTOGRAPHS BY HENRY DILTZ

SAM AND the band all drank while he slept!

njoying a tour of Australia in 1974.

I had some friends meet me at the airport from time to time...

May 1974: a memorable time for fan Jane Charnock, seen here outside the White City Stadium.

Jane's ticket for the show, and her David Cassidy badge.

MEL BUSH ORGANISATION LTD.
presents
DAVID CASSIDY
AT WHITE CITY STADIUM
WOOD LANE, SHEPHERDS BUSH, W.12
SUNDAY, 26th MAY, 1974
From 8 p.m. - 10.30 p.m.
GATES OPEN 6 p.m.
£2·20
№ 4911 STANDS AND TERRACES OTHER THAN GRASS AREA
TO BE RETAINED FOR PASS OUT PURPOSES
SPECIAL NOTICE
Patrons are requested to make sure that they obtain the OFFICIAL PROGRAMMES and POSTERS which are only ON SALE INSIDE THE STADIUM.

PHOTOGRAPHS BY JANE CHARNOCK

Performing live at the Melbourne Cricket Ground. Not a bad crowd!

PHOTOGRAPH BY HENRY DILTZ

PHOTOGRAPH BY DAVID BRIDGER

Me with Dicky Leahy and David Bridger, celebrating success.

With my manager, Ruth Aarons.

My arm around my dear Auntie Ruth...

PHOTOGRAPH BY HENRY DILTZ

I heard those words and I went numb. Echoing through my thoughts was all of the anti-drug rhetoric I'd been told for years. All those things people had said about drugs killing you were true. I should have known something like this was going to happen.

All of our old friends gathered at his funeral. Some made small talk with me before it started, trying to say something nice about me having a hit record. They said it didn't sound like me. It didn't sound like my voice or my style. One said it didn't do me justice. *Who gave a damn?* At the time the only thing that was important was the body lying in front of us.

Kevin's father was looking at us, and maybe at me in particular, sort of glowering. He didn't say anything to me about it, but my friends and I knew he was thinking that we were to blame for Kevin's death. I may have been some guy with a TV show and a hit record now, some guy who was being written up here and there as a new star, but Kevin's father knew the real me. He knew that it could just as easily have been – and maybe *should* have been – me rather than his son in that coffin.

With Kevin's death, a chapter of my life closed. Drugs had already begun losing their fascination for me, and now I just felt like avoiding them altogether. I was so shaken by Kevin's passing. He was such a talent and a true friend. I still think of him a lot.

After Kevin's funeral, I focused on my work. I was determined not to put anything into my body I shouldn't. No cigarettes, no pot, no drugs at all if I could help it. The work was the main thing. I was just going to work very hard. Just keep running, boy. Keep running.

8 *Teen Beat*

I had never read the fan magazines, the teen magazines. I knew some, like *Tiger Beat*, had been around for ages. Others seemed to come and go. But I let them take all the pictures they wanted. At first it was kind of a kick to see myself on a magazine cover. And, of course, I answered all their questions. Where did I live? Where did I shop? And so on.

That seemed fine, until I walked into the Canyon Country Store after work one night and they told me they had been inundated with nearly a thousand fan letters addressed to me care of the store, simply because one magazine had just printed that I shopped there. And some of the letters the fans wrote were alarming: 'I'm your long-lost brother . . ., 'You were adopted, I'm your real mother . . .' Twisted!

Once the show went on the air, it became hard for me even to get into the studio in the morning. In the fall of 1970 there'd routinely be 40 or 50 fans crowding the entrance. Some of the more aggressive girls would bare their breasts, some would follow me while I drove home after working all day. There were girls who'd spend days and nights outside the studio, some even sleeping there. I'd try to smile pleasantly, but I was thinking, *Go home, do something with your lives, don't stand here all day, every day waiting for me.*

Danny Fields (co-editor *16* magazine): David was the perfect teen idol. He had everything. He was in a rock and roll band in the show. He was cute and smart and he was extremely cooperative with the editors of *16* long before I got there. He was always a *mensch*. I appreciated his unhappiness at being thought of as a 16-year-old dumbo when he was 19 years old and the opposite of a dumbo. I understood his frustration because he really wanted to act. David was very talented. He was an excellent and very funny person, a great mimic whose talent was not allowed to blossom on that show, except his talent for being cute. He knew what was wanted of him and he delivered it.

With all of the publicity exposure, it became impossible for me to go in a store or even walk down a street without being stopped by people. At first I enjoyed the sheer novelty of having fans. Quickly I began to sense problems ahead. When you're young, you always believe your dreams will come true even if you don't know how. I had seen my career turning out very differently. I foresaw that my father would be proud of me and I would work in the theatre and become a good working actor. Success would simply be recognition of my talent. Being famous was not my goal. My dad was very pro paying your dues and I think part of him felt like I hadn't paid enough dues and that I hadn't struggled enough. My struggle lasted only two years as opposed to his 20 years of hard work. I had no idea people would react the way they did and that my career would go the way it did.

The teen magazines, which were whipping up frenzied interest in me with their articles, were also running ads telling kids to send in their money and join the official David Cassidy fan club. Or buy David Cassidy love musk. Or David Cassidy love beads. A whole group of these teen magazines was beating the drums, informing the youth of America that David Cassidy was now *it*, the new star they should idolise. Watch his show! Buy his records! Buy anything associated with his name or likeness!

Charles Laufer (publisher, *Tiger Beat*): David first came on my radar when I saw him do an auxiliary part on the *Marcus Welby, MD* TV show. He played a sick kid who got cured and he did a good job and I thought, *Yeah, he looks good*. At the height of his fame we were receiving literally thousands and thousands of letters a week for him. David was by far the biggest teen idol.

The Partridge Family and David Cassidy mail-order items we sold were giant sellers. One of the first things I did was buy another safe. It was very lucrative. *The Partridge Family* was head and shoulders above *The Monkees*. David was The Partridge Family. He was the driving force of *The Partridge Family*. He was the meat and potatoes for *Tiger Beat*.

From acting to performing in concert, he could do anything. I thought he had more acting talent than any of those teen stars including Presley. David was a teen idol but he had the talent to back it up and that's why he still lasts.

Probably six months into *The Partridge Family* being on the air, I called Chuck Laufer, who was the owner and publisher of two teen magazines – *Tiger Beat* and *Rave*. He also put out *The David Cassidy Magazine*, *The Partridge Family Magazine* and ran the fan clubs and all of the rest of it.

I went into his office and said, 'I can't live like this any more. I want you to take me out of your magazines. Take me off your covers.' And he looked at me and laughed, in a kind sort of way.

He said, 'Son, you're very naïve. I'll tell you what, you're a nice kid. We paid a lot of money for the rights to your name.'

I said, 'You didn't talk to me about it.'

And he said, 'I didn't have to. You're what makes our business work. We've waited since The Monkees for you. You can either just strap yourself in and enjoy the ride or make it difficult for yourself and we'll do what we want to anyway, and it will be uncomfortable for all of us. And Screen Gems might see it as counterproductive. So you make the choice. This business is what I do and you have no control over it.'

So I went along with it begrudgingly. Again, I had no control. And it depressed the hell out of me.

Sharon Lee (editor, *The Partridge Family Magazine/Tiger Beat*): Nobody had a magazine like *The Partridge Family Magazine*. Immediately it had 250,000 readers. Since the magazine was sanctioned by the network and delivered what the kids were looking for, I'd go on the set three or four days a week for a year and hang out with David in his trailer. We hit if off really well. After filming was over, we'd go have dinner at Steak & Stein. Then I'd go to the studio with him and I'd watch them record The Partridge Family songs. The music was more important to him than the show. It always was. That's my impression. Even then, he wanted to record different kinds of music, not silly songs.

My friends were brutal about me being in the teen magazines. They laughed at me and tortured me beyond belief. To them, I was a joke. They'd say, 'Who does David dream about and why is he drooling on his pillowcase?' Those magazines were made for little kids.

Laufer was using his magazines to build me up, to fire up

further interest in me, because he'd acquired certain marketing rights from Screen Gems. All the readers who sent in money to join the David Cassidy fan club were – whether they knew it or not – putting money into his pockets, not mine. I never saw a cent. If he could help create enough interest in me to justify publishing new magazines devoted exclusively to *The Partridge Family* – and he had acquired the rights to do just that – it would mean that much more income for him. If fans were willing to spend the little money they had on David Cassidy bubble gum or beads or anything else, that was all right by him. If kids were convinced they had to be David Cassidy fans to be 'with it', he would reap the rewards. Essentially what he said to me boiled down to, 'Look, David, I'm a flesh peddler. You happen to be the flavour of the month.' Little did he, or I, know that month would last three years.

I felt this man was a parasite, growing rich off the public interest in me. He eventually told me, 'Since I've been in the business, you are the biggest single money earner for us. You've generated the most mail of any single person who has been in the business.' He said that the Elvis fan club was the biggest at one time, then the Beatles, and then mine took over the top spot. Eventually, I think it was the Bee Gees that knocked me off.

Considering all the publicity I was getting, I'm sure a lot of people assumed I was making a bundle. But in the fall of 1970, as a star of a popular TV show, I was receiving only the $600 a week I'd originally negotiated, out of which, of course, my agent took ten per cent, my manager took fifteen per cent, and so on. That was it. I received no advances or royalties for making the records. The only guaranteed work I actually had at that point, despite the long-term contract I had with Screen Gems, was one half-season – 13 episodes – of *The Partridge Family*. As public interest warranted, the show would be extended, one half-season at a time.

At the studio I certainly wasn't given star treatment. If I complained about one thing or another, I'm sure the execs considered me 'difficult'. Their attitude was summed up by this remark, 'You'd better tow the line or we'll go out and pull another David Cassidy off the rack.' They made it perfectly clear they considered me – initially, at least – just some interchangeable cog in the grand machinery that they'd built. But I knew the public was responding to *me*, to what *I* had to offer. I wanted to be shown a certain amount of respect.

I tried to talk to them about some of the songs they wanted me to sing. When I heard *Doesn't Somebody Want to Be Wanted*, I finally flipped out. I didn't like the song and I didn't like the vary-speed vocals. Again, it was, 'We don't want you to be *you*. We don't want people to know *you*.'

I hated the idea that they wanted me to talk rather than sing in the middle of it. That talking-over-the-music routine was old when Elvis did it on *Are You Lonesome Tonight?*

I said, 'This is crass commercialism. It's hype. It's jive. It isn't me.'

Wes Farrell freaked out. 'You can't do this!' he shouted. I had no say in what I was to perform; I was just supposed to follow orders. I'd never been good at following orders.

I almost quit the show over the issue. They brought my manager and agent down to the studio. It turned into a nightmare. They actually stopped the shooting of *The Partridge Family* so that my manager could talk to me.

She insisted, 'David, you've got to do that spoken thing.'

I said, 'I'm not doing it, it's the kiss of death.'

Everybody got involved: the head of Bell Records, the head of Screen Gems, the head of Columbia Pictures Industries. It was like, suddenly, I was some big problem to them because I didn't want to do this one thing. I was saying, 'Look, I don't believe in it. I don't think it adds anything to the record.' And they were saying how many more copies they'd be able to sell if I'd talk. That was the bottom line.

They put the pressure on me until I caved. I recorded it exactly the way they dictated. It was horrible. I was embarrassed by it. I begged them not to release it. I still can't listen to it. And, to make matters worse, Farrell used his trick of altering the tape speed to make my voice sound higher than it really was.

But the public loved it. That record wound up on the *Billboard* charts for 12 weeks, peaking at number six, and *Cash Box* had it on the charts for 13 weeks, peaking at number one. Bell Records sold nearly two million singles. I still get requests to sing that song today.

A sitcom with music is more complicated to film than a standard sitcom. And the presence of so many young and inexperienced actors in our cast meant the show took even longer than normal to shoot. In the beginning it would take us six or seven days to complete shooting one episode, and then the cycle would start right up again. I was glad when we seemed to find our stride and could complete an episode in five days. I imagined I'd have weekends free. Yeah, right!

If I had any free time, it soon became clear that I'd be expected to work to promote the show and the records. In the fall of 1970, I went to my first autograph signing, in a store about an hour from Los Angeles. Until I stepped through the door, I couldn't see that there were thousands of kids waiting for me. I'll never forget the screams they let out the moment they saw me. That was the first time I'd ever heard anything like that. I was stunned. I spent three hours signing autographs and only got to half of them.

It was like that every minute of every day. I couldn't get into a venue, I couldn't go anywhere without signing autographs and having photographs taken. It was overwhelming. I never thought signing autographs was fun, although I've always appreciated my fans. I really respected Paul Newman when he made the decision to stop, saying, 'I'm not doing that any more. I've done it for 30 years.'

I've signed my name thousands and thousands of times over the last 35 years. I continue to do it because I know it means something to people and I care about them and appreciate what they've contributed to my life. At every concert, I sign probably 50 to 100 pictures backstage for the promoters, their friends, the sponsors and all the rest of it. And I won't just sign my name. I like to personalise every autograph. For one thing, I like to connect with the person, and I don't want to see one more thing of mine on eBay.

Ruth didn't know anything about the record business or the teen idol business; she'd had no experience with that. Her clients were all older, respected, established figures in the industry. When she saw those screaming fans at that first autograph signing, she began to realise just how big my career could be. None of her other clients had ever elicited screams like that from fans. Ruth felt that young fans were reacting to me in a way that was unique. The $600 a week I was receiving for the TV show was insignificant, she concluded. She began focusing on the rock concert business as a potentially greater money-maker for me.

With hits like *Proud Mary* and *Bad Moon Rising* in 1970, Credence Clearwater Revival was the hottest American rock group around. One day Ruth told me, 'Credence Clearwater just gave a concert that was huge – they got $50,000 for one night. I'm going to get *you* $50,000 a night.'

I thought, *What, is she crazy?* I'd never sung in public. And with the TV show eating up all my time, I wouldn't even have time to prepare an act.

The first concert booking she got me – an 8,000-seat auditorium in Seattle, in October 1970 – was for $8,000. True, that wasn't $50,000 but it sounded astronomical to a guy who was making just $600 a week. I couldn't help thinking, *My only previous performing experience has been limited to friends' garages and rooms, jamming on the blues and numbers by Led Zeppelin, Cream, Hendrix – absolutely nothing like what I'll be expected to do now. What am I going to play?*

Other bookings began pouring in, unsolicited, due to the popularity of the TV show and records. In two weeks my first Partridge Family album had gone platinum, which meant it had sold one million copies. In Seattle, *I Think I Love* You was a number one hit and by that time *Doesn't Somebody Want to Be Wanted* had sold something like a million and a half copies. I had two hit singles and the first Partridge Family album and my fans knew every track. Ruth said I could count on spending every weekend doing concerts – two a day.

Ten days before my first concert, I didn't even have a band. I asked Steve Ross, my old garage band cohort, to join me. I told him he'd have to start learning Partridge Family songs *fast*. No problem! I figured it would be great to have buddies on the road with me.

A guy named Richard Delvy, whom I'd met through Bell Records, was hired to save the day, and he became my musical director. Richard hired some studio musicians, including drummer Ed Green and bassist Emory Gordon – really great players – to back me up. We put together a good-sized road band, including a few horns, plus three back-up singers, who also could serve as a warm-up act for me if need be: Kim Carnes, Dave Ellingson and Brooke Hunnicut. My good friend Sam Hyman was hired, too. He quit his job as an assistant film editor to become my merchandise guy, which, in the beginning, was just selling posters. I think there were 600 posters made for the

Seattle show and they were gone in the first hour. He was overwhelmed. We were so innocent.

Sam Hyman: I made the proposal to him that I manage his merchandising so I could travel with him. The poster was huge. I take great pride in that because I went through thousands of photographs and just used my gut. Later, I think we produced 10,000, and they were selling quickly. It was a killer picture, you know, because he is so photogenic. He very seldom took a bad picture. That poster was the top-selling poster until Farrah Fawcett's. Everywhere we went, we would usually sell out of merchandise. There was also a programme, a little photo album and then there were love stickers, that kind of stuff. The vendors would always say, 'I have never seen anything sell so fast and so much. Do you have more?'

Dave Ellingson: We got a call from Richard Delvy, who said, 'Hey, do you wanna do this tour?' He told us we had to stretch the show and asked if Kim and I could open. We never had a situation where you walk out and the entire sports arena yells in unison, 'WE WANT DAVID!' Kim and I just kind of looked at each other and went, 'Oh, this is gonna be fun.'

For his first show, David did great. He had a big supportive band of really good players. He had background singers and he had horns and so he was able to strut and go out there and do his stuff. He was well taken care of with a good show around him. He just came out and nailed it.

We travelled to our first concert dates with 16 people, including the musicians, singers, road manager and an equipment guy. I thought that was a lot, but eventually I wound up carrying some 30 people on my tours, including security guys.

I was too busy with the TV show to work on an act. I figured we could do every number from *The Partridge Family Album* (which enjoyed a phenomenal 68-week run on the *Billboard* pop album chart, beginning 31 October 1970). To fill out the bill, I could do songs popularised by Crosby, Stills & Nash and Buffalo Springfield, and maybe a little blues. I figured the kids would be going, 'What's that? And who cares?' because that material was from before their time. But I really only had about an album's worth of Partridge Family material to use, so what choice did I have?

For the first date, Ruth, Wes Farrell, and seemingly everyone from the record company flew up. It was a big event. Seattle was sold out and it was madness. It was the first time I'd heard mass hysteria. I was petrified because I'd never played a live show before. I didn't know what I was doing, but instinct took over. I only had one rehearsal, and that was in front of Kenny Lieu, who was taking photographs for *Tiger Beat*, *The Partridge Family Magazine* and *The David Cassidy Magazine*.

I was nervous to begin with and it didn't help that Seattle was hit that weekend by the worst storm in ten years. For a while we weren't even sure any planes would be flying into the area.

I was backstage when Kim and Dave opened the show. When the lights went out after their performance, the whole place went crazy. There was all this screaming from 8,000 girls and boys ranging in age from about seven to 17, with most around 13. I remember the emcee addressing the audience: 'Give me a D! Give me an A! Give me a V! Give me an I! Give me a D! What does that spell?' And all of these kids screamed 'DAVID!' and generally went berserk.

I was in an outfit that had just been made for me. I bounded out on the stage and was hit with so much light that for a moment I couldn't see anything. All those kids had cameras and they all wanted pictures. It created a startling, spectacular effect for several minutes – thousands of those big old Sylvania flashbulbs popping off.

My heart was pounding. I was sweating profusely. My energy was really flying. The first song was *I Can Hear Your Heartbeat.* A good rockin' song – high energy. And it builds. Just three minutes long – perfect for an opener. I needn't have worried about whether the kids were going to like me. They were screaming – and in some cases fainting – before I got my first note out. I rushed through the show. Everything was going 150 miles an hour. I felt overwhelmed by the strength of the reaction I was getting.

Richard Delvy: I think we had about a week to get a show together before his first concert in Seattle. I put together an Elvis Presley type of show for David: lots of singers, lots of brass, just a knockdown band. The shows in Seattle and Portland went great. The places were packed. David and the band performed great. No one knew what was gonna happen but it worked out very well.

After those shows, David's touring agency, William Morris, realised that he was a viable live act and felt he was a star. They began booking him and we were playing shows every weekend across the country. I had to wear ear plugs at the show because the little girls would scream so loud that it would hurt your ears. It was so high-pitched that it drove you nuts.

I couldn't hear any of my vocals. I couldn't hear my guitar and my amp was turned up to ten. To try to sing when you can't hear yourself is impossible. I'm sure I sang a lot of songs out of tune because I couldn't hear the band. The audience never stopped screaming; I never stopped flying. That's all I remember. That's the thing about kids in their early teens. They're out of control with their emotions. It's insane. When they love you, they let you know it. If they don't love you they let you know that, too.

I think there were some parents in the audience, but not many. It was too loud for them. Most of them were out in the parking lot, waiting for it to be over. So many kids were stomping their feet to the beat and jumping up and down, you could feel the vibrations. The hysteria hit me like a drug. My adrenaline was working overtime. I could hear the girls closest to the stage screaming at the top of their lungs, 'David, I love you!', 'I want your baby!' They began throwing stuff at me. And when the spotlights are on you, you can't see anything coming until it hits you.

I didn't say much more than, 'Thank you, thank you very much.' I just raced through it, from one number to the next, in a style a lot funkier and a lot faster than on the album. By night's end I was hoarse from trying to scream to be heard. I was really drained; my whole body started feeling sore because I'd expended so much energy. I gave everything I had.

Sam Hyman: David was nervous before the first show. He kept turning his back to the audience and working with his band. He couldn't hear. It was his first time being in that kind of venue. He didn't do a bad job and he wasn't forgetting lines. The sound mix was kind of mushy, but the fans didn't pick up on it. David's performance was a natural, intuitive thing that he had. You know, it was like the first time Elvis put his guitar on and was straightening it out and his hips moved and the fans all screamed. And he went, 'Oh, that's interesting.' He moved his hips again and they screamed again, and he realised, 'Oh, OK, I got it.' And that's kind of how it happened with David. He learned as he went along what worked. I think any good performer does. Once he got going and could relax a bit so he could then communicate with the audience, it evolved into a decent show. It was not a gimmick show. There were no fireworks or smoke, just basic lighting, a band, back-up singers. For his audience, it was an evangelical experience.

I was skinny to begin with, but I must have lost three or four pounds every time I went out on stage in those days. I still lose weight when I perform. My body was still sore the next day and I had to do it all again at a show in Portland in the midst of this hurricane. It was an insane weekend. Ruth patted me on the back with an almost maternal pride, as if to say she knew that her boy could do it. It's an amazing high when you're the focal point of thousands of people screaming 'I love you!' at the top of their lungs. They had no idea how much that meant to me. It's a jolt of energy. I wish everybody could understand what it feels like when people love you that much.

The die was cast. In a matter of days, my guarantee went from $8,000 to $10,000 to $12,500. Eventually, I got as much as $ 25,000 and $50,000 for bookings – gigantic figures for the early 70s. At one point, after the second or third year, I was getting as much as Elvis, and in some cases even more. I knew it, and Elvis knew it, because we had the same agents.

Elvis called Sam Weisbord at William Morris, who relayed the conversation to me. He said something like, 'Who's this kid stealing all my thunder? He's making as much money as I am.'

On weekends I'd often fly out to dates in the Midwest. I remember being picked up at the airport for one Ohio date in a 1959 Cadillac hearse; I think the local mortuary owner was the only guy with fancy cars for rent. We played big auditoriums, which got bigger as time went on. I couldn't have worked any harder than I was working. Every minute of every day of my life was booked. And I wasn't even sure how much I was really making. It was expensive carrying all of the people I carried. But money wasn't why I was doing it. I didn't know or care about the money.

On Mondays I'd get back to *The Partridge Family* set and tell

Danny Bonaduce and Susan Dey how the concerts had gone. They were both popular as well, Danny because he played such a feisty, wisecracking kid and Susan because she was so great-looking and idealistic, but theirs was a much different experience from mine. They didn't have the screaming fans and all of these magazines going gaga over them.

The first time they got to share in what I was experiencing came when Susan, Danny and I flew out to Cleveland for the city's Thanksgiving Day parade. We'd been booked as grand marshals before our TV show even went on the air, but I don't think anyone could have anticipated how quickly the show would have created this kind of hysteria.

We got to downtown Cleveland and led the parade riding in a fire truck. The event turned into sheer pandemonium. We had to get on our hands and knees and duck because people were trying to grab us. By the end, an estimated 60,000 to 80,000 kids were following us down the streets of Cleveland, screaming and yelling. No thought had been given to security, to how we were supposed to make our exit when the parade was over. No one had anticipated there'd be any fuss over our appearance. Ah, the power of television and records! At the end, when we had to run 20 feet from this fire truck to a waiting room, it was really dangerous. People were nearly trampled.

There were times, during my tours, when I was afraid for my life, because I saw fans turn into a mob, and a mob can't easily be controlled. I knew the fans loved me – they didn't want to kill me – but their emotions were at fever pitch. And they all wanted a piece of me.

That parade was the first time I'd had my clothes ripped. That was the first and last time I ever went anywhere without people whose job it was to get me in and out safely. I think the parade was a turning point for Danny. That's when he saw me as having the fame he wanted. He started really looking up to me from that time. He was very young, maybe 11 or 12, so it made an impression on him.

And the fan madness just kept escalating. It had seemed like a lot when there were 40 fans crowding around the studio every morning. It grew to where there were hundreds of them. Who were all these people getting up at six in the morning just to see me? I couldn't really go anywhere in public any more without being hassled.

I needed to get away, so I took a week off. Steve Ross and I hiked in the forest of Big Sur. We spent three days doing absolutely nothing but getting in touch with nature, living *au naturel*. It was really cool, the antithesis of Hollywood. We lived off the land, bathed in a stream.

When it was over, we hiked back to our car and drove down to the Big Sur lodge, a rustic place that had no customers when we arrived that afternoon. We had beard growth, our hair was filthy. We washed the dirt and mosquito oil off our hands and faces so we could at last sit down and have something proper to eat. Oh, baby, was I ripe!

We sat in a back corner of this huge, empty cafeteria. Because of the fans, I had become completely paranoid about being in public. So I sat facing the wall, reading the menu, thinking how I didn't want the waitress to notice me. I just wanted to be a regular guy. I kept my shades on even though it was dark in this joint.

Steve ordered for us. I breathed a sigh of relief at not being recognised. I turned and saw that a camp bus was pulling up in front of the lodge. A hundred or more Girl Scouts came rushing out of the bus and poured into the cafeteria.

There's no way these girls are not going to notice us. We're the only patrons. We're 20-year-old males. These are 11- and 12-year-old girls, who would notice any young guys, especially hippies with long hair. And my friend Steve was an attractive guy; girls called him 'cute'.

I kept thinking that if I was recognised, aside from the pandemonium that it would create, all these girls would leave and tell everyone they knew, 'We saw David Cassidy in person, and he's really gross!' I was thinking, *David Cassidy simply cannot be this person. He cannot be seen like this.* I'd built up the persona of this David Cassidy guy that the public knew from TV and, even though I didn't particularly relate to that character, I had to protect him. Realising I was now a role model, I took it very seriously.

I inhaled my tuna fish sandwich as quickly as possible, facing the wall and trying to look down. The girls kept looking in our direction, whispering and giggling, because they'd spotted a couple of young guys.

I put my hands up to cover my face and started coughing and sneezing. I kept pretending to sneeze as I hurried all the way from the back of the room and out the door. By the time we were safely in the car, we were laughing hysterically, so glad to have escaped with our lives. And I kept thinking, *This is insane. My whole life's become a charade. I'll never even be able to go camping again!*

Dave Ellingson: I remember once David walked into his dressing room and went into the bathroom and there was a girl hiding in the bathtub behind the shower curtain and as he came in she jumped out through the shower curtain and just scared the shit out of him.

The fans weren't just hanging around the studio any more. They'd found my house. We had so many fans hanging around the place, neighbours were complaining. We had to move. We found a house off Sunset Plaza Drive that cost us $1,500 a month. Sam paid the same as before, around $150 a month.

He couldn't afford any more. I knew he'd contribute more when he was able to. Sometimes Steve lived with us, too. He would be in and out. He'd go off for a while to check out an Eastern religious guru or something, then he'd come back and stay with us. Somehow, the fans found out the new address pretty quickly. Some would sleep outside my gate all night. I had to draw the line. I was extremely hostile. I had so little privacy, I needed to protect it.

9 Eight Days a Week

I must have played the role of Keith Partridge pretty convincingly, because everyone believed I really was that guy. Keith was a happy-go-lucky 16-year-old with no bigger worries in life than which girl he could get up to his favourite make-out spot, Muldoon's Point. He was carefree, relaxed and shallow. Throughout the course of the show, he never really seemed to grow older or more mature (although by the final season, I finally persuaded the producers to let him go to college).

We shot the show on the Columbia Ranch, which has since become the Warner Ranch, on Sound Stage 30. Almost everything was constructed on the sound stage: all the bedrooms, the kitchen, the living room, the stairs that led to nowhere, and any new set we might have needed. The performance sequences were shot there as well; they would just change the backdrop and we'd put on our crushed velvet outfits.

The Partridge Family house is still on the Warner lot in Burbank, near the house where the TV series *Leave It to Beaver* was shot. Down the street, the building that was supposed to be the public library on that show served as our school on *The Partridge Family*. VH1 did a *Behind the Music* in 1998 and we took a walk around *The Partridge Family* house. I had nothing but good memories.

Even though I wanted to, I didn't suggest a storyline until the end of the first year, when I still only had six lines an episode, which seemed ridiculous since I was getting 25,000 fan letters a week. It took the producers and writers a while to figure out what to do with me beyond singing one song a week.

Keith evolved as the airhead that Danny took advantage of. I was the straight man for Danny Bonaduce. He and Dave Madden, who played our manager Reuben, were the comedy, Shirley was the conscience and Susan Dey was the feminist, Laurie, who believed in causes and was committed to social change. Laurie and Keith had a love–hate relationship – she was always taking up causes and all Keith did was make sure his hair was cool, play guitar and, therefore, get chicks. The show inspired a lot of guys to play guitar.

The essence of *The Partridge Family* is family. Playing together. Travelling together. Simple conflict. Simple resolution. The simplicity and innocence of the show and the portrayal of a close family is what appealed to audiences. It made people feel good. I think every kid fantasised about having a family like that.

Bernard Slade: A lot of the stories were from real life. There was an episode where the family's dog gets involved with a skunk. That happened to our dog. That happens a lot in situation comedy – you remember something that happened to you and you use it in a show. We tried to give each member of the cast their own spotlight. Each would end up with their own story, although the two younger kids were not that experienced, so you couldn't really give them leads. It was pretty much divided between David, Shirley, Danny, Susan and Dave Madden.

My own existence was hardly as carefree as Keith Partridge's. From 1970 to 1974 I worked like a machine. On Monday we'd rehearse the TV show, do a read-through and block. Tuesday and Friday we'd shoot. Most mornings, we'd come in at half-past seven (though on Mondays they let us come in at ten). We wouldn't be finished until seven at night. Photographers were often on the set, shooting us for magazines while we rehearsed or filmed. During our so-called lunch breaks, I'd have to do interviews; I couldn't just relax and eat. For most of the year I'd go straight from the sound stage to the recording studio, where I'd work until about midnight. In 1971 I started recording solo records under my own name for Bell Records, while still making Partridge Family recordings.

Almost every Friday night or Saturday morning I'd fly to wherever I was doing my weekend concerts. By then, I had my own airplane, flying all over the world and playing to 60,000–70,000 people at a time. I was out of town until late Sunday night or very early Monday morning. So I'd often get to *The Partridge Family* set a little late. If I could steal even 15 extra minutes of sleep, it was worth it.

Dave Madden: David was just wearing himself out. In the second year of the show they gave him even more to do as an actor. He was going out and making probably 20 times the amount of money doing concerts than he made on *The Partridge Family*. It made coming into work and getting into make-up and doing those silly lines pretty ludicrous to him. But David handled his success as a TV star and teen idol extremely well. He handled it better than I would have, had I became famous at the age of 21. If I had started showing up on the cover of *Life* and *Time*, I'm sure it would have just about destroyed me.

Because of the younger kids and the nature of what we were doing, we'd be behind all the time in the first year. By the second year, they had it down, and the network had given us enough money to film the musical number on a fourth day. Thus *The Partridge Family* cost more than any of the other shows on television. Most half-hour shows done at Screen Gems and Columbia Pictures at the time were three-day shoots – shows like *Bewitched*, *I Dream of Jeannie*, *Leave It to Beaver* and *Father Knows Best*. The performance day, when there were extras and the audience, was my favourite because there were young, beautiful girls who would come and visit me in my dressing room afterwards.

It was the musical numbers that ultimately made the show unique and more than just a sitcom. But it cost the studio, and to say they were cheap would be an understatement. They wouldn't spring for a seven-dollar pair of sunglasses for me. They had a budget and you couldn't go two dollars over it. It was like pulling teeth getting them to pay for anything.

A lot of the time, they would use an Arriflex camera, which didn't have the capability to match my lip-synching to the music. I looked like an idiot and it would drive me crazy. It was bad enough that I had to play with people who couldn't play.

It was all so ludicrous. Here I was working with studio session greats and on the set I would have to show Susan Dey and Danny Bonaduce how to look like they were playing. The first thing I said to Danny was, 'You don't *strum* the bass. You play notes.' To make it even worse, he was given a bass that was obviously way too big for him, but the producers never cared about details like that. None of the others knew anything about their instruments, through no fault of their own. They were actors, not musicians. The strings on the guitars I was given were seven years old and rusted. There was never any thought about having me play live, so I didn't have them change the strings, so they didn't think I'd use it. When I did, though, it sounded terrible. Screen Gems wound up giving me all of the guitars that were left from *The Monkees*.

Paul Junger Witt (producer/director): We had to film the musical sequences in a very short amount of time, with a lot of relatively inexperienced kids. David and Shirley were the real musicians. We spent a great deal of camera time on David and Shirley for those sequences because they knew what they were doing, but we had to go to the other kids occasionally and it was tricky stuff.

Within the cast there was a love and an appreciation for each other that was very deep. Shirley Jones created an exceptionally warm atmosphere on the set. If many of us came to feel we really were part of a family, it was because of the tone that Shirley set. She taught me how to accept fame at such a young age and how to deal with it. She set an example by how she conducted herself and how she treated people. Everyone revered her – not just because she was an Academy Award-winning film star, but because of her personal qualities. Even the crew treated her with obvious love and respect, and we're talking about hardened veterans who'd worked on one TV show after another. She's as warm and genuine in real life as she appears to be on TV. She kept me grounded.

Shaun Cassidy: The fact that David was cast in a television show with my mom was surprising. I thought it was great, but at the same time it was weird; the odds of that happening are very slim. The idea that my mother was doing a TV show was novel enough. My mother had always done movies. I loved it because she would be home more. I had no idea how successful *The Partridge Family* would be and how big a deal David would become. I remember visiting the set and thinking that Susan Dey was the most beautiful girl in the world. I vividly remember wanting to be a part of *The Partridge Family* but my mother wisely said, 'You must wait until you're done with high school.'

To some of the crew I was just some punk actor who was making their lives more difficult because of all the screaming girls trying to get on to the sets. I'm sure I was kind of cocky in those days. They thought I was demanding. One of them called me S.S. – Super Star. I can hear him now: 'Certainly, S.S . . . Yes, sir, Super Star . . . Whatever you say, Super Dave.' If someone was hassling me, I just figured it was because I was skinny, young, rich and successful. I knew a lot of people hated me because of my success, including some critics.

I had received some great reviews for the dramatic work I'd done before *The Partridge Family*, but as soon as I became a sitcom star, the critics dismissed me. They'd say, 'Pretty face, no talent.' I took a lot of lumps. The more popular you become, the more they put you down.

I made guest appearances on TV shows including Dick Clark's *American Bandstand* and *The Glen Campbell Goodtime Hour*. I wasn't exactly thrilled about being invited to guest star on a Bob Hope special, but we sang together, joked around, and traded mock insults. What could you expect? After all, he played golf with Spiro Agnew. But the show turned out OK.

I was on hand when *This Is Your Life* saluted Shirley Jones. They brought on both her real family (my dad, my brothers Shaun, Patrick and Ryan and me) and her TV family. And my dad and I appeared on the *The Merv Griffin Show*, singing *Danny Boy* together. I suspect it irked him that both his wife and his son were now bigger TV stars than he ever was, perhaps partially because he had turned down the role of Ted on *The Mary Tyler Moore Show*, which had become one of the biggest hits on TV. When he did guest appearances on talk shows, he was as likely to be asked about his famous wife and son as about himself. After working so hard all his life, I think he began to resent that. And me, in fact.

Shirley Jones: Jack always said he was not envious of David's success, but he was appalled at the way he got it. Jack didn't really appreciate or respect the rock star syndrome. He couldn't stand the whole screaming teen idol thing. I have a feeling that had David made it on Broadway, Jack would have had a little more respect for his success. Jack used to say that what David was going through was like being 'a monkey in a cage'. That's truly the way he looked at it, even though I think he respected David's talent.

Sandy Stert Benjamin (associate editor, *Tiger Beat*): David wanted to make it on his own without feeling he was there for having a famous last name. One of the times that became crystal clear to me was in November 1971, when I wrote the script for a little turquoise cardboard record we sent out to the fan club. When I scripted it, it said something to the effect of, 'When I got out of school I wanted to follow my parents into show business.' David struck through the words 'follow my parents into show business' and changed it to 'get into show business'. He really wanted to prove he was his own man.

As my own career took off in various directions, I also found I had less and less time available to study the scripts. With concerts, guest appearances on other television shows, promotional activities, recording sessions and whatnot, my schedule was absolutely jam-packed, so I'd learn my lines in the mornings, during my 10 or 15 minutes in the make-up chair.

And as I became more successful, I did more and more screwing around on the set. I had so little fun in my life, I needed some outlet. I was working all the time. I would get punchy towards the end of the day. I'd say things like, 'Are we rolling yet? We are? Can you see I'm picking my nose?'

I'd occasionally drink a little, but I steered clear of drugs throughout *The Partridge Family* years. I could not possibly have used anything and done all that I had to do back then. I tried to behave professionally. I respected professionalism.

The Partridge Family was often looked down on as merely a cute little show, but it was very well executed. Bernard Slade, who dreamed up the show in the first place and wrote some of the scripts, went on to become a successful playwright and screenwriter. Producer Paul Junger Witt went on to produce such hit TV shows as *Benson*, *Soap*, *The Golden Girls* and *Blossom*. Story editor and producer Dale McCraven, a really funny guy who had previously worked on *The Dick Van Dyke Show*, went on to do *Mork and Mindy*, *The Betty White Show* and *Perfect Strangers*.

Mel Swope, who was initially an associate producer on the show after serving in the same role on shows like *The Flying Nun* and *The Monkees*, became the producer in the second season when Paul left. After our show, he became a producer on *Police Story* and ended up winning seven Emmys for it. He was Executive in Charge of Production for *Fame* and *The Outer Limits* and went on to do about a hundred quality made-for-television movies like *The Taking of Pelham One Two Three* and *12 Angry Men*.

A pretty extraordinary group of actors were guests on *The Partridge Family* in supporting roles. When you watch the reruns, look for appearances by Rob Reiner, Louis Gossett, Jr, Farrah Fawcett (she did a walk-on with one line), Jaclyn Smith, Richard

Pryor, Jodie Foster, Ray Bolger, Richard Mulligan, John Banner, Mark Hamill, Annette O'Toole, Pat Harrington, Harry Morgan, Noam Pitlik, Jackie Coogan, Michael Ontkean and Meredith Baxter.

The members of the cast became familiar faces to all America. Here are some of my impressions and recollections of them.

Dave Madden, who played our bumbling manager Reuben Kincaid, was a very good comedy actor who'd appeared on *Rowan & Martin's Laugh-In* and *Camp Runamuck*. I liked working with him. Sometimes I'd be doing a scene with him and he'd mug – his face was like rubber. We had a friendship, but we didn't become really close. There was definitely a generation gap there.

Dave Madden: David Cassidy, in essence, was *The Partridge Family*, not from an acting point of view but from a singing point of view. He was the factor that made it all work. Sitcoms are sitcoms, comedy is comedy. But it was the music that was the primary driving force of the TV show's success, and that's all because of David. David and I had a lot of fun together. We had scenes where we had laughing fits and it would take us 15 minutes to get through two lines. It was craziness, but we all had a lot of fun together. There's a tape of *Partridge Family* outtakes that shows some of the silliness that went on.

Susan and I were basically contemporaries. Susan was a sister, friend, confidante and girlfriend without being a lover. I really valued our friendship. We could talk about anything and we supported each other. We started working together as teenagers and by the time it was over we were adults. She had gone through a couple of long relationships that were very serious and I had gone through many short-term relationships that weren't.

Susan became very thin. She starting living on carrots and her skin turned noticeably orange. I would look at her and say, 'Susan, you've got to eat something besides carrots.' I think she had an eating disorder. At the time it was called the 'Barbie Syndrome'. She was desperately afraid of gaining weight.

She got involved in a relationship with story editor Dale McCraven. They lived together for over a year. He had hair down to his butt, a full beard and wore a headband and hippie clothes. He looked like he was right out of Haight-Ashbury. She was 18 by then; he must have been 40. She obviously always looked for a father figure because both her husbands were many years older than her. She used to talk to me about problems she had in her relationship with Dale. I don't mean to suggest it was a bad relationship; they were the kind of problems that crop up in any relationship.

She went to Europe with Dale and when they came back we noticed that she had gained all this weight. Our mouths dropped open. Oh my God, she had tits! She must have gained 20 pounds. And 20 pounds on a girl like her is a lot. It was 20 pounds she needed to gain. I was happy for her. My relationship with Susan was rooted in real love and support.

The two littlest kids in *The Partridge Family* cast were Suzanne Crough, who played my sister Tracy, and Jeremy Gelbwaks, who played my brother Chris. They weren't expected to do much more than just look cute.

Jeremy was at a very bad stage in his childhood. He was an obnoxious, almost hyperactive kid. He'd come to the set and run around making jet noises, crashing into people. He couldn't say a line and had personality conflicts with every person in the cast and the producers. He left the show at the end of the first season. His parents moved out of the area and that was pretty much the end of his show biz career.

Brian Forster replaced him. I got to know Brian a little better.

Acting was in his blood; his mother, father, stepfather and grandfather (Alan Napier, best known as the butler Alfred on TV's *Batman*) were all actors. Brian had acted in commercials before joining the show. He worked very hard with a drum instructor so that it would look like he was actually drumming when we mimed our musical numbers. He and Suzanne Crough had a bit of a romance, but it never progressed beyond simple kisses, I'm told. He says he got his first French kiss on the set of our show, from a young guest actress.

Danny Bonaduce wound up getting a lot to do on the show, because he was funny. He had a lot of personality. He had a tremendous need to be accepted and liked. He had to be 'on' all the time. Obviously, he didn't get enough attention at home. Danny was a pretty wild kid, and his father was a pretty violent guy. He beat him regularly. We were all very concerned about it. Dan would come to the set in the mornings looking completely dishevelled. He'd look like he'd been run over by a truck.

Danny was really starved for love. He needed a role model. He was maybe 11 years old when we started doing the show and he started looking up to me, imitating my mannerisms. He also started having problems socialising with other kids. When we weren't filming the show, he'd go to a regular school and he didn't fit in there.

He deserved better than what he was getting. I saw him acting out his need for love. He started smoking at 11 or 12, hanging around with all these misfits. I saw a little of myself in him. Whenever someone told me what to do I'd do the opposite, and Danny was the same way. He'd bring these loser friends of his to the set, 14, 15, 16-year-olds. Bikers. You could practically see it tattooed on their foreheads: seven years to life, armed robbery. You could see it coming.

On the show, Danny was always trying to act older than he

really was. And in real life, he wanted everybody to think he was cool. He lost his virginity when he was just 13, with a young woman who'd come to the set hoping to meet me. I could see he was going to have problems. I remember talking to Susan and Shirley about it; we were all concerned and we pulled together. There was a real closeness, a bond, between Susan, Shirley and me. Although Danny liked being with me, he was actually closer to my younger brother Shaun's age, so Shirley would take Danny home so he could spend a little time with Shaun.

Shirley: Danny Bonaduce was a pain every now and then because he was the snotty little kid. And I had to settle him down. At one point, we all decided that Danny was getting a little too risqué and out of hand. In one of the scenes, we were supposed to bring in a pitcher of milk and put it in front of him during a breakfast scene. We all got together and decided that Susan was going to pour the pitcher of milk over Danny's head. And she did.

Like the younger kids in the cast, Danny was absolutely terrible when it came to remembering dialogue. Dave Madden once did this scene with Danny up in a tree house and it took them 36 takes.

'I swear,' Dave Madden said to me, 'if Danny messed up one more time, I would have thrown him out of the tree house.'

In one show, Danny and I had a scene together where we were supposed to pull up in front of the house in the family's bus, get out and say, 'Hey, Mom,' or something simple like that. Danny made a mess of it two or three times. I said, 'One more time and you're out of this scene.' The fourth time he screwed up, I said, 'Get on the bus!' I threw him on the bus and, on impulse, drove right off the Columbia lot, into Burbank.

Once I drove off, I realised I had this power, this freedom.

Suddenly I was driving down the street. Car horns were honking and people were shouting, 'Hey, there's David Cassidy and *The Partridge Family* bus! There's Danny Bonaduce!'

Danny, of course, was thrilled that I was that bold, that defiant. It was one of the worst examples I could have set for him. Breaking rules, and even the law, was something Danny got very good at as he became an adult.

10 The Reluctant American Idol

I felt my life changing rapidly. It's hard to convey how big the teen idol phenomenon got. America's youth was being conditioned to believe that I was the hottest young actor and singing star around. The dream guy that every girl was suddenly supposed to want. Sometimes it was ridiculous. Walking on the Paramount Pictures lot one day, I was spotted by a couple of the girls from *The Brady Bunch*. When they saw me, they dropped to their knees and screamed. It didn't matter that they were featured in a popular TV show themselves. In fact, they were already on television the year before, when I was just an unknown scuffling for enough work to pay the rent.

Throughout most of the first year, it was exciting to be the object of so much attention, even though the girls were simply idolising a magazine cover. My career was escalating at an amazing speed and I was getting more fan mail and more money for personal appearances. *The Partridge Family* show steadily picked up viewers during the first season and attracted even more of an audience for the second season. And even though I wasn't drawing a salary that was commensurate with star status, the public was certainly treating me as the star of the show. By 1971–2, I had the highest Q rating (a rating which reflects a performer's likeability quotient) of anyone on television.

My record sales were huge. My very first record, *I Think I Love You*, won the National Association of Record Merchandisers' award for being the biggest-selling single of 1970, even bigger than *Let It Be* by the Beatles, who broke up that year. I was beginning to understand why the Beatles stopped playing live. Just getting in and out of a venue was so stressful; it was insane.

In the spring of 1971, Bell Records released *I'll Meet You Halfway*, the third Partridge Family Top Ten hit single in a row. I took pride in those record sales, even though I wasn't receiving a dime in royalties. The success helped me to continue to believe in myself. Everything was really rockin'. I felt like I was on a huge rollercoaster that was just going up, up, up, but I couldn't help feeling that some twists and drops were certain to follow.

The fans clustering outside the studio gates morning and night were becoming a problem for me, though. To try to avoid them, I started to go in and out by different exits; there were three or four gates I could choose from. But inevitably, one or two of the fans would start following me. That became a major pain. Losing them was really hard.

So I had to start meeting someone every morning about six blocks from the studio gate. I'd leave my car there, lie down on the floor in the back of this other fellow's car and ride in through the gates unseen. It became an incredible hassle. And some fans still managed to sneak into the studio to try to meet me.

Security at my home became an issue, too. There were women showing up, unannounced, uninvited, at all hours. You might think this is every male's fantasy come true. And I'm not going to claim I turned down every opportunity for fun and games that was presented to me – far from it – but I wanted to maintain some sense of control over my personal space, over my life. I'm basically a very private person and I was losing my solitude.

If I went out to eat at a popular restaurant, it seemed like the moment I'd get some spaghetti in my mouth some guy would be standing next to me, demanding, 'Come on, come on, give me an autograph. Let me take your picture. It's for my kid.' And if I didn't give fans what they asked for they'd sometimes stomp off saying I was a jerk. I was happy to discover a couple of restaurants, like the Imperial Gardens in Hollywood, which would put me into a private room so I could eat without being disturbed.

At heart I was still a teenager, but I had adult responsibilities. I really wasn't ready to deal with financial concerns; I'd had no education or preparation in that area. I figured my manager could take care of such matters for me, but Ruth had never really been a money-oriented person. She'd always taken care of building her clients' careers. She was interested in the creative side of the business and had generally let her brother take care of money matters. Unfortunately, he died shortly before my career had taken off and she found other people to manage her clients' money. I didn't worry much about who was handling mine, although in time it would become painfully clear I should have. I just had so many other things on my plate.

And I didn't feel like I could go out to a local bar or anywhere for a diversion. I had a responsibility to my fans and I had to be careful about where I was seen going, what I was seen doing. I knew I had fans who looked up to me and I felt a responsibility to be something of a role model. I always felt I had to be careful where I went and what I did. These fans expected me to have answers for everything and I was uncomfortable with that. I had enough trouble coping with the stress in my own life, without having to be anyone else's guru. You may find this hard to believe, but I actually had fans who would tell me, 'I do whatever you do,' or, 'I moved to Los Angeles just so I could see you.'

For the TV show and concert appearances, I wore whatever ridiculous outfits I was told to – some 'mod' crushed velour outfit or a skintight white jumpsuit (often made by the same guy who was making them for Elvis). Those were simply costumes. When I wasn't performing I liked to wear jeans, a ripped T-shirt and tennis shoes. That was the real me – a pretty gritty, earthy person. The problem is that when you work 18 hours a day perpetuating a public image, the real person gradually gets lost. He vanishes. And that's what I felt was beginning to happen to me.

It became harder for me to do some things that once were so natural. I'd be invited to some old friend's birthday party and I'd look forward to going and relaxing and just being myself again, like in high-school days. But when I'd get to the party, the whole focus would turn towards me, the 'star'. And I didn't need that! I'd been the focus of attention all day. I needed to be left alone. 'It's *your* birthday!' I'd say. And, 'No, I *don't* feel like getting up and singing for everybody tonight. We should all be singing *Happy Birthday* to you.'

It was wearing to have people I met casually want to talk to me just because I was a success. New acquaintances would say they felt like they already knew me because they'd been watching me on TV and reading articles about me and I'd have to explain to them that I wasn't that guy on *The Partridge Family*. They didn't know me at all. Not the real David Cassidy.

There were some fans who were obviously unbalanced. I'd get letters from girls who seriously thought they had some kind of relationship with me, even though I had never seen them before. They would write things like, 'David, you're going to have to stop all of this. I know you've been seeing other women. You have to remain faithful to me. And you really must send me the money I've asked for *now*, or I'll be forced to come after you.' I couldn't help wondering if they really might come after me.

There are still many people like that following me. There are a number of people in the world who believe that I'm destined to be their husband, lover, partner in life, their main financial support. Clearly those people are not dealing with reality. I think that kind of negative attention is part of the price you pay when you become a fixture in certain people's consciousness. Fortunately, I never got a serious death threat, although there were many boyfriends who were jealous and tried to impress their girlfriends by threatening me.

The fans were taken in by the posters, the dolls, the records, the music, the magazine covers, the idolatry. They couldn't get past that. They saw me as a phenomenon, not a person, and part of my pain and frustration was that I was never able to show them the real me.

Danny Fields (co-editor, *16* magazine): David's frustration was real. It was daunting for him that other people couldn't distinguish him from the role he played. He wanted to be taken seriously as an actor. He wanted to do some acting that he could get his teeth into. That was very difficult because if that confounded or contradicted his established TV image, that would be poisonous. The producers didn't want him starring in a movie as an axe killer and then coming back to play Keith Partridge. He confronted the producers more than once saying, 'I can't do this any more.' They would say, 'If you pull out, there's no show and if there's no show, we'll have to lay off the wardrobe department, the make-up department, the director, the cameraman, your stepmother.' So he had to just keep on doing it. When people would yell, 'Hey, Keith!' that really rankled him, but he'd have to smile back.

Once, I was booked to play an auditorium some place in southern New Jersey. I arrived 15 minutes before I was supposed to go on and went into the trailer that was to serve as my dressing room. I got out of my street clothes and I was standing there, naked, looking for a place to take a leak before putting on my stage costume. The primitive trailer didn't have a bathroom and all I could find was a plastic cup. Suddenly, I heard these little squeaky high-pitched sounds coming from under the vanity. For a moment I was thinking, *What is that? Mice? Rats?* Then I heard the laughter. I saw eyes looking at me through an opening in the vanity. It turned out that two girls had been hiding in the trailer for 21 hours, waiting to meet me. They stockpiled fruit drinks and bananas under the vanity. And now they're unable to stop giggling at the sight of their idol, naked, trying to piss into a cup. I just lost it. I flipped out. 'Get the f*** out of here!' I threw the cup of piss, shouting, 'Here I am, babe! Is this what you expected?'

I wasn't the only one being pestered by fans. In the first year that *The Partridge Family* was on the air, my mom moved back to West Orange, New Jersey, to take care of my grandfather. He had lived quietly in that same modest house his entire adult life. My mom told me that kids were coming around, ringing the doorbell all the time and generally driving my grandfather nuts, because they knew that was my old house.

So how do you control kids who are 13, 14, 15 years old? You can't slug them if they get out of line, but you can't let them run all over you, either. Security on tours became an issue and many meetings were held about the problem.

I didn't want my security people to be too heavy-handed when maintaining crowd control. My concerts would draw some very young kids and I wanted my people to be really careful, really gentle with them. But the very young fans could become frenzied and destructive, much more so than the ones in their late teens and 20s who were more in control of their emotions. They could have scratched my eyes out as they were reaching grabbing at me just to touch me. In fact, I was hurt more than once, and as recently as a few years ago.

The concert bookings just kept pouring in, and the crowds and the money kept getting bigger. My theatrical and concert booking agents never had to solicit bookings for me. They just answered the phones and booked me on as many dates as possible. The more I worked, the more money they made. They took their ten per cent commission on my gross earnings and were very happy. One agency eventually made $800,000 in commissions from me. Think about it: I had to earn $8 million for them to net that $800,000. I was a kid who didn't know any better, so I went along with it and didn't question anything. I mean, $800,000 just for answering the phones! I had the world's highest-paid answering service.

And I was working to the point of exhaustion. When I had to travel for a concert date, I'd get out of bed at the last possible minute, throw some things in a bag and go. I'd take no money with me. Even when I began touring abroad, I'd carry no cash. I didn't need it, because I was never asked to pay for anything. Ultimately, of course, I paid for it all, financially, physically and emotionally.

I was glad to have Sam and Steve as friends, especially when I toured. I trusted them implicitly. It helped having them around to share experiences with me. We all lived well, of course. I had no money worries then. Money seemed to be no object.

Sam Hyman: Being associated with the David Cassidy hysteria, I got to live out a lot of my fantasies. I felt like I was with the Beatles: travelling around the world, flying in helicopters and other bizarre stuff that most people can only dream about or read about in magazines. I actually had the best of both worlds during that time because David had to be secluded. We would go to a city and we'd have to lock him up while the rest of us went out. So I could experience some of the frills of fame with him and yet be a normal person, which was very important. He didn't get to experience normal life. He couldn't go to a 7-Eleven or go through a grocery store line. How does someone stay in touch with the world like a normal human being?

I was forced to move again in 1971 because too many fans were invading the privacy of my home in the Hollywood Hills. It turned into chaos up there. I'd arrive home and find people living in my house. Or throwing a party. There'd be chicks in the pool, in the house, some of them naked, trying to look inviting. Sam and Steve enjoyed the fruits of my success, but we knew we needed a place with more security.

I bought an old stone house, with a guest house behind it, out in Encino, a suburb of Los Angeles, in the San Fernando Valley. It had been built in 1925. It was on two and a half choice acres of land near the reservoir on White Oak Avenue, and it included a huge orange orchard. There was plenty of space there for Sam, Steve and me. The house was expensive, but thanks to all the concerts I was doing, I could afford it. Michael Jackson's family lived out that way too and Jimmy Webb lived up the street. At one time, I'm told, Clark Gable kept a mistress in the house. In more recent years, it had belonged to Wally Moon from the Los Angeles Dodgers and Chad Stewart from the folk-rock duo Chad and Jeremy.

Some of my belongings seemed to have been lost or left

behind in the moving process, but I generally didn't worry much about possessions. I figured almost anything could be replaced. There would always be more tours to do, more money to be made. The one item that disappeared that I really regretted losing was the gold record I got for *I Think I Love You*. I never really coveted awards and never put any of my gold records on display. But still, I would like to have that first one.

I loved the Encino house. It was a great crash pad for me and my friends. Rustic, really beautiful, old hardwood floors. The place had a casual kind of funk to it. It had no air conditioning; in the summer we'd just throw open the windows. It felt almost like camping out. The area was still very rural back then. We even had sheep in the meadow above us. We put up an electric gate with a buzzer so I could get some privacy. That helped for a short while, but people quickly found out where I was living. So many strangers would press the buzzer, that a lot of times I'd simply disconnect it.

I even assumed an alias – Jackson Snipe. I got a telephone answering service, but I didn't tell them I was David Cassidy. To them, I was simply Mr Jackson Snipe. When my friends would phone me, my service would answer and call me, saying, 'Mr Snipe, I have so–and–so on the phone.' And, if it was someone I wanted to talk to, I could say, 'OK, put them through.'

I also had a direct phone line at the Encino house. I gave no one that phone number except Ruth and my mom. They were the only people who didn't have to go through the service. I needed to be able to shut everyone out.

It felt like the only time I could really be me was when I was alone in my room. The only time I had to myself was when I slept or took a crap. And there wasn't much time to get the sleep I needed. If I didn't get six hours, and I often didn't, I'd be irritable. Filming *The Partridge Family* actually occupied only about half the weeks of the year. I'd tour every weekend while the TV show was in production. When the show would go on hiatus, I'd tour without pause for weeks at a stretch.

When I was on the road, we had things timed as tightly as possible. If we were flying anywhere within the continental U.S., my roadie would be at my house in a limo just 32 minutes before the flight. If we hustled, we could make it to LAX in time. We'd have the radio on in the limo. I loved hearing them play my records. But I was so worn out I'd usually fall asleep before the limo even made it from my house to the airport.

At first, I could walk through airports like any ordinary citizen. But as the TV show grew in popularity and my own following grew, I couldn't do that any more; my presence would cause too much commotion. So it was arranged that when I flew anywhere, the police would meet me on the tarmac and escort my limo to the back entrance of whatever hotel I was staying in. In the early days, the band and I would stay at the same hotels until we attracted too much attention. It finally got to a point where some hotels simply wouldn't take me. They didn't want all the aggravation.

Henry Diltz: Very often they would put the band in one hotel and David in another to try and throw the fans off. The girls would be outside the hotel room singing and calling for David and poor David was stuck in the suite. He couldn't leave. He was definitely a prisoner. We couldn't go out until nightfall, after those little girls had to be home.

I had always tried not to take life too seriously, but things were now getting out of hand. I feared I was losing myself with this whole David Cassidy thing. Weeks turned into months. I realised I hadn't had a moment to think, *What do I feel like doing?* I didn't want to just get up and function, perform, learn my lines, do the show, do the interview, do the photo session, make the plane, get in the car, get to work on time. I was becoming some crazed machine.

Before the first season of *The Partridge Family* ended, my body began breaking down from overwork. When you're under stress and completely exhausted your body has a way of telling you that you need to rest. I had serious problems with my gall bladder. At just 21 years old, I was one of the youngest patients the doctors said they'd ever seen with that problem.

One Sunday night, when I got back from doing a concert, I felt a little funky and went right to bed. At about 2.30 a.m. I woke up screaming. I passed a gall stone. The pain was intolerable. I've never felt pain like that in my life. I started banging my head against the wall to knock myself out. It took 45 minutes for the doctor to get there. I had a big lump on my forehead by that time.

They knocked me out with a shot of Demerol. They put me on this diet: no spice, no fat. I was eating toast and oatmeal and nothing else. I was on it for a couple of months and I really got skinny. I didn't weigh much to begin with, maybe 125 pounds, and I got down to 112 pounds. I was a rail.

Then, after we'd begun the second season, I had another attack, for which I had to be hospitalised. By the time they cut me open and removed my gall bladder, my liver had been affected and I'd become jaundiced. That was really a close call. I'm very fortunate they got it out in time.

While I was in the hospital, things got really nutty. It was on the news that I'd been hospitalised, forcing the production of *The Partridge Family* to be suspended. Fans gathered outside the hospital and down in the lobby and started to send me gifts and cards – thousands of them. One fan broke through security and was heading towards me in intensive care. There was some scare about the fan wanting to put something in my IV. All I can tell you is for the two weeks I was in the hospital, it was a circus. Fans, family, media, me on Demerol. Flying. Just flying.

Six weeks after the operation, I returned to work. It was big news that I was working again. In addition to working on the show, I kept doing concert dates. I broke the record at the Garden State Art Center in Holmdel, New Jersey. It was the biggest single day's business ever. The box office take was huge. Running more on nerves and adrenaline than anything else, I did six shows in one weekend. When I got back home, every muscle in my body was a mess. I felt like I'd been hit by a truck. But I dived right back into working at the same pace I'd kept up before the gall bladder operation. In some ways it was even more intense. I started a heavy public relations schedule, doing five or six things each day, almost as if we were making up for lost time.

I was trying to regain my overall strength. I got my weight up to 114 pounds, 116 pounds. But I was still just skin and bone. I developed a small tumour on my back. It was removed. My face began breaking out in infections, which could not always be hidden with make-up. I suspect the infections made it even easier for some viewers to identify with me. I can imagine teens worried about their acne saying, 'Look at that. Keith Partridge has pimples, too.' I was put on antibiotics, but the facial infections remained a recurring problem throughout the second, third and fourth seasons of *The Partridge Family*. The fundamental cause of them, I'm sure, was simply stress. I was burning out.

Around this time, my friend Steve was becoming diet and

health conscious and started fasting. He got me interested in it, too. I figured maybe the gallstones, the tumour, the infections, were trying to tell me something. I went on a total non-fat diet. I stopped eating meat. We all started eating natural food. I wanted to feel really cleansed, really pure.

I took about two months off at the end of 1971 and beginning of 1972. I couldn't sustain the pace any more. I had to take a break or I would have lost my mind. I vacationed in Italy and France, in towns where I could go unrecognised. *The Partridge Family* hadn't reached there yet, so I could travel like a normal guy. It turned out to be a great experience for me. I read a lot, meditated a lot. I stayed at little inns. No one knew me anywhere. I love to be alone. I thoroughly enjoy my own company. It was just great. I recharged my batteries.

Then I was to head to England, where the show had been airing and our first Partridge Family album was just released. Ruth was to meet me at the airport, along with people from my record company's British office. The radio and newspapers had mentioned I was coming and the record people thought it conceivable that a hundred or so fans might turn up at the airport.

Flying in, I was thinking, *I've never been to London before; this is going to be great.* I wasn't thinking about being David Cassidy the 'celebrity'. I was totally out of that mindset after spending time in France. I got off the plane and there were all these cops and people standing around. I thought, *What's going on here?* Some official, pointing his finger at me, shouted, 'Mr Cassidy! You're the one that's caused all this!'

I said, 'Excuse me? Are you talking to me?'

He said, 'We can't even bring you through customs.'

I asked, 'What are you talking about?'

He said, 'You can't go through passport control.'

And I certainly couldn't. There were far too many people.

Thousands of fans had shown up. There was no time for me to worry about getting my luggage, they said. More people had turned out at Heathrow for me than ever turned out for the Beatles or The Jackson Five. It was insane. I wasn't even successful there yet.

The authorities rushed me through a part of the airport that was presumably secure, but somehow somebody spotted me and fans started screaming at the tops of their lungs. People started stampeding. They broke through barriers. The authorities urged me frantically, 'Go, go, go!' We were running down steel stairs; we sounded like a herd of elephants.

Suddenly, I started laughing uncontrollably, hysterically. The cops were looking at me like I was a real fruitcake. They began pushing me, saying, 'You don't understand this! There are thousands of kids out there, and they're going crazy! Move! Go!'

The whole madness just hit me like a ton of bricks. I'd come to Europe to get away from all of this. The cops threw me into the back of a Daimler. Ruth was there along with Dick Leahy, the managing director of Bell in England. And we took off with a police escort. Dick said, 'Hello, David. Welcome to London.'

They had me doing press interviews throughout my whole stay in England, from the moment I'd wake up each day until I went to bed. In a week I became a big national name. It was overwhelming. My album went right to the top spot.

David Bridger (U.K. promotion director and artist relations, Bell Records): We knew David was a superstar. He had the full aura of a pop star. We use the term far too much these days. David was in a total and utter class above everybody else.

When he came to England on the first promo tour it was totally and utterly amazing. He could not go anywhere. His popularity was compared to the second coming of the Beatles. There had been nobody from America that had come to England in such a blaze of glory until David.

I stayed at the Dorchester Hotel. By the end of the week, there were 15,000 kids in front of the hotel, stopping traffic on Park Lane. It was on the news. The unusual thing about the English fans is that they would sing. From about seven to ten every night, they'd be serenading me outside my hotel. For teenagers to be out alone that late, with badges, buttons and banners, singing all my songs – it was incredible.

You couldn't get in or out of the Dorchester. Fans were getting crushed trying to push through the revolving doors. The hotel management was aghast. The idea that I was causing all this commotion was totally unacceptable. That was the last time I would be able to stay at a London hotel for the entire 70s. No hotel would have me after that.

Dick Leahy (managing director, Bell Records U.K.): It was total insanity at the airport. There was a terminal with a roof terrace and there were 10,000 fans just hanging off this terminal to welcome him. I worked with The Bay City Rollers and The Osmonds and I witnessed the Beatles phenomenon. The young kids in England just loved David Cassidy. He was massive in England. Huge. He was the biggest thing in the U.K..

Top of the Pops was a huge music programme on TV back then. Bill Cotton, Jr was the head of BBC Light Entertainment, which aired *Top of the Pops*. He phoned me and explained why he was banning David Cassidy from the studio. He was worried about the security and worried about the thousands of people that followed David everywhere. If he booked him on the show, the whole place would be overrun by young fans.

I visited many different places in the U.S. and abroad while I was doing my concert tours, although I can't say I actually saw many of them. For security reasons, it was often necessary for me just to stay put in my hotel room when not performing. If I were to even try to walk through the hotel lobby, fans might riot. I began feeling more and more removed from the band, my friends, from the world. I became isolated.

As the tours became bigger, the lonelier I got for someone's company, yet the more I found myself sitting in my room watching TV while the rest of my entourage was partying. Everyone and everything had to come to me. That was when it became a difficult issue. Who could I bring into the inner circle? Is this person trustworthy? What is this person's motivation? I started to become more and more hyper and anxious as things evolved.

I didn't know what to do. The whole thing was gaining momentum weekly, daily. I was getting more famous. I was becoming less and less myself and more and more this guy whom people perceived as Keith Partridge.

I no longer trusted anybody. Everyone I met wanted me for sex, or for my money, or they just wanted to make themselves feel more important by hanging out with someone famous. It became very difficult to trust anybody other than friends like Sam and Steve. I distanced myself from almost everyone else. It took me a long time after *The Partridge Family* years to regain trust in anyone.

For a long time, I had disliked people's reactions to me. I was embarrassed when people started screaming just because they saw me. And the more famous and successful I became, the more shows I did and the bigger the arenas I was playing at, the more difficult it all started becoming for me. I felt I suddenly understood why the Beatles had broken up, why they were saying they never wanted to go out on the road again, regardless of public demand. I really learned the downside of being a rock star when *I* became the deal. No matter how pleasurable it might be for that one hour of the day when you were performing on stage, the other 23 hours of the day were impossible to cope with. They were hell.

11 Brown Rice and Tetracycline

It's bizarre but true that once I became really famous, virtually the only real contact I had with people outside my immediate circle was with women who wanted to have sex with me. They'd come into my inner sanctum for a little while and we'd talk. I'd talk to them about the most mundane things. They'd say, 'Oh, you wouldn't care about my job . . .' But I did care. They became my last connection to the real world. I'd ask things like, 'Where do you go for fun? What do you do? What's it like when you stand in line at the bank?' There was no way for me to know these things. I didn't live that kind of life.

As soon as people started to talk to me, they'd find out I was not that guy on the TV show. I had adult thoughts and sexual fantasies. Part of the game became the fact that I could do anything. I could have anyone I wanted. I mean, come on, who wouldn't get turned on by that?

The dialogue became the aphrodisiac. The fact that they wanted me. I felt sexually aroused by their wanting to please me, wanting to satisfy me, wanting to touch me, wanting to be intimate with me.

I genuinely liked some of them. There were women I got to know well. It was great to have a real conversation with someone I didn't work with. I like listening instead of being the one who had to do the talking all the time. Then it was a matter of living up to their sexual fantasies.

We'd be in my room, one-on-one, and I'd say, 'Tell me how you fantasise about me.' I'd want to know, 'How did you end up in my room? What did it take for you to go out and buy a ticket, or come back to the hotel and sit and wait, or chase the car I was in? What motivated you to do those things?'

In truth, I knew it wasn't *me* they loved; they really didn't know me. I was trying to find out, *What made you idolise this creation that you think you know through the media?* Could they have glimpsed something of the real me and been attracted to that?

I've always been very comfortable with my sexuality. I really love women. I think they're beautiful. I find them enchanting creatures. I enjoy being with them. I enjoy their attention. I enjoy giving them attention. The difference between me now and me in my early 20s is I now enjoy *giving* a lot more than I enjoy receiving. Back then, I was more self-centred. More chauvinistic.

I never had to hit on women. I didn't have to. Women would come up to me all the time and say things like, 'Hi, want to have sex with me?' I always liked that blatantly honest approach. No b.s., right? Ah, it makes me miss the 70s just a little when I think of how wild a time it was.

Sex was just sex. It was there. It presented itself to me numerous times during the course of the day, and I could take advantage of it or not. Pick anyone. Who would you like to meet? Who would you like to sleep with? I was 21 years old, I was always ready, and they were all so willing. *Yeah, I can live with this . . .*

My brothers call me 'Donk'. It's their nickname for me. One fellow even published a book on the Hollywood scene and included a reference to my being 'blessed'. I decided that if I *had* it, there wasn't any point in just keeping it in the holster all the time. I'd have to let it out. And let it out I did.

I had many sexual encounters. Did I do anything any red-blooded man in his 20s wouldn't have done if given the opportunity? The most beautiful women in the world were calling me, saying, 'I've got to see you. Please let me see you.' And they would come up to my room.

As the pressures of my career mounted, I felt like the sex was compensation for not being able to lead a normal life. At least I could be the real David Cassidy in my bedroom. There, the real David Cassidy could live, and live well.

To me, the act of sexual intercourse represented a serious commitment, which oral sex did not. I could indulge in the fantasy with talk and oral sex, without feeling I'd really committed myself in terms of time or emotion. So I almost always avoided sexual intercourse in these casual encounters. I had to feel a real connection before I'd sleep with someone. I still held on to this romantic concept that intercourse should mostly be saved for more meaningful relationships. Well, OK. Maybe not *meaningful*. But at the very least I'd need to know her last name.

If I slept with a girl, she would have to stay for a while. She might even want to stay the whole night! This was not something I usually wanted. In addition, you risked knocking her up. Nobody wore rubbers in those days, so I felt I had to be very careful if I actually had intercourse. My friends and I also took antibiotics constantly. We lived on brown rice, sex and tetracycline, which we figured would protect us from getting venereal diseases.

One of the most celebrated groupies of the era, known as Barbara the Butter Queen, came to the arena when I played Dallas. If you were a rock star – or close to one – Barbara the Butter Queen sort of went with the territory. She was legendary. She serviced countless rockers of the 60s and 70s. I'd heard her name in connection with Joe Cocker, the Rolling Stones, Donovan and others. The guys in my band and crew just gasped when they heard that Barbara the Butter Queen was actually coming to do them all. They were actually shaking with anticipation. I was sort of fascinated by the whole groupie thing. I mean, back then, you could actually become famous for performing fellatio. Yes, and a performance it was. What a concept!

Barbara got into all the gigs for free because she would blow all the promoters and the guys at the gate. Everybody knew her. She would blow everyone along the way, in order to get to the rock star. So democratic of her.

When she arrived at my three-room hotel suite, where we were having a party after the concert, she looked about 27 or maybe even 30. She was no kid. She looked tired and spoke with a heavy Texas drawl. She was not a beauty, not even attractive, and nor were the two younger girls – her apprentices – she brought with her. She looked us all over, the whole band and crew, and announced, 'I'll take the star, the dark hairy one [Sam] and the guitar player. My girls will divvy up the rest.' She had been through all of this so many times before. She made some small talk about how she thought rock was dead and she had seen its glory years. She was a joke. This wasn't gonna turn me on.

One of her girls decided she would take the horn section and the other would take the rhythm section, or something like that. The girls were actually very shy; they obviously hadn't had anywhere near the experience Barbara had. But some trumpet players had brought up a couple of other chicks to join in the action.

Barbara picked up the phone and called room service. 'Can we have a pound of butter, please?' And up came a silver tray piled with tubs of butter! That was her gimmick.

Barbara and her girls went about the business of going down on everybody. I would not do anything in front of my whole entourage; I was still much too private a person for that. But I felt comfortable with Steve and Sam. After all, we'd been friends for years and shared a house. So the three of us went into my bedroom with Barbara.

She took one look at me and said – trying to flatter me, I guess – 'Oh, wow, man, you've got it all over Mick Jagger.' Then, before I got too cocky, she turned to Sam and said, 'Oh, wow, man, look at all that hair. I'm in love with you.'

She brought out the butter and put it all over Sam. You know what butter smells like when it's hot? Steve and I began watching television while she was doing Sam and I said to Steve, 'Pass the popcorn.' He fell over, dropped to his knees.

It was all over for us. Steve and I rolled out of the room. It was hysterical. The whole place smelled like old buttered popcorn. Funky. Very, very funky.

One night at the house in Encino, Sam and I and a few friends were getting pretty drunk when we heard the buzzer at the gate around midnight. Steve answered it. The rest of us listened as some girl none of us knew started talking sex to Steve over the intercom.

We were falling down laughing. Steve and I decided we'd walk down to the gate. The girl wanted to see me, of course, but by this point she felt as if she knew Steve because she'd been talking on the intercom with him. By the time we got there, she was already down on her knees, her face pressed right up between the slats of the gate. She did us both under the stars, right through the gate.

I think back on it and think I must have been mad! Had anybody – a stranger, a cop, *anybody* – driven down White Oak Avenue that night, they would have seen this girl giving blow jobs through the bars of my gate. We could have all wound up in jail. But once again, the Good Lord shined His light . . .

I guess it's safe to say that at that time a lot of fans would have done anything for me. I'll admit I did things that I now think were degrading for the women involved, and for that I'm ashamed.

I'm not sure how I felt about all the adulation I received. You're always trying to convince yourself that you really are worthy of it. But are you? Come on, no one is. There were a lot of other guys who were more handsome and talented. I happened to come along in the right vehicle, at the right time.

On tour, there'd be all these girls hanging around the hotels. The guys in the band and the roadies would pull in girls who were looking for me. Sometimes those guys would tell the girls they'd have to have sex with them first if they expected to ever meet me. I had no way of knowing that was going on. I didn't want people to take advantage of their power and do things like that. But that was the deal, and I learned later that there were plenty of girls who were glad to comply.

I had a guy travelling with me who had only one job to do: hand me my guitar when I needed it for one number in my concert and then take it back from me when I'd finished with it. I can remember this one huge outdoor daytime concert. I'd reached the point when I was supposed to do the number with the guitar and the fans were screaming and yelling, eager for me to get on with the show. I was looking around frantically for the guitar, ad libbing, 'Thanks, and now for my next trick . . .' *Nothing.* Finally, I spotted the guy who was supposed to be handing the guitar to me, way off to one side of the parking area, his pants down around his knees, having sex with some chick leaning on an open-back truck. And you want to know something? I didn't fire him. That's how loose things were.

We had a name I coined: 'Squeaky Clean [which was me] and the Dirty All-Night Boys'. In fact, I wanted to make an album under that alias. Steve and I were going to do some of the stuff from our garage band days, all that really hard, stoned-rocker stuff I loved before getting trapped into *The Partridge Family* bag.

Sometimes it became a contest between a couple of the guys in my entourage to see how many girls they could pull for me. They thought they were impressing me or something, or somehow proving their masculinity by rounding up a lot of girls quickly. But it usually made me feel terrible. Empty. What was I supposed to be, some sex machine servicing the groupies of the world? It was uncomfortable, feeling I had to live up to others' expectations that I'd be some superstud because I was a star.

I can remember one night in particular. These guys had rounded up seven different girls. They had them waiting for me, undressed, in the outer room of my hotel suite and they'd send them into my bedroom at ten-minute intervals. You want to know what I did with all those naked girls in my hotel bedroom that particular night? Nothing.

I can remember the first girl coming in, awkward and uncomfortable, standing nude at the foot of my bed saying, 'Well, uh, hi. I, uh, guess you sort of know what I'm here for.' Yeah, I got that. And then suddenly it hit me and I was totally turned off. I thought of my roadies out there in the other room, so proud that they could get these girls up here like this. I felt somehow emasculated by the whole situation. I felt like a sleaze.

I'm sure there are some of you out there who are reading this book who might strongly disapprove of promiscuity, who will say I used women. You're right. I did. But it wasn't always clear to me who was really using whom. I was usually the one being pursued by fans who wanted me much more than I wanted them.

Once, Sam brought a girl home who turned out to be a real nutcase. She was obsessed with me. It turned into a rather difficult situation because Sam thought she was in love with him. But she lied to him to get into our world. She used him, but he really dug her. That was awful.

He'd met this girl on one of our tours. She was really dirty – I mean literally, she had dirt all over her hands – but there was something about her. She just reeked of sex. And Sam fell for it, big time. She really got under his skin. He brought her around. Showed her off. Then she got drunk one night on the road and started crawling into my room. She was banging on my door, crying. I wasn't interested. A couple of my guys grabbed her and took her downstairs. Sam couldn't look me in the eye. He tried to rationalise the situation, saying, 'Well, she was drunk.' I said, 'Yeah, but she *was* trying to get into my room. That tells you something.' He was really hurt by it and a little angry with me.

Even when I was 20, I wasn't attracted to 16-year-olds. I went for older women, 30-year-olds. I was well aware of the difficulties Elvis and others had had due to involvements with underage girls. And I was also concerned about the possibility of inflicting trauma on someone who was just too young.

It was not always easy turning down those temptations. I can remember one 14-year-old who wanted to have sex with me, but I wouldn't do it. I felt like such an old square declining her offer. She was a virgin and one of the most beautiful girls I've ever seen. I told her I didn't want to be the one to take her virginity. 'Save it, baby. Your time will come soon.'

> **Sam Hyman:** There were a lot of women, an extraordinary amount of women of all ages. It used to astonish me the power of fame and celebrity and what many women would subject themselves to. They might be in a committed relationship, they might be married, and they would throw themselves at him. For a one-nighter they were going to just throw their morals right out the window. The number of women used to astonish me. There were certain cities where everybody got lucky.
>
> Being young guys, of course we would take advantage of the situation. David couldn't actually go out and get the women. We'd have to kind of scout around for him a lot. But sometimes there were parties you went to after a show and girls would actually throw themselves on him. It was like being a kid in a candy store. Boy, this was a great fringe benefit of touring. You thought your whole life was going to be that way and then all of a sudden you get back to reality.

I had some male groupies who would also hang out around the hotel or wherever I was, waiting to see me. Some transvestites, some gay guys. I always liked seeing them. They were always interesting and amusing. I never treated them any differently than I did the female fans. Except I'd only sign autographs for them!

Part of the bizarreness of being a teen idol, a rock star, a TV star is becoming the focus of people's sexual fantasies – both male and female. I used to feel flattered when I'd hear that a friend had gone into a gay bar and heard half the guys saying they'd slept with me. I thought it was funny. I've always figured it's a compliment when someone says they're attracted to you. Gay friends would say to me, 'Hey, I hear you've been spending a lot of nights at the Rusty Nail,' which was a popular gay bar. Right! As if I had the energy or the time to go out to any bars after work! But there'd be that kind of gossip. To borrow a phrase from Dustin Hoffman, the first time I realised I had made it was when I walked into a bar and heard I was gay.

I never wanted my fans to be disappointed in David Cassidy. That was a tremendous weight on me. There were things about me that they believed that weren't true, and I didn't want to burst their bubbles. I was torn, because I wanted to be myself, but then I couldn't live up to their expectations.

I was painted to be this White Knight, this perfect guy, and the truth about David Cassidy is he was and is flawed, just like everybody else. My friends used to say, 'Your drugs are women and sex.' And that was true. I'm not ashamed to say it, although I can't say I'm proud of it. I never discussed the people I was dating. I never exposed anybody. I never taped anybody. I never did anything sick, you know? I wasn't cruel. It was consensual. It was fantastic. I was fulfilling people's fantasies and they were fulfilling mine.

In the 70s, the Playboy Mansion was beyond the beyond and I thought it would be interesting to check it out. I was taken there by two beautiful women in their 30s. When I got there, there were naked Playboy Bunnies running around and they were more than anxious to meet me. This was probably in 1972. There were only a few men in the world who were permitted to go up there and I became one of them, although I wasn't nearly as frequent a visitor as some of the others, only because I was working almost every weekend. I walked into the Grotto and a number of Playboy Playmates screamed as if I'd walked into Madison Square Garden.

That night I felt compelled to live the American Dream as

every boy would have. I got to know all four of the girls that night, intimately. And I got to know them again on a couple of different occasions. Wilt Chamberlain, one of the superheroes of basketball, made the greatest mistake of his life by telling the truth about his sexual exploits in his autobiography. I met Wilt there; he was one of the guys in the entertainment business who were welcomed by Hef. It was Hef's palace and his world and we were just living in it for a while. I loved the fact that he was genuine and generous about his home, providing food, women, movies and anything else you wanted. And I will defend him because he deserves to be defended as a guy who is living what every man in our culture has dreamt of. He was willing to risk everything he had and go on the line to do what was, in the 50s, not socially acceptable. In the 60s that lifestyle became very acceptable, and then came AIDS and political correctness. Hef's not somebody who cares about being politically correct. I liked him. Most women see him as being the poster boy for the anti-feminist brigade. But he loves women. For a decade and a half, my way of life rivalled his.

As my fame grew, I became even more reclusive. It was a big responsibility living up to my image so I retreated into my shell. I was scared that if people really got to know me, they wouldn't love me as much. How would they really feel about me if they found out I wasn't this superhuman I was built up to be?

For a couple of years during the run of *The Partridge Family*, I went to see a psychiatrist every Monday night. I wanted help so I could deal with the kinds of stress that were too great for me to handle alone. I was particularly bothered by my inability to form lasting friendships with women.

Sam Hyman: I was fortunate to have nice girlfriends and some long-term relationships. David and I would sit down and talk and I'd say, 'Man, I wish I had the Midas touch like you. You can have a hundred girls in a hundred days if you want.' And he would say, 'Man, I wish I had a long-term relationship like you.' Here was a young man who was vying for the love of his father and not getting it, and wasn't able to have a meaningful relationship. It took him a long time to mature emotionally in that way. I don't care if you're famous or not, having that life partner is such an important part of one's life.

12 Pooka Shells and Stolen Identity

I gave interviews all the time, but the teen magazines wrote what their readers wanted me to say, not what came out of my mouth. They could ask, 'What do you think about most?' And I could've said, 'I like getting sex in my dressing room in between takes.' And they would've said, 'David would like to walk down the beach alone and read poetry with that someone special he's yet to find. You could be that person.' That's funny. I had no time for a walk on the beach. There was never any of that. They were all fabricated stories for their readers.

Sandy Stert Benjamin (associate editor, *Tiger Beat*): Because of the volume of magazines we were putting out, plus the fact that the people who were around long enough, like David, were in every issue of every magazine, you had to fudge a bit. We had to get the material out there without having to call them on the phone or be in their face every five seconds.

He and Susan Dey did an advice column called 'David and Susan

Tell It Like It Is' and I was writing that. If anybody paid attention to any of the advice in there, hey, I hope it worked out for them because I was trying my best. I was a teenager myself – just fresh out of high school when I was hired – and was actually the youngest one on staff at the time.

Ann Moses (editor, *Tiger Beat*): The headline on the cover of the January 1971 issue of *Tiger Beat* was 'David Cassidy Quits'. Now what's the story about? We'd been protecting David for six months or a year because he chain-smoked. So in this story we had a picture of him smoking from one of our photo sessions. It was the first one we ever published. We would never normally publish a picture of a teen idol smoking. We were a part of their whole image. So the story, which went on for two pages, was about how he had quit smoking. I don't call that a fabrication, I call that taking one sentence and making it into a two-page article.

We had a headline, 'David's Struggle with Death'. Our photographer, Kenny Lieu, went with David and Sam Hyman to Hawaii. David was into scuba diving and he ran out of air underwater and they buddy-breathed 'til they got to the surface. But, of course, the headline is, 'His Brush with Death'.

Sharon Lee (editor, *The Partridge Family Magazine*/editor and editorial director, *Tiger Beat*, 1972–84): The articles were based on one kernel of truth and then were expanded pretty dramatically. That's how all the teen magazines operated. You'd get an interview and use parts of the same interview over and over. You'd take something that David said and just elaborate on it. A lot of it was quotations that you just made up and some of the people didn't even care. For instance, we ran a column by Susan Dey and she never even looked at it. We were very creative as writers. We'd have idea sessions. We'd clip things from newspapers, titles that sounded good. We'd look at a photo where David looked really sad and think, 'What can we write about to go with the picture?' We'd come up with the idea that his heart was breaking because he didn't have free time. Then we'd write our story based on that idea. It was true, he didn't have free time. We had to deliver stories that would capture the readers' attention. We'd have to be creative and really descriptive. Instead of saying, 'David walked into the room smiling,' it's 'David walked into the room with the light glowing on his hair and his eyes sparkling and his lips open ...' You had to make it *dramatic*.

Sam Hyman: I did a monthly column for *Tiger Beat* but I didn't actually do the writing. I'd tell the writer something like, 'OK, this month we did this. Why don't we talk about how he got a new car?' After a while it was pretty lame. He was such a big star and he had to have so many stories written about him that the articles would just be a bunch of fluff, like: David goes on a picnic with his old friend. But the kids wanted to know as much about him as possible. And the magazines were portraying a very squeaky-clean image. You're portraying an image and you perpetuate it and you've got a machine behind you to let everybody think this is what it is. It's the same today. It drove him nuts. He couldn't wait to break away from it.

On television I may have been playing a 16-year-old, but my fans knew I was really older. For one thing, the teen magazines would make a huge deal out of my birthday. Every reader knew when I turned 21 on 12 April 1971, because Chuck Laufer threw a 'surprise party' (translation: photo op) for me. His magazines published photo after photo of Sam Hyman, Steve Ross and me opening presents and reading cards. One typical posed photo showed Sam 'surprising' me by dumping boxes of cards from fans over my head. The caption assured everyone that I had read each and every one. That sounded much better than what really happened, which was that the Laufer Company, which was licensed to handle my fan mail, simply recorded the names and addresses of everyone who wrote to me so they could be added to their mailing lists, and the mail disappeared. I never saw any of it. But, those youngsters would then be solicited to purchase other David Cassidy and *The Partridge Family* memorabilia, as well as subscribe to Laufer publications. Nice work, eh? Clearly, I never saw any of the fan mail, and I certainly never got any money out of it.

Other birthday party photos showed Laufer magazine editors giving me supplies of cashews and 7 Up (which the magazines relentlessly reminded readers was my drink of choice). Another photo showed me hoisting what could have been mistaken for a large glass of champagne if you didn't read the caption, supposedly quoting my own words: 'Time out for cake and 7 Up, and a toast to you for making this the happiest birthday of all. I never expected such love from you. How can I thank you?' Another caption had me insisting that this Laufer-organised event was 'my all-time best birthday'. Yet another had me accepting a poster from Sharon Lee, editor of the Laufer publication *Tiger Beat Spectacular.* The caption quoted me as responding, 'Gosh, Laufer's editors are so wonderful.' Gosh, that sure does sound like me talking all right.

And the editors informed the presumably lovesick young readers nationwide, 'David wants all of YOU to know that he loves you very much and without your love he couldn't have known happiness.' And, 'David wishes he could give YOU a hug and a kiss to let you know how much he appreciates your thinking of him.'

Even though I didn't really have any use for them, I was touched by the care fans took in sending me gifts, particularly the handmade ones. I got a lot of those, I suppose because most fans realised that I was already a millionaire. A fan who sent a really great birthday gift knew she might even be lucky enough to see her name in one of the magazines. They'd print a line saying, 'David is going to use the hand-knitted Afghan sent by fan Eileen Fry of Bellmar, NJ, as his bedspread,' and other fans would rush to send similar gifts.

One person who really should have been cognizant of my age – but, fortunately for me, was not – was the lawyer for Screen Gems (or its parent company at the time, Columbia Pictures Industries), who drew up the contract signing me to them.

You see, when I signed that remarkably one-sided contract I was under 21 years of age and so, as a minor at that time, the contract would only have been valid had either my father or my mother or another legal guardian signed it. But they just assumed I was an adult. They didn't check. That one little oversight would wind up costing Screen Gems a lot of money.

The show went into production with me being paid just $600 a week, little more than scale (the very lowest amount they can pay anyone). They promised to give me modest raises in subsequent years. With that contract, they believed they had acquired all the rights to my name, voice and likeness for seven years. At some point, however, someone from Screen Gems finally realised they'd made a mistake and that the contract was not legally valid. The work I'd been doing for Screen Gems and its affiliates, including Bell Records, was not under contract at all.

Rather sheepishly, they asked if they could just get one of my parents to sign the contract so it would be binding. Ruth, of course, knew better than to allow that. Now, for the first time, we clearly had the upper hand. She went in to see them on my behalf. By this point, the show had been running for more than a year, my record sales were in the millions, I was on the covers of magazines. I was *the* hot young dude. Screen Gems and Bell Records needed me.

Ruth told them, 'Look, you've treated this person badly. You're making millions of dollars off David Cassidy and are paying him just $600 a week. I want you to remove his name, his voice and his likeness from everything unless you are willing to make him a profit participant.'

The first time she said it they freaked. Never before had anyone shown any guts with these people. I mean, they raped everybody who ever worked for them. The Monkees received nothing compared to the money they earned for the company. But that was standard in the industry at that time. Who got the profits? The corporations. Screen Gems and Bell Records stood to make hundreds of millions of dollars off me, yet they were content to pay me less than they would have paid guys in middle management. Ruth said she wouldn't stand for it. She was about to change the rules of the game.

Bob Claver (executive producer, *The Partridge Family*): Ruth renegotiated a contract that he (David) was entitled to. The studio was expecting the worst. She could have asked for almost any amount of money but she didn't. She had the power to have had the show taken off the air but she didn't. She was a wonderful, honest, forthright intelligent person . . . a rare bird.

In the end I wound up owning a piece of the *net* profits, which at that point was unprecedented. Columbia Pictures and Screen Gems had never given up a piece to anybody. My base salary shot up to $4,000 a week. That was a lot of money in 1971! And as a token of their appreciation, Screen Gems also gave me a new Corvette, a classic move in Hollywood and the record industry. A performer is expected to feel grateful for the wonderful gift and to be less inclined to check carefully whether he is being paid fairly. I took the bait.

Under the contract I had originally signed, I was not to have been paid *anything* for making records – that was to have been part of the work for the salary I got. Ruth insisted I'd now have to be paid royalties for my records too. We settled on the following terms: for all the records issued under my own name (and the first David Cassidy single, *Cherish*, was on the *Billboard* charts for 12 weeks, beginning 6 November 1971) and all *Partridge Family* recordings, I'd receive five per cent of the net profits to $500,000, six per cent to $1 million and seven per cent thereafter. This was a very good royalty rate in 1971; today it would be three times that.

Ruth also insisted that I participate in the profits derived from all *Partridge Family* or David Cassidy merchandising, that is to say, anything that Screen Gems licensed using *The Partridge Family* or David Cassidy names or likenesses, from a poster to a lunchbox. Sounds good, right?

Ruth further insisted that the period the contract covered be shortened from seven years to four years. After four years, we figured we could probably negotiate an even better deal, or I could go elsewhere and do better. Screen Gems took the attitude that they had made me a star, just like they had made The Monkees stars, and that I was raping them. They felt that I was becoming too big for my boots. Screen Gems had helped launch my career, but now it was me that the public wanted. I had a notion that *The Partridge Family* TV show might even be holding me back. I didn't want to be tied down for seven long years. I wanted greater freedom to express myself as a creative artist. I wanted freedom to do whatever I chose after four years. And I wanted to be paid. I could envision my career continuing to grow in subsequent years – concerts, records, TV and films. Ultimately, I got most of the terms that I asked for.

I still wound up being paid a lot less money than I should have been. Ruth simply didn't have experience in the record business or merchandising. She'd certainly never represented an 'idol' before.

One mistake we made when renegotiating was that we agreed to accept a percentage of the net profits. We should have insisted upon a percentage of gross income. With clever accounting, a record company, for example, could claim that even if they grossed hundreds of millions of dollars on my recordings, their net profits – and consequently the royalties they had to pay me – were actually surprisingly small. At one point, when we suspected that Bell Records was not paying me all that it should, we had an audit done which indicated they owed me an additional $400,000. They then grudgingly gave me about half of that, which I accepted, knowing that if I fought them in a long court battle, I'd spend a fortune in attorneys' fees.

I earned virtually nothing on merchandising – a total of $15,000, even though every time I turned around someone was marketing another product bearing my name. They were making the money, not me. But Ruth and I were barely aware of what was going on in the merchandising field and we let millions of dollars slip through our fingers. If we got a report that only 6,000 David Cassidy posters had been sold in a certain period, at very little profit, we didn't challenge those figures. By the time Ruth was managing my brother Shaun's career in the late 70s, she was much more knowledgeable about merchandising deals and watched the money much more carefully. I think Shaun made a million dollars from the sale of posters and related items, even though his career as a pop star didn't last as long as mine.

Shaun Cassidy: As with David, Ruth managed me, too. I learned by David's example. Very, very few people go through the experience he went through, and certainly having two people in the same family go through it is incredibly rare. Having been able to watch him and see what was thrown at him and see how he managed some things and couldn't manage other things, was probably the best education

> I could have had. I think the consequence of that was I never expected it to last very long and didn't take it seriously at all. It was like a novelty. The greatest challenge I had was trying to figure out what I wanted to do with the rest of my life, when at 21 I was married and kind of retired. I didn't have bitterness about it and didn't feel that I'd been used up, all of the things that I know David experienced. Unfortunately, when I was going through it, he was in that bitter place. I couldn't really talk to him about much.

Everyone I knew respected Ruth Aarons for her wit and her knowledge. She'd come from an important theatrical family. I just naturally assumed that she and the business manager she had hired to look after me knew what they were doing. I was really impressed that she got me a salary of $4,000 a week for the TV show. You have to remember, I didn't have anything when I started out. In 1969, my total earnings for the *year* had been no more than $3,000.

So I was delighted, in 1971, to be getting more than that each week. Salaries in show business, generally, weren't anywhere near as high then as they are today. The biggest star in television at that point – James Arness, who'd been starring as Marshall Dillon in *Gunsmoke* since the mid 50s – was only making around $18,000 a week. And at that point, I believe that was the longest running show on television. The most Shirley was ever paid for a motion picture was $250,000. Ruth assured me that between my TV show, records and concerts, I could certainly count on making more than that figure each and every year.

I was making so much money overall, particularly from my concerts – I could gross $50,000 or more in one night – that I didn't worry that I might be getting short-changed here or there. How much could I spend, anyway? And when? All I did was work. Besides, I was not a materialistic guy.

> **Sam Hyman:** David is not an extravagant person. And in those days, he was not extravagant at all. I had to talk him into finally buying a new car. He bought a Mercedes, which cost $12,000 in those days. He drove it for like a day or two and immediately gave it to his mother. He was not into 'stuff'.

Screen Gems had initially established a budget of about $120,000 per episode of *The Partridge Family*. If my salary had to be upped to $4,000, that was no problem for them. *TV Guide* reported in 1972 that, due to the success of our TV show, records and the assorted merchandising spin-offs, one Screen Gems bigwig was now referring to the brand as '*The Partridge Family* money machine'. *The Partridge Family,* declared *TV Guide,* was 'practically a branch of the U.S. Mint'.

I guess I never heard those reports. I was too busy touring, filming, recording and answering – for the umpteenth time – the same dumb questions from interviewers. Almost everyone wanted to know what I ate, what I drank, what I looked for in girls ('honesty' was my less-than-completely-honest reply) and how I liked working with my stepmother. One interviewer, who'd been around the block more times than most of the others, had a more pertinent question to ask, even though I didn't grasp its significance at the time. Veteran *New York Post* columnist Earl Wilson didn't ask me any of the usual nonsensical questions when we met in March 1972. The thing he wanted to know was, 'Who's taking care of your money, David?' I told him, 'A business manager and accountant. I'm investing in oil . . .'

13 The Soundtrack of My Youth

On *The Partridge Family* we had an assistant director named Chris Morgan, who is the son of the wonderful character actor Harry Morgan. Chris had worked on a couple of Elvis's films and he knew Elvis personally. Chris was one of the great practical jokers of all time. He would go to great lengths to suck you in. And he and I had this ongoing daily sparring match to see how we could mess with each other. That was one of the few things that I had as a release – humour.

One day, the phone rang on the set while we were doing a blocking session in rehearsal and Chris walked over to the phone, answered it and said, 'Oh, hi, Elvis.' Then he said, 'Hang on,' and he turned towards me. 'Uh, Elvis is on the phone for you,' and the whole set goes, 'Ooooo, David is gonna talk to Elvis.'

I knew it wasn't Elvis. I was positive it was just another one of Chris's practical jokes. I picked up the phone and said, 'Hey, Elvis, baby. How are ya, man?' And a voice that sounded like his said, 'Hey, baby, how are ya?' And, still thinking it was a prank, I was like, 'Oh, I'm fantastic, man. We're just blockin' a scene here.' And he laughed and said, 'My daughter's a big fan of yours and would love to come and meet you,' and I said, 'Sure, bring her on Thursday. Great to talk to ya, Elvis.'

I walked away from the phone and announced, 'Yep, that was Elvis and I told him to bring his daughter and his wife to the set.' Two days later, we were on the set and, very dramatically, the doors to the sound stage, which were at least 40 feet high, opened. In pulled a black limousine and out stepped arguably the most beautiful child and the most beautiful woman I'd ever seen – Lisa Marie and Priscilla.

Lisa Marie was about four years old, a platinum-blonde child with big blue eyes. Priscilla, then in her early 30s, was drop-dead gorgeous. I was sitting there thinking, as most men would, *This is maybe the most beautiful woman I've ever looked at. Look at that magnificent face*. I understood how he would want the most beautiful woman and how no one else would have been worthy of her. And there I was with my mouth open. Chris Morgan was standing there with a big smile on his face and all I could think was, *Oh no, I made such an idiot of myself.*

So I called Elvis and said, 'Listen, I know you know Chris.'

And he said, 'Of course I know Chris and I know he was messin' with you. He called me and told me.'

Lisa Marie Presley: I was a huge fan of *The Partridge Family* and I did go to the set. They were in the middle of taping. I was probably three or four years old at the time. I was told that I was comfortable enough with them and felt connected enough with them that I got up from sitting on my mom's lap and ran on to the stage while they were taping and jumped into Shirley Jones's lap. They had to stop the taping. I loved *I Think I Love You*. In fact, on my *Now What* CD, the intro on *Raven* is my three-year-old voice singing *I Think I Love You*. You hear my mom saying, 'Sing it right' and I just thought that was funny. And the 'ba-ba-ba-ba' in the beginning is the intro for *I Think I Love You*. My mom would always tape me singing and send it off to my dad when he was on tour.

Elvis was very complimentary when I finally got to meet him. I went up to his house in L.A. I came away from our meeting liking him a lot and feeling so sorry for him and also frightened to death. He had so much talent but he allowed somebody else to take over his life. There was a sadness about Elvis that I recognised in myself. He too surrounded himself with friends. I knew all about the hysteria and madness he had gone through. So we had a unique sort of connection. When the Beatles first came to America, they wanted to meet him; they probably felt the same kind of connection with him.

Meeting Elvis that time was like seeing myself ten or fifteen years from then, sad and lonely. I couldn't get it out of my head. This was a guy who was smart. He was funny. He was very cool. Yet he had sold his soul to do the teeny bopper movie *Clambake*. I loved him as a guy and as an artist and I respected him more than just about anyone, but I wouldn't have sold my soul to the devil and he did. And the devil was the Colonel. That's the saddest part. I know that Elvis regretted it every day of his life, but he was loyal.

During that time, I also got to know one of my musical heroes, John Lennon. When he split with Yoko and was with May Pang, I spent some time in L.A. with him. I first met him at Elliot Mintz's house and spent a little time chatting with him. We subsequently had dinner together a couple of times. We'd go to the Imperial Gardens so we could be in a private room where no one would bother us.

Later, I flew back to New York twice and spent a little time with Yoko. She is very bright and I liked her a lot. I think she was treated unfairly by the media and the public. She provided a real grounding for John and a place to feel safe. She loved him for who he was, not because he was a Beatle. I later found the same thing with my wife, Sue.

May Pang: Elliot Mintz said to John and me, 'I want you to meet David Cassidy.' I said, 'David Cassidy? Cool, I love *The Partridge Family*!' Besides, I thought he was cute and thought it would be fun. John knew who David Cassidy was and knew his background. John was a big movie buff and admired David's father, Jack Cassidy, and his stepmother, Shirley Jones.

John was looking forward to meeting David. He understood what David was dealing with as a teen idol. My girlfriend, Arlene Reckson, was our houseguest in L.A. and wanted to meet him too. So John, Arlene and I went to meet David for lunch at Carlos & Charley's. Arlene and I were talking to David a lot. I guess we were paying too much attention to the new kid on the block. It didn't help matters when a little girl came over and asked for David's autograph and not John's. She was too young to recognise John. That was quite funny; it must've bruised John's ego slightly.

We had a great lunch. David and John were talking about the different projects they were working on. Here you had John Lennon, who went through everything imaginable with Beatlemania, and David Cassidy, who's riding the crest as the current teen idol. They compared notes about the toll of stardom and they shared a common bond. John really liked David and David seemed in awe of John and was very respectful and reverent.

When it came to ordering food, David said, 'I'm gonna have the eggplant parmesan,' and I said, 'Oh, that sounds good, I think I'm gonna have that too.' And then Arlene said, 'Oh yeah, I think I'll have that too.' So there were three of us who ordered it. Unbeknownst to me, John was getting upset and made a point of ordering the ravioli. I didn't realise that John was starting to get jealous; he kept it under wraps pretty well.

We spent some time together at Elliot MIntz's house, and after David left, John and I headed off to A&M recording studio, where John was working on his *Rock 'n' Roll* album. He had had a couple of drinks at lunchtime. No sooner were we in the studio than John announced, 'The session's cancelled!' I asked, 'Why?' He said, 'I can't fuckin' do this!'

We went home and he's screaming that I was flirting with David Cassidy. I said, 'What are you talking about?' And he said, 'You ordered the same meal!' I said, 'What?! And so did Arlene. What does that mean?' And then John ranted, 'What about that song he sang to you?'

I had just recorded a song called *Mae* for my *Dreams Are Nuthin' More Than Wishes* album. I whipped out my guitar and sang this sweet little song for John and May. Interestingly, John wrote a song called *Jealous Guy*, which was John talking honestly about how he could get jealous.

May Pang: Then, like clockwork, Yoko called and he told her about it. John told me Yoko said, 'Of course she was flirting with David Cassidy, she doesn't wanna be with you.' I'm thinking to myself, *Thanks for fuelling this fire, Yoko.*

After a good night's sleep, John realised that I wasn't flirting with David. He calmed down and apologised to me. John spoke with David on the phone later that day and everything was cool.

During the last year of *The Partridge Family*, 1974, John continued making the *Rock 'n' Roll* album. I saw Elliot all the time and John and I would pass messages back and forth to each other through him. John came over to my house in Encino on New Year's Eve in 1974 or 1975, when I had just finished my world tour. Susan Dey was there and I had fallen asleep at around midnight on her lap. Elliot and John showed up and they had been out drinking and celebrating. Susan woke me up and said, 'David, I think there's a Beatle in the house.'

After slurring a few words to each other, John and I decided to play some music. So we went into my music room, where I had all my guitars, and we sat on the floor and I began playing the Beatles' song *Any Time at All*. It was one of my favourites. That and *Mr Moonlight*. And John was like, 'Oh, I can't remember that.' He had written hundreds of songs since then. So I sort of re-taught him the chord structure. We sang it together and I did Paul's part. It was like being a Beatle for a moment. I was fulfilling a dream I'd had since I was 13, learning Beatles' songs on my first guitar after seeing them on the *Ed Sullivan Show*. You don't forget some of the first songs you learn.

We started playing rock 'n' roll songs, stuff by Chuck Berry like *Nadine*. John loved all that Chuck Berry stuff and he knew it much better than I did. It didn't sound very good, we were drinking, laughing and just stumbling through a lot of it. I played him a song I had just written and he started playing me stuff that he was working on. He was into this rock 'n' roll thing from the 50s, the sound he had grown up with. He played the Dave Edmunds song *I Hear You Knocking*. I'd been working on *Be-Bop-a-Lula* at the time and he loved that I was into that kind of stuff. John recorded it on his *Rock 'n' Roll* album. We had a musical connection.

I had an interesting relationship with John. I related to him because of his abandonment issues and his creativity. He was kind enough to give me insight into what I was about to go through. He'd been there and done that and was in the process of demystifying himself.

Once, while we were having lunch together, he invited me to come to A&M Studios where he was recording the *Rock 'n' Roll* album. He asked me if I wanted to play with the other musicians. I did go but it was so crowded and almost every great guitar player you can think of was there. Harry Nilsson, Cher and lots of other people were there, too. At the time I didn't want to be part of the circus. I only stayed for around 15 minutes, although in hindsight I probably should have played.

John told me all the stories about his studio days. It was around this time that Phil Spector, who produced some of the album, came in dressed like a Nazi, calling himself Hitler, flailing a gun and even shooting it off. He was out of his mind.

John had a fabulous sense of humour. He was more dedicated to the things he believed in than anyone that I can think of. He wasn't seduced by greed. We only spoke briefly about Paul and his comments at the time were, 'Yeah, well, you know, that's just Paul.' I think John was deeply hurt by their differences and the fact that their partnership wasn't a partnership. He felt the competition with Paul, who would come in with 15 songs and want to record them all. John told me, 'I don't want to be in, you know, "Paul & the Beatles". I don't want to be a sideman for Paul. It's not what I want to do any more.'

John Lennon had a very strong influence on me by giving me advice on how to start trying to live a normal life again. How do I find a way to walk down the street or go to a restaurant and not be paranoid? We talked a lot about that. There were certain things that I could say to him and he could say to me that no other people on the earth could understand except perhaps the other Beatles and Elvis.

I was in England doing promotion for my *The Higher They Climb, The Harder They Fall* album in 1975 when I met Paul McCartney. He invited me and Steve Ross, who was playing guitar for me at the time, to Paris to watch the last rehearsal for the Wings over America tour. They did the whole show on that huge stage with all the special effects just for Steve and me. Two nights later we went to the actual concert and were invited up on stage and played with Paul and Wings.

Jimmy McCullough, the lead guitarist in Wings, came over to the hotel one night during that time and got incredibly drunk. He smashed the television set and broke his hand and I had to call Paul and tell him that Jimmy was with me and that he had been taken to the hospital. They had to postpone their tour for six weeks or so and I think Paul somehow blamed me. Jimmy was just out of control and, because of his alcoholism, he went nuts. He ended up killing himself.

Back in L.A I saw Paul a few other times, at a party I was at with Ronnie Wood ('Woody') just after he joined the Rolling Stones, and Bob Dylan. I was also invited to the Hollywood studio where Paul was finishing up an album in Hollywood. I think it was probably 1977 or 1978 and I had just finished working down the street. He played me a song they had just recorded. I think it was *Venus and Mars*. Listening to him finalising a track was really great, because he is arguably one of the great talents of all time.

I also had a chance to hang out quite a bit with the Beach Boys. I went to Brother Studios in Santa Monica once or twice and played with Carl Wilson. I hung out with Brian Wilson and worked with him at his house, at Gerry Beckley's house (Gerry was in the group America) and at my home. We messed around playing. Brian was not recording any more. Ricky Fataar, who was in the Beach Boys for a long time before he left, was working with me. Ricky is one of the most talented human beings, and one of the greatest drummers. He's been Bonnie Raitt's drummer for maybe 20 years now.

In 1991, I played some stadium dates with the Beach Boys. One night Carl and Bruce said, 'Come and hang out and sing with us,' and I did. Ricky came and sat in and played drums. Playing those songs with those guys was cool. Along with the Beatles, those were the guys who created the soundtrack to my youth.

14 No Time for Love

A lot of women I met struck me as opportunists. They were using me to advance hoped-for acting careers, or perhaps they were interested in me for my money. That ain't the real stuff. I was looking for something more.

Of all the actresses I dated, there was only one I fell for, or thought I had. Only one I wanted to have a lasting relationship with. Meredith Baxter. She was a few years older than I was when she made a guest appearance on *The Partridge Family* and we began dating. If you can call it that. She'd just got divorced from her first husband and was living in a little house in Burbank with her two young children, trying to make it on her own as an actress. I really carried a serious torch for her. I never told anybody about it except Susan Dey, Shirley and a couple of other close friends. Meredith was a beautiful woman – warm, intelligent, independent, kind of a hippie at heart, like I was. She liked music and would sit around and play guitar. She was also much more mature than

I was. I may have been 21, but emotionally I was still a teenager.

We were very secretive about our relationship because I didn't want to tip off the tabloids. We usually went to Meredith's house or mine. I was going through one of the worst periods of my life. I had so little free time that days and weeks would often go by without my seeing Meredith at all. I was just a working machine.

When I was able to be with her, we had a great time. I thought I might be in love with her. I'm sure she didn't realise how much I cared about her because I was away so much of the time and that was frustrating for me. But I was on such a roll in the rest of my life that I just went with the flow. I figured that eventually my life would grow less hectic and then we could really get to spend some time together. Wrong again. Instead, my life grew more hectic.

After Meredith and I had been dating for about a month, I got home from work one Friday night – I was supposed to go on the road early the next morning – and got a call from Ruth.

She said, 'I want you to pack up. You're leaving your house.'

I said, 'What are you talking about?'

'In about fifteen minutes there's going to be someone from the FBI at your gate. Go with him. This isn't a joke. There's a legitimate kidnapping threat.'

Perfect.

The Los Angeles Police Department had been tipped off by a very reliable source that two guys planned to kidnap me and hoped to collect a multi-million-dollar ransom from my family and Screen Gems. I immediately thought of the worst-case scenario: *they're going to kill me.* I moved out of my house and into the Holiday Inn on Highland Avenue. Initially there were

FBI agents in the room on one side of mine and the LAPD in the room on the other. For extra security, I hired a bodyguard who lived in my room.

We didn't want to let anybody know what was going on. I simply had to bring this guy with me everywhere I went, as if he were some good ol' friend. Problem was, I didn't know him. He never said much; he just stuck to me like glue. If I got up to go anywhere, even to the john, he'd walk along with me. He'd stand outside, casually keeping an eye out. He was a muscular fellow, the bodybuilder type, in his early 30s. And I was this rather slight, androgynous-looking, long-haired 21-year-old (my stand-in on *The Partridge Family*, if you can believe it, was a girl). Everyone at work was convinced we were lovers. 'David's gone around the bend!'

I restricted my activities. To minimise my vulnerability, I went almost nowhere except to work. I took things one day at a time. The days turned into weeks. I was in agony.

The only public function I went to in that period was the annual Golden Apple awards presentation. They told me beforehand that I had won a Golden Apple. The ceremony took place at the Beverly Hills Hotel, and all of Hollywood was there. The police and FBI were especially fearful that an attempt to kidnap me would be made there, where maintaining security was difficult. This would be the day they'd make the snatch.

At the hotel, there were waiters and doormen who were really FBI agents or LAPD. I was so scared that I was going to be kidnapped that when I got up to accept my award, I was shaking. I was looking at everyone in the room like, *Maybe these are the guys who are out to get me.*

Accepting my award, I said just two words, 'Thank you.' That was it. And I'm usually a pretty verbal guy. But I just walked off. And I had dressed in a jean jacket, jeans and a T-shirt, everyone else was dressed up. The audience must have thought, 'That's it? "Thank you?" What a stiff!'

At one point during the awards, I had to get up to go to the bathroom. There were 27 people who got up simultaneously and followed me there. I didn't know who was trying to protect me, who might be trying to get to me or who was just trying to take a leak.

I fantasised about the day when this mess would be over with and I could pick up with Meredith where we'd left off. I was so weighed down with my own problems I really wasn't thinking what she might be going through.

I'd never lived in the real adult world. I'd gone straight from fooling around as a teenager, living with my parents, to the highly artificial world of TV stardom. Here I was, having to live with this bodyguard instead of with someone who mattered to me, like most people my age.

My life as a pop star was like being in a hurricane most of the time. As if someone had completely ripped up my sense of reality and said, 'Here, try this on for a while.' No one could really get near me any more. I'd become this guy, living in fear in a Holiday Inn, accompanied everywhere by this nondescript, tall, silent, muscular guy.

And what did I think would happen once this whole kidnapping thing was behind me? I guess I thought that I could resume touring, doing TV and making records and somehow maintain a successful relationship with Meredith Baxter. Yeah, right.

I wasn't mature enough to see that the kidnapping threat wasn't the real problem. I could confide in Meredith and longed for a real relationship, but I was not emotionally equipped and, frankly, I was too young for her, both emotionally and intellectually.

There wasn't enough free time in my schedule to have a

relationship with myself, let alone with another human being. But I just couldn't grasp that. I was totally lost.

Finally, after about a month had passed since I'd first been told there was a pending threat, everyone assumed the would-be kidnappers had given up. I had seen no signs of danger. Maybe it had been a false alarm all along, or maybe they'd been scared off. It took me a while to believe that the threat was over and I was safe, but finally I let the bodyguard go and tried to get things started up again with Meredith.

Her life had moved ahead without me. While I'd been worried about possible kidnappers, she'd fallen in love with someone else. The producers of *The Partridge Family* had hired Meredith and David Birney to co-star in a new series called *Bridget Loves Bernie*, and I learned she'd started having a relationship with her co-star.

Meredith and I spent one final weekend together after they became involved, which I'm sure David Birney never knew about. Then Meredith broke off the relationship with me for good. It was hard for me to accept. Even though there were millions of people who loved me and worshipped me and wanted me, I needed something more.

Meredith and David filmed their TV series in the studio right next to mine. I'd see them together every day. It broke my heart. Eventually, of course, they got married (and some years later divorced) and after a while I got over her.

I continued to fantasise about having a real relationship, about going out in public on a date without having people going stupid over me. Maybe I hadn't been college material, but I began to envy my old high-school classmates who'd gone on to college. I even envied people with 'normal' jobs. Either of those paths seemed preferable to the one I'd taken. I started longing to have any other career but my own. It may sound absurd now, but it's true. There I was, rich and famous, a star, wishing at times I could be some thoroughly ordinary, anonymous guy instead. I'd dream about what it would be like to work at a real man's job.

15 Congratulations, Here's Your $15,000

Whenever I stepped out on to the concert stage, I liked to think my sole purpose was to entertain people. I was serious about my show. I wanted to be the best entertainer I could.

TV Guide, for one, perceived my role in the business differently. They said that in my public appearances I served in effect as a shill, not just for *The Partridge Family* TV show, but also for a seemingly endless supply of products bearing its name or mine. I hate to admit that was true – certainly it had never been my intention to become anything like that – but in a way that is how it was.

The industry found me highly marketable and exploited my appeal to the maximum. My face was used to sell pictures, posters, magazines and even special stamps for fan mail. It appeared on cereal boxes – General Foods paid a great deal to Screen Gems for that right. I had no say in how my name, voice or likeness was used, or what products I appeared to be endorsing. That was all handled by Screen Gems. They wanted to get everything they could out of the craze for David Cassidy and *The Partridge Family*.

There were *Partridge Family* colouring books, comic books and David Cassidy music books. By mid 1972, Popular Library had published a dozen *Partridge Family* paperback novels, the bestselling of which reportedly sold a million copies. I never saw a dime. Popular Library paid five per cent of the cover price of each item to Screen Gems. There were *Partridge Family* paper dolls, regular dolls, diaries and astrological charts. School children could carry David Cassidy lunchboxes. Their older sisters could spend their summers lying atop beach towels bearing full-length portraits of me – those were a popular premium offered by Hi-C fruit beverages.

Screen Gems tried to tell my manager that licensing items really wasn't a very lucrative business, but reports in the press suggested otherwise. I was supposed to get 15 per cent of all revenues from licensing my name or likeness or that of *The Partridge Family*. I never did.

With great fanfare, Kate Greenaway Industries, a reputable, established children's clothing manufacturer, introduced a *Partridge Family* collection (for which, the press reported, they agreed to pay Screen Gems a licensing fee of $10,000 a month for 15 months), to be marketed with the message 'David Cassidy will love you in these Kate Greenaways.' Greenaway advertising director Alan Jackson noted, '*The Partridge Family* is what's happening in America today.' Greenaway vice president Neil Goldberger said, 'David Cassidy is the love object of thousands of ten- to thirteen-year-old girls. We hope these young ladies will be equally as excited by our *Partridge Family* collection as they are by him. After all, if you get a girl at six, she's a customer 'til ten or eleven.' And so on.

Companies marketed a *Partridge Family* game for the whole family, a David Cassidy plastic guitar for boys and a Susan Dey sewing kit for girls. Buyers of the latter were encouraged to 'make an outfit for David Cassidy'. With seemingly any product they could find some way to trade on my name.

I took a little vacation in Hawaii, and while I was there I strung some shells together on a string. I was photographed wearing that homemade necklace. The next thing I knew, magazines were talking about how much I loved to wear those pooka shells and ads began appearing telling kids that if they'd just send in their money, they too could soon be the proud owners of a necklace like mine. At my concerts I'd see thousands of kids who had proudly bought these necklaces, even though by that time I was no longer wearing anything like that myself. I thought it was hysterical at first, all of these kids copying me. Then I thought it was disgusting, the way kids were being conned into buying things they didn't need. I looked around and thought, *What have I done?*

What really pissed me off is that I had no control over the quality of the merchandise. They could make anything that had my name on it – cheap perfume, an unimaginative toy, even a David Cassidy pillowcase (so girls could, in effect, sleep with me) – and sell it. That was really disturbing. There were massive sales of this stuff all over the world, England, Germany, Belgium, Hong Kong, Japan, Australia. Columbia Pictures and Screen Gems grossed untold millions of dollars. I got a token sum of – are you ready? – $15,000. Once. Yep, that was my share.

My manager tried to get financial statements from them, but with all the clever accounting it looked like no one was making any profit. We were very unsophisticated about merchandising and had no idea how many units of any item were selling. *The Partridge Family* phenomenon was unprecedented, so we had nothing to compare it to or learn from.

The Partridge Family show first aired in the U.S., Canada and Hong Kong in the fall of 1970. By early 1971 it was also being seen in Central America, the Caribbean, Brazil, Thailand and Japan. By the end of that year, they'd added England, Ireland, Spain, Portugal, Peru, Chile, Colombia, Zambia, the Philippines, Australia and New Zealand to the list. And by early 1972, *The Partridge Family* was also being shown in Greece and some of the Arab world.

Screen Gems said yes to anyone who wanted to license the use of my name, likeness or *The Partridge Family* name for any product. The gag around Hollywood was that the only opportunity for exploitation that Screen Gems had missed was auctioning off the gallstones I had passed. A lock of my hair was a more common written request from fans. One company's proposal to market genuine locks of my hair sealed inside plastic was, I'm happy to say, turned down, I later found out.

The letters I read from young fans often had a plaintive innocence. One girl explained her interest in me this way: 'I thought you sounded like a nice person. And I really don't meet up with nice people.' Another youngster confessed: 'I always dreamed I was going steady with you, but now I blush whenever I think about it. I heard you are 20 years old.' Fans vowed their eternal love for me, revealed that they'd written my name with theirs all over their notebook covers and had plastered their school lockers with photos and clippings about me. One fan wrote: 'I hope my letters have been getting to you. I'm just wondering because I haven't gotten any back from you. If you think I have a boyfriend, I don't . . .'

I'd get 20,000 to 30,000 of these letters a week. So many of the fans actually seemed to expect me to write back to them personally. Instead, they'd receive invitations from the Laufer Company to read *The Partridge Family Magazine* (by mid 1972 they were peddling 400,000 copies a month at 50 cents each), join the official David Cassidy fan club (by mid 1972 they had 200,000 members, paying $2 each per year) and purchase assorted photos and posters priced to fit any budget. The company would encourage fans to send an extra 50 cents if they wanted 'rush handling' and countless girls in the throes of puppy love, imagining they'd be making contact with me that much quicker, would gladly cough up the extra four bits. It would have been more honest if they'd simply printed: 'Please enclose an additional 50 cents for Chuck Laufer.' All of those extra 50 cents sure added up for him.

Laufer was an interesting character. I didn't care for him myself because I knew he viewed me as someone to make money off, but I have to admit he knew the teen idol business better than just about anyone. He had quit his job as an English teacher to launch one of the very first teen fan magazines back in 1954 and had soon followed up with others, realising he could just as easily run photos and stories about a pop star simultaneously in four different publications. His timing was perfect. In the mid 50s rock and roll was just coming in and an affluent teen market was emerging in America. Kids were spending money on records, movies, clothes and more. They wanted their own heroes to give them a sense of identity as a generation, and he tapped into their desires. By the time I came on to the scene, he had the business of exploiting teen heroes down to a science. He told me that we were each good for about a two-year run before the magazines started hyping someone new. By then, we'd be overexposed and the readers would be eager to look at a new face.

He explained to reporters, 'There *has* to be a teenage idol, but girls outgrow them. When they're 11 to 14, they can have a nice, safe love affair with somebody like Davy Jones, Bobby

Sherman or David Cassidy. By the time they are 16, they're having dates and they don't need them any more.'

My career still seemed to be building in intensity. In 1972, the TV show was in the top 20 and my concert grosses were huge and growing. I felt like I was *the* guy, yet when I'd talk to Laufer he seemed to be all but anticipating that soon my career would begin to slow down. He'd been running me on his magazine covers every issue since mid 1970. Public interest in me, he admitted, was feverish, but he felt that fevers had a way of suddenly breaking.

Although there were no signs yet that my popularity was beginning to wane, Laufer said he was already looking around to see who might replace me as the next teen hero. And once I'd been replaced, he believed, I'd be history. He'd seen the pattern played out so many times before. He reminded me how Bobby Sherman had been practically created by television. His frequent appearances on *Shindig* had led to a featured role on *Here Come the Brides* (1968–70). But when that TV series went off the air, his concert bookings and record sales dramatically fell off. The producers of *The Partridge Family* tried to revive interest in Sherman by having him guest star on our show and then spinning off a new series for him, but it didn't work. I thought it was sad.

Dave Madden: Bobby Sherman's photo would be the entire cover of *Tiger Beat*. Then all of a sudden David Cassidy's name popped up on the bottom of the page. Then David Cassidy's picture shows up and then it got bigger and bigger and bigger. Pretty soon it was as big as Bobby Sherman's and they appeared side by side. Then Bobby Sherman's picture started to shrink. It was hysterical to look at. It shrank to the point where finally all it said at the very bottom of the magazine cover was, 'Bobby Sherman says, "Don't forget me."' And then his name disappeared altogether. I told David, 'We're

> going into our third year of the show and your picture is gonna start getting smaller.' He said, 'You're right,' and sure enough, we watched it happen. In the third year of *The Partridge Family*, Donny Osmond's name appeared, just like David's name had. Then a very tiny picture of Donny Osmond appeared and it got bigger and bigger and the cycle continued. They were side by side and then David's picture got smaller and smaller and then it said, 'David Cassidy says, "Don't forget me."' The same line. *Tiger Beat* had it all planned out. It was a formula. David thought it was funny, too.

I told myself my popularity was much bigger than Sherman's had been. My career was going to last. I mean, Sidney Skolsky, one of the oldest and most respected of the syndicated Hollywood columnists, had declared flatly (5 February 1972): 'David Cassidy is to today's youngsters what Elvis was to his generation's youngsters.' I believed that to be so.

To any reporter who was astute enough to suggest that Laufer was probably making a lot of money promoting me in his magazines, he moaned that he was also spending a lot of money. In mid 1972, he figured he was paying 30 people to work on me – writing about me, photographing me, opening my fan mail, processing mail-order requests, and probably special folks to just count the money. He had considerable overheads and had to give Screen Gems a cut of everything he made off me.

Laufer's biggest competitor was the late Gloria Stavers. He used to say to me things like, 'If *only* we could merge, we could *control* the teen market.' Her top publication (with a circulation in 1972 of 1.2 million) was the rather classy *16*. She, too, did record-setting business peddling David Cassidy-related products (for which she paid Screen Gems a five per cent licensing fee), hyped via house ads. She had made money off other teen heroes before, but nothing like what she was making off me.

As she told one reporter in 1972, the David Cassidy Love Kit, available exclusively to her readers, was 'the super-biggest thing we've ever had. I ought to know. I created it.' Costing $2, the David Cassidy Love Kit included one life-sized, full-length portrait of me, one autographed poster which was *three times* bigger than life size, one photo album covering my entire childhood (I loaned priceless original childhood photos to various magazines, most of which I never saw again), the supposed story of my life (considerably cleaned up), no fewer than 40 wallet-sized photos, a special 'love message from David' and – Stavers' master coup for the truly ardent David Cassidy fan – a 'lover's card with his name and yours'.

When the *New York Times* asked me why I thought I had become a teen idol, I answered carefully.

'Who can say why one person is singled out? Maybe because of the way I talk or look. Possibly because I'm uncomplicated, clean. There's no threat involved.'

Man, that sounded deep, didn't it?

I got sick of the endless photo shoots and of seeing my face everywhere. Posters were being hawked outside every arena I played. Most of those posters were unauthorised and I received no money from their sales. Anybody could take a photo of me from the pages of a fan magazine and use it to make posters. One journalist said he could imagine my high-school guidance counsellor taking one look at my face and saying, 'I'd advise you to go into the teen idol business.' I grew weary of photographers requesting things like, 'And now, David, can you give us your pouty look?' And I'd do my finger-down-my-throat routine.

But I didn't know how to simply say no. So my body began saying no for me. The skin infections on my face grew increasingly worse. We tried heavier make-up, which didn't always work. Some days my rather tactless road manager would actually tell the press, 'David can't see anybody today. No photos! His acne is really bad.' And the British press would make little cracks about my 'spots', as if to say, 'He not only sings for teenyboppers, he's hardly much more than one himself.'

Even I was amazed at how much the interest in *The Partridge Family* and me grew. We were nominated for Grammy and Golden Globe awards, none of which we won. Our show and music weren't quite credible enough; they were too commercial, too kid-oriented. That I got nominated for Grammys seemed pretty extraordinary to me, considering that before I was hired for *The Partridge Family* I had never even had aspirations of becoming a recording artist.

16 From the Sublime to the Ridiculous

In 1972, I broke the attendance record at the Steel Pier in Atlantic City, doing three shows in one very long day. That's the venue that had been made famous by the diving horse trick years before. It was old and very obviously unprepared for a show like mine and the crowds.

From the time I arrived in town, there were 50,000 kids absolutely jamming this pier waiting for me. There was only one way on and one way off the Steel Pier and security was almost non-existent. They had two guys at the artists' entrance at the stage. It was a joke.

For the first show, at around midday, I arrived and left via an ambulance. That sort of worked. The crowd parted enough so that the ambulance, with lights flashing and sirens blaring, could get through. But some fans guessed I was inside. My cover was blown and I got grabbed a few times getting from the ambulance to the backstage entrance. We knew we couldn't use the ambulance again.

For the second show, we needed to be more creative. I walked the entire length of the Steel Pier, right through the crowd, disguised as a woman. I put on my usual hip-hugger jeans, but instead of my sneakers I slipped into a pair of clogs. I put on a wig, glasses, lipstick, rouge, the whole deal. It scared the hell out of me when I glanced in a mirror and didn't recognise myself. As I checked myself out in drag, I thought, *Damn, I actually look pretty good.* It worked like a charm, but I nonetheless hated disguising myself as a woman.

By the third show, in the evening, I hid my hair under a hat which I pulled down over my face, put on a pair of shades and raised the collar of my windbreaker up as high as possible. I walked with one of my publicists, a girl name Bryna, as if we were a couple. I put my arm around her. I looked right at her as I walked. I think we even kissed a little. Nobody paid attention to us as we worked our way through the crowd. My heart was pounding because the fans were packed all around me. I was actually touching them, rubbing shoulders with them. Finally, when I was just a few steps away from the stage door, somebody spotted me and grabbed my hat. My hair came tumbling down and everybody could see it was me. Instant insanity! Chaos. Screaming. I managed to make it inside the building, slam the door shut and yell for security. If it had happened a few seconds earlier, I would have been dead. The fans were on poor Bryna, who hadn't made it inside the building.

Kim Carnes: I remember one show in Detroit. It was an outdoor gig in the summer and it was really, really hot. All the kids in the audience were pushing each other to get closer to the stage and girls were getting crushed. Standing on the stage, all we could see was a constant flow of bodies being handed over the heads of the crowd to get them out of there. These were girls that had fainted or passed out or had the wind knocked out of them. All night long at the hotels, the girls walked up and down the halls, knocking on doors trying to find where David's room was.

Sam Hyman: Because he had that very distinctive shag haircut, he had to hide the hair with a hat, put on glasses too and I believe at times we used a beard. As for decoys, we would get a nondescript automobile that had lots of room in the back. David would be soaking wet from his performance and we'd put him on the floor, give him a towel, cover him with blankets and then send the limo out one way and this car out the other way. It's very claustrophobic when a car gets surrounded by a thousand people. People are pressing against the windows and you see the glass starting to bend, like it's going to break. Or the fans start jumping on the car and you see the ceiling coming down. It's very scary.

Henry Diltz: Very often, I would be in the back seat of the decoy limo and all the girls would be screaming thinking it was David Cassidy. And then, behind them, would come some delivery truck with David in it wearing a deliveryman's outfit with a big hat pulled over his eyes. He did that a lot.

When we were travelling and in airports, sometimes his disguises would be so elaborate that you would say, 'Oh my God, look at that guy with the great big straw hat and the huge sunglasses and the overcoat. That's got to be somebody famous.' Sometimes he would try a little bit too hard, you know?

I always tried to get out of a concert hall before the fans realised I'd left. I'd do my last number, fly off the stage and make it to a waiting car while the band was still playing and the audience was still roaring, hoping for another encore.

I got used to breaking box office records at my concerts. I filled some of the biggest stadiums in the world. I broke the Rolling

Stones' record of five consecutive shows at Wembley Stadium. I did six or eight sold-out shows there.

The first time I went to England, everyone in the press was great. They loved me. I was unknown, new and they treated me like a hero. The colour supplement of the *Evening Standard* put my face on the cover with a headline reading simply, 'Welcome David Cassidy'.

I had no idea what England was actually like until I went back in 1984, when all of that early 70s public hysteria over me was just a faint memory. I had never been through Heathrow Airport as an ordinary person until then, although I'd been there six times.

On my second trip to England, about a year after the first, the hysteria of the fans was even greater. After the Dorchester fiasco on my first trip, no hotel in London would take me. So my manager had rented the yacht that Liz Taylor and Richard Burton had rented when no hotel would take their dogs.

You know what my fans did? They jumped into the filthy, freezing, contaminated Thames. There was pandemonium. On every dock, there were cars, boats. I had to be picked by a police boat, which took me to a dock where they'd have a car and security waiting to take me to the television studios for my appearances.

David Bridger: The yacht was parked in the middle of the Thames just down from Tower Bridge. We arranged with the Metropolitan Water Police department to come to the boat and pick the party up any place along the river within a five-mile stretch. Every evening I would come out on deck. There was a launch slip and we'd have five, six, seven hundred kids lined up there. They'd all stand on the edge of the wharf and I'd come out with a big old bullhorn and say, 'Good evening, everybody!' And they'd say 'Good evening, David!' I'd say, 'Hey, guys, would you like David to come out and say goodnight?' and they'd scream 'YES!' David would come out from below deck and this incredible noise from the fans would echo across the river. On a couple of those occasions, kids dived into the water and we had to have the police boat pick them up.

Sam Hyman: At that time, the boat we were on was the largest privately owned yacht in England. It was like 110 feet and we each had a stateroom. We were not roughing it. The Thames was so polluted that if you went into the water you had to have your stomach pumped. We stayed between Tower Bridge and London Bridge and there'd be patrols of shore police in these little boats that would go along the docks to keep the kids from jumping in, even though some of them did. We would have to go to a different dock each day to be picked up or dropped off. The fans lined the shore until late at night.

It's boating protocol that the largest ship in the area has the right to have its flag raised first. There was a big Navy ship in the area that had precedence over us to show its colours. The Navy guys were jealous that all these girls lining the banks of the river were screaming, 'We love you, David!' So they would yell insulting things at us. 'David's a fag, right?' And, so one night we said, 'This is bull. We've got to get back at them.' The crew on our boat felt like, 'Hey, how dare you say that about our mate David? He's a good bloke.' So we came up with a plan to steal their colours. Two of the crewmen dressed in black and snuck on to the Navy ship while we watched. They went into the wheelhouse and stole the colours of the ship and then came back and presented them to David. At that point, they realised their ship had been breached. This is the British Navy. Sirens are going off and they're going crazy and we thought, 'Oh, this is gonna be interesting in the morning.' We couldn't wait to see what they did when they tried to raise their colours. They ended up leaving the harbour that night.

This time around the press wasn't quite as kind to me. They tried to find little things about me to criticise. They wanted to hit a nerve. I think they began to feel resentful of the fact that I was an American doing so well in England and maybe taking away some attention from British pop attractions who'd dominated the music business for years.

Dick Leahy: In England the press concentrated on the phenomenon, not David's music. The music press in England, *Melody Maker* and the *New Musical Express*, was into Rolling Stones type of rock. They dismissed David's music, but put him on the front pages because he sold newspapers. Musically, he was never treated like the Beatles or Stones. I could sense David's dissatisfaction with that. It was like being treated like a piece of meat. Forgetting the phenomenon, David Cassidy was a very good singer.

One thing that was frustrating to me was that writers rarely seemed to write thoughtful critiques of my show, or even bother to review my talent or the material at all. They were more interested in covering the spectacle: the money I was making, the fans I was drawing, the number of people who fainted or were injured at my concerts – almost anything other than how well or poorly I performed.

Some British and American writers began to put me down because I appealed to younger fans. I grew defensive. So what if my records were aimed primarily at 13- to 16-year-olds? Why is it that adults believe their taste is more meaningful? I still don't buy that one! When critics belittled me, saying I appealed only to kids, I felt they were putting down my fans, not just me. And most of us, if we admit it, are still kids at heart and are just playing at being adults. I know I am. I always empathised with my young fans.

What I tried to get across was that our teen years are no less significant than other periods of our lives. I think teenagers are often treated as second-class citizens. Adults say dismissively, 'Oh, you know it's just puppy love, it doesn't mean anything.' But when you're 13, it's the most important thing in your life.

I came to understand, too, that even the lightweight pop songs I recorded could have an enormous value to my fans. Songs like *I Think I Love You* and *Cherish* may have been dismissed by some adults as simplistic, but I know that millions of teens, whose sexuality was just awakening, found those songs really articulated their feelings. I gave voice to emotions associated with adolescent relationships.

Partridge Family singles, given great exposure by our show, sold millions. *I Woke Up in Love This Morning* made *Billboard*'s Top Pop Singles charts for 11 weeks from 14 August 1971. *It's One of Those Nights (Yes Love)* did the same for 8 weeks from 18 December 1971. *Cherish* was also the name of my first solo album. I wanted to record some material that was more me, although I knew that I had to stay within the parameters of *The Partridge Family* and that Wes Ferrell was ultimately going to be in control of the material. I was pretty much trapped by the Wes Farrell/*Partridge Family* lock and key.

I thought *Cherish* was a really good song when Wes presented it to me. And it turned out to be a really good record. When I perform it now I do it a little bit differently, a little more acoustically, a little more organically. A few years ago, when I returned to touring, I asked members of my fan club which songs they would most like me to perform in concert and *Cherish* was their first choice by a huge margin, which shows how timeless it is.

I called Tony Romeo when I was looking for songs and he wrote *I Am a Clown.* Tony knew me well and saw what I was going through and put it to music. It describes the circus that my life had become, with me as the clown. It was a huge hit around the world, especially in England.

My First Night Alone Without You was a song written by Kin Vassy, who was a friend of Kim Carnes and had been in The First Edition with Kenny Rogers. Kin stayed up all night at the piano and wrote this magnificent song that is so emotional and powerful. I think the record is fantastic, but the pop strings background vocal part should have been more one-on-one, more raw.

Mike Melvoin: The sound on those records moved from saxophones to flutes. That was one of the hallmarks of David's solo arrangements. They were more orchestral, less band. It was more grown-up. The rhythm section on David's solo work was more transparent, less electronic sounding, more mellow.

The first song I ever wrote and recorded on my own without anyone's permission was *Ricky's Tune*. I wrote it in about five minutes the day before I was about to go on a tour. *Ricky's Tune* is about a wonderful, sad, lost boy who's saying goodbye to his dog. The dog is a metaphor; it was about saying goodbye to a relationship that I couldn't have, saying goodbye to someone who didn't exist, but who I wished could have been there. I closed my eyes and imagined what it would be like to be in love, to be connected with someone. The song just fell out of me. As soon as I wrote it, I decided I was going to record it. I held on to it. I played it a few times on the tour, came back and booked a little eight-track studio. I also recorded two other songs I had written much earlier. I got a few musicians together, went in this little studio and played guitar and sang the demo. Alas, the tape no longer exists.

The *Cherish* album went gold. It made the charts for 23 weeks (peaking at number 15) from 12 February 1972. The single sold nearly two million units. And I was giving sold-out concerts in the biggest halls, arenas and stadiums in the world, like the Houston Astrodome. The level of success just blew me away. I was swept up in it. To become that famous all over the world was pretty phenomenal. To capture the imagination of a whole generation of people is a difficult thing to do. Very few people have had that kind of impact.

I knew there were some people who hated me as a performer, who viewed me with utter contempt. They were entitled to their feelings. People seemed to either love me or hate me. Fortunately for me, the percentage that did love me loved me a lot. There's an old saying in the business that if you get one per cent of the population to really love you, you're the biggest star in the world.

My second album, *Rock Me Baby,* charted for 17 weeks, peaking at number 41. After *Cherish,* I had three more solo singles in the charts in 1972: *Could It Be Forever?, How Can I Be Sure?* and *Rock Me Baby.*

Rock Me Baby was more of a departure. It was more me. I was becoming more and more difficult to keep under lock and key, in a musical sense. At that time, I was so successful that I finally said, 'Hey, look, I want to make a record that's more to my own taste. You guys are making millions of dollars on anything that has my name on it, at least let me do something I like.'

Rock Me Baby is a good pop song that scared the hell out of everybody because I said the words 'get down' in it. All of the entities involved in the David Cassidy business thought, *Uh oh, he's being sexually explicit.*

I wrote *Two Time Loser* about a relationship that I had that was never really a relationship, but I imagined it was. It was the first song I wrote on the piano that went on to record.

I loved The Young Rascals' song *Lonely Too Long* and I asked to cover it. Eddie Brigati and Felix Cavaliere from The Young Rascals are two of the great musical influences of my teenage years. I thought they were just about the best American 'pop' band. They were called a pop band only because they had pop hits, but they were heavily into R&B and soul.

Some Kind of Summer, written by Dave Ellingson, was a big hit. Kim Carnes, Dave and I were hanging around one day and he picked up a guitar and started playing it. And I said, 'That's a great song.' I still love it.

Dave Ellingson: Kim and I were in. I got the idea for the song, *Some Kind of Summer* while Kim and I were driving back to Los Angeles from San Francisco in the summer. We were visiting the promotion man working on her first album. It was a road song. David did a great job with the song. We were thrilled that he cut it.

Song for a Rainy Day is a nice song that Kim and I wrote. *Song of Love* and *Soft as a Summer Shower* were Wes Farrell additions to the album, in an effort to try to lock me into *The Partridge Family* bag.

I chose to cover *Go Now* by The Moody Blues. When Denny Laine sang that song, it was so soulful. The song itself has a really British, soulful rock sound and I've always loved it.

How Can I Be Sure? is another Young Rascals song. It wasn't a hit outside the U.S. when they cut it in 1967, but it brought back so many memories of that era for me. It was a pretty big hit for me – Top 20 in the U.S. and Top Five virtually everywhere else it was released in the world. I love the song, still sing it, and will probably continue to do so. It's a singer's song. Eddie Brigati is one of the great American vocalists, in my opinion. If he and Felix Cavaliere had been born in another era, they would have been like Mario Lanza. They had such great chops.

Their voices together were magic, kind of like Paul McCartney and John Lennon. They had this unique quality together that was extraordinary.

I knew that what I was doing was more important than my more cynical critics realised. Sure, I could find flaws in the music myself. I felt wrenching conflicts about having made it as a music star without having picked, much less written, most of the songs I recorded. This pang grew. But I was also aware I was bringing light into a lot of people's lives. And while I didn't always feel worthy of all the adulation I received, didn't always feel I was the best person the fans could have picked to worship, I also knew I was far from the worst. It was better that they were placing me on a pedestal rather than some hostile, anti-social jerk. Privately, I may have complained that I was more complex than the image the public had bought into but, if kids had to have a hero, it was a good sign that they responded to one perceived as positive and honest.

Critically, it was impossible to win acclaim. But the appreciation of the fans spoke volumes and kept me going. To a point.

Playing Madison Square Garden, the biggest indoor venue in America's biggest city, New York, may have been my most prestigious public appearance to date, but one thing that made it especially important for me was that among the 20,000 people in attendance was my 83-year-old grandfather, Fred Ward. I still get choked up when I think about how proud he was when he saw how popular I had become. He got so carried away with the audience reaction and my show that he stood up, this old man in his 80s, and started clapping and cheering for me. It breaks my heart that he's no longer with me and yet it thrills me to think that he got to see that. For his last birthday, I sent him $5,000 in cash, which is probably what he made in ten years. He worked during the Depression and he made very little money. He couldn't speak when he got the money; he'd never seen anything like it. And my mom, I knew how proud she was of me. It blew them all away.

Shaun Cassidy: David's show at Madison Square Garden was alternately exciting and terrifying. I'd never been to a rock concert. I was there with my little brothers and my mother. You're thrown into this sea of screaming adolescence. It was a sea that I would find myself in years later. As a young kid, I worried about David. Watching your brother at the centre of the hurricane was scary. It wasn't fun. It seemed like it had nothing to do with him. It was about the kids having their moment, it was an outlet for them. But David was a great performer. He was much more animated than I ever expected. I'd never seen him dance around and all that stuff. It was alternately exciting and alluring because when you're 13 and all the girls are screaming, it seems like a good job to have. But as I found out later on, when I went through a similar experience, you are actually so disconnected from it. It's what the Beatles talked about. They stopped touring because it wasn't about their music. It was about the phenomenon. Nobody could hear their music.

David and I were closest in age but he was still eight and a half years older and that's a big spread when you're a kid. I loved it when David came over to the house because it was an adventure – and I had a big brother.

Patrick Cassidy: His live show at the Garden was surreal. I remember I couldn't hear anything. The screaming was so loud that the actual songs could barely be heard. The minute he walked on stage, the minute he did any sort of movement or gesture toward the audience, the whole auditorium erupted. I remember being in a traffic jam of insane, screaming girls. I gained a lot of attention because he was my brother. I mean, going to school and trying to be a regular kid, there was no way that was gonna happen when your brother was such a superstar.

The Madison Square Garden concert was a huge event. Bell Records put up billboards in Hollywood announcing to the world at large (and the entertainment industry in particular) that I would be playing the Garden, 3,000 miles away, and then almost immediately plastered on to the billboard the message: 'Sold Out!'

The concert took place on 11 March 1972 and received extensive media coverage. *Life* magazine's managing editor, Ralph Graves, noted that before I appeared there was a one hour warm-up period featuring other singers. Those singers, whom he didn't seem to feel were worth mentioning by name, were Kim Carnes and Dave Ellingson. He added that having a warm-up for me 'was about as necessary as warming up an arena full of starving tigresses before throwing them a single Christian'. Graves said he'd never heard anything like the audience's frenzied response to my performance. 'You have to imagine the roar of a crowd at the moment Frazier knocked down Ali, while at the same moment Bobby Thomas was hitting his famous home run that put the Giants in the World Series, while simultaneously George Blanda was kicking a game-running field goal in the last five seconds, just as Ben-Hur was on the last lap of his chariot race. Now put all that sound together on tape and play it without respite for an hour, not forgetting to raise the pitch . . . The young girls in America have absolutely perfected the pitch up to a high C shriek. My middle-aged eardrums were in shock after the first five minutes.' Graves added that his 12-year-old daughter told him, 'I'll remember this day all the rest of my life.' It made me smile, that one.

The showbiz bible *Variety* got to what it considered the most significant thing about the event in the first paragraph – from that one concert I had grossed a whopping $130,000. In 1972 that was a huge take. As for my performance, *Variety*'s judgment was that 'Cassidy's well-choreographed act consisted mainly of waving his rear (in tight white pants) to his adoring public.' They said I fronted to the orchestra for one instrumental number at my 'wiggling best'. But they admitted the squealing teen and pre-teen girls seemed thrilled by every moment, even my mumbled introductions to songs, like when I told the audience that *I Think I Love You* described 'how I feel about you'.

Lillian Roxon of the *Daily News* noted that at the Garden I was 'wiggling like Monroe in *Niagara*', although she felt I 'was not one half as comfortable with it as, say, Michael Jackson . . .'

The *New York Post*'s pop music writer, Alfred G. Aronowitz, fumed about my performance: 'There is something obscene about selling sex to pre-pubescent little girls as if it were apple pie . . . The way David swung his torso around, there was no question that he knew what those girls wanted to see.'

The *New York Times* assigned both a feature writer, Angela Taylor, and a music critic, Don Heckman, to cover my concert. Taylor reported that Madison Square Garden security guards had never seen anything like my frenzied fans. She noted it was startling to hear a second grader yelling, 'I don't care if he's old. He's beautiful. Give him to me!'

Heckman declared the event was 'less a concert than a symbolic announcement of what pop music might become'. He described me as 'the current idol of almost every 13-year-old girl in America' and said, 'Cassidy is a still-developing singer with a pleasantly bland voice and notable absence of rhythmic vitality . . . But the significant element here is sensuality and theatre, not music.' He said I left 20,000 fans thoroughly satisfied, but added he suspected that their devotion to me 'had more to say about the manipulative powers of television and recording than it did about David Cassidy'. Maybe so. But here's my take.

In America, performing at Madison Square Garden is the pinnacle for any artist, and apparently I sold it out faster than anybody. It's even bigger than the Melbourne Cricket Ground, at which I broke box-office records. I was the highest-paid person ever to play there. I sold more merchandise than anyone had ever sold. But to me, the show was a personal triumph only because of the people who were there for me – my mom, my grandfather, my dad, my brothers.

I remember 'my people' were thrilled by all the publicity the Garden concert generated, not to mention the huge box-office gross. Of course, we had some unexpected expenses to contend with. My frenzied fans managed to destroy six limousines.

When the concert was finished, I ran off the stage and two burly security men wrapped me in an army blanket and threw me in the trunk of a Toyota. They sent limousines out which fans followed, while the Toyota headed off, unnoticed, in another direction. By the time the fans realised they'd been tricked, it was too late; I was gone.

About four blocks later, we stopped. I hopped out of the trunk and got into the back seat. All the hotels in Manhattan were swarming with fans looking for me; none of the good hotels in Manhattan would take me any more, although my band still stayed in them. I, on the other hand, was driven instead to some dump out in Queens, a cheap motel, where a room had been reserved for me under an alias. Fifteen minutes after starring in the most publicised concert in the world, I was dropped off – still wearing my white jumpsuit, which was drenched in sweat – at a shabby motel. I didn't know where I was. I had no money and no clothes except for what I was wearing. I stayed in the bathtub for an hour and a half, alone. I waited for someone to call or come and get me. I didn't know where anybody was. I understood why Marilyn Monroe couldn't get a date on Saturday nights. I lay there and thought, *What am I doing this for?*

17 I Love You, You're Famous, Now Go Away

The perception that Shirley Jones was my mother drove my mother crazy. She was tortured by it. Shirley had nothing to do with it; it was the media. A couple of times I had her included in articles to say, 'This is my mom,' to appease her, so she wouldn't be so distraught all the time. She would read these articles about me and my family that were, of course, completely untrue. So my fame became torture for my mother as well as my father.

My mother was more embracing of my success than my father. But being around either one of them was very uncomfortable and unpleasant for me. My parents wanted success for themselves so desperately that they couldn't be happy for me. The way they felt and behaved towards me made me feel rejected. I spent a lot of my life trying to make both of them happy, trying to be a good boy, trying to be someone they would be proud of, trying to get their unconditional love. But I couldn't make them happy, no matter what I did.

Sharon Lee (editor, *The Partridge Family Magazine*): Jack wanted to be big and instead his son became the big star and that was hard for him to accept. David's mother, Evelyn, did a column for us that I wrote. I interviewed her for hours and she gave us some baby pictures. We had to make sure we listed her as actress Evelyn Ward. So, again, it was a situation where the son's fame overpowered both parents. David had a good relationship with Shirley Jones and I think subconsciously that bothered his mother. It seemed like Shirley was the most supportive of David whereas the father was contending with him and the mother wished that success had happened to her as well. So here's the son on the cover of magazines, a teen idol, a recording and TV star, and he had parents that were jealous of his achievements.

Shirley Jones: It was clear to me that David himself was really suffering when he was going through the teen-idol syndrome. Being the sensitive and basically private person David is, it really got to him. The type of success David achieved proved to be very difficult, not just for him but for everyone who was around him. Jack was bothered by the fact that David hadn't worked long enough for everything he'd achieved. And he knew that kind of success often didn't last. David's mother also had difficulties as a result of his fame. One of the terrible problems his mother had was that everybody seemed to believe I was David's mother. Most people believed it then; most people still believe it today. His mother was not very happy about that, nor could I blame her. And having to go see him under an assumed name and all that crap that was necessary in order to avoid fans and the press; there had to be hordes of police and security men around him – that was also terrible. David became a prisoner of his success. I wouldn't want anybody to go through that. Just think of what David went through. You make a lot of money, you have a lot of success, but it's all so fleeting. That's hard on a young person. Especially when, unexpectedly, you find it's all gone. David's success was rough on the whole family. It was rough on his brothers, having to be the brothers of the great teen idol.

I asked Shaun how he experienced my success and how he thought I might have changed as a result of it.

Shaun Cassidy: When it all began to happen for David, I was only 11, so I was too young to have a great deal of insight as to who David was as a person. I mean, I didn't even know David sang until he did *The Partridge Family*. Up until then, my perception of David was simply as my half-brother who I hung out with. And I loved hanging out with him. I thought he was a good older brother to me when he was around. He teased me a lot, like I'd tease my younger brothers. I loved going places in the car with him.

Then suddenly he was acting on this TV show. And don't forget, *The Partridge Family* was not just any TV show. It was very popular and it was considered very 'wholesome'. So there I was, this kid whose mom and brother were starring in this wholesome show. And David's music was invariably described as 'wholesome', too. So I acquired a *Partridge Family* kind of image by association. And, believe me, when you're a kid going into your teens, as I was when David's fame was reaching its peak, 'wholesome' is not a cool thing to be. So I pushed hard to go the other direction, to establish a different identity with my peers. And I made it clear my musical tastes were Led Zeppelin and The Stones. When I was 13, I had dreams of someday going into music, but The Partridge Family sound was the last thing I would have wanted to emulate.

From my point of view, the most important change I noticed in David as he became successful was that he just wasn't as accessible.

Timewise, he just wasn't available as often as he had been before. I didn't feel really close to him. He became much more insular.

Looking back with the wisdom of an adult, I'd say that when success happens to anyone as early as it did for David – or, a few years later, for me – it can be damaging, because you end up being surrounded by a lot of sycophants. And that was certainly the case with David. The same thing happened to me, too. Had I been older, more experienced, I could have said to David something like, 'Don't wrap yourself up in Graceland here.' He definitely had a bit of that going on.

As I became more and more famous, my father and I saw less of each other. Things had never been great between us, and my success only seemed to add to the tension. Every kid wants his dad to put his arm around him and say, 'Great goin', son. I'm really proud of you.' I never got that.

Sam Hyman: Just the way Jack presented himself, I think there was that intimidation factor, father to son. You know, the son could be real tough when we were together with friends, and then you get with the dad and you become the little boy. Jack would say things about David like, 'You're just lucky. You were at the right place at the right time and you have the right look.'

My dad didn't have the capacity as a human being to show real emotion, and I can now forgive him for that. For years he was upstaged by his wife. And then came 1970, and he became known as Shirley Jones's husband and David Cassidy's father. It drove him round the bend. In his heart, I'm sure he was proud of me; he genuinely *did* care about me. But his ego was bent out of shape. However, just because his feelings were hurt, I wasn't going to kowtow to him like a child, the way my brothers did.

Shaun Cassidy: My father, by nature, was a very competitive guy. I don't think you should ever be in competition with your children. I think you should only be supportive of your children. But I think what is viewed by some, including David, as only jealousy was also a lot of conflicted feelings. I think my dad was also feeling protective of David. My dad saw the career David had in the early days as one that would be very short-lived and tough to recover from. I think he was feeling competitive, but I also think he felt, *What's gonna happen to my son when he's 21?* I can only say that now with the objectivity of having children who are young adults.

David didn't live in our house. He had the extra challenge of being a guest, visiting a new family that he probably often felt threatened by. Competitiveness is common in a lot of divorced families. When kids are shuttled back and forth there's resentment. I'm divorced and I have children who've grown up in two households and even if they love both sets of parents, it's a pain to have to pack up half of your room every two weeks or in the summer and move to another place with another group of friends and new rules. All of those things are challenging and complicated and painful. The dynamic that David experienced with my father isn't as unique as perhaps David thinks it is. It's only unique in that it was projected on to the world stage as a result of David's success and my father's success.

David wanted what we all wanted from our father, which was more of a dad. My father was not a good parent. He was not a practising parent. He wasn't a guy who really enjoyed the company of children. When my parents finally divorced, I never got a sense that anything was much different because he'd be in New York for periods of time or on the road. A lot of David's issues related to my dad are his fantasy of what he thought he might have been missing. I don't know that he missed as much as he thinks he did.

By the early 70s, my father was drinking like a fish every night. Although he denied he had an alcohol problem, he obviously did. He lived his life in a constant state of denial. There were times when I overdid it, but my drinking never became a problem for me like it was for my dad. And he had a mean streak in him that surfaced when he drank.

That's why I was glad I never really lived with him. Whenever I was with him for a few weeks while growing up, I found him an impossibly strict disciplinarian. He was so overbearing, I vowed I'd never be like him when I became a parent. And I've tried hard to keep that vow. Shaun has turned out to be a very good parent as well. Perhaps we're both overcompensating because of what we suffered as kids.

My dad had such selfish household rules. He'd have silent periods when he didn't want to be disturbed. In the morning you couldn't make any noise and wake him up. Four boys, right? When he wasn't working, he and his friends would likely stay up until 3 a.m. and it was likely he wouldn't get up until noon the next day. You try to tell kids they've got to be quiet all morning because daddy needs his rest.

The funny thing is, he could never see that he had any problems. By the early 70s he was convinced I was the one with the problems. He'd complain to reporters that he didn't have access to me, that I'd gotten too big for my britches and was surrounding myself with hangers-on who barely knew who he was, that he couldn't get to see as much of me as he wanted to. Yeah, right! Like he'd ever wanted to see a lot of me. He couldn't conceal his resentment of my success. *New York Daily News* gossip columnist Robin Adams Sloan reported (13 July 1972) that Jack Cassidy was 'basking in reflected, teeth-gritting envy' of me, adding, 'They say if you want to make friends with Jack nowadays, don't say anything to him about another show business star, little David.' Yep, that was my dad.

One reporter tried to get me to say whether I thought my father or I was the star of the family. I responded curtly that I didn't consider myself part of my father's family, that his family consisted only of himself, Shirley, Shaun, Ryan and Pat.

I wasn't the only one having difficulty getting along with him. Before the year was out, newspapers were reporting that Shirley Jones and Jack Cassidy had agreed to a trial separation. Their marriage sputtered along, off and on, for a few more years before finally collapsing. He was slowly destroying everything around him. The years of alcohol abuse, combined with his mad behaviour, caused his life to begin to unravel.

I wasn't deliberately trying to isolate myself from my family or anyone else. Running an international career involving television, records and concerts was exhausting. The only reason I was making millions of dollars was that I was working hard, doing as many shows as I could. During a two-year period of time, I was the highest-paid solo male artist in the world. I was playing huge venues. I could work one night and take in $70,000 or more.

I talked to Ruth numerous times every day. She was the only person I talked to so frequently; no one else had access like that. I was closer to her than I was to my parents. We had a business together, Daru Enterprises, Inc. ('Daru' came from the first two letters of my first name and hers.) My career was so unlike that of anyone else she'd ever handled before and she'd never been involved with commercial success like mine, so she was learning a lot as she went along. The record business was all new to her. She had to hire several other people just to work on my career. Directly or indirectly, I was supporting a lot of folks, but I had no cause to be concerned about money at that point.

I trusted Ruth's judgment. There are mixed opinions about her. I thought she was great – a unique, in many ways bizarre human being who lived and breathed show business. She always championed me and was a close ally of mine. A number of people, including members of my family, don't agree with my assessment of her and in fact actually came to hate her. My mother, for instance. I think she was simply sorry that I didn't spend as much time with her as I did with Ruth. Even Shirley eventually decided to leave Ruth because she was being slowly drugged and taken advantage of by her doctor, thus reducing her clarity and effectiveness. But I loved Ruth and would have done anything for her. I thought she was right on top of things. And she was, until the last months of her life. Talking to her wasn't the hassle talking to my parents could be. And I didn't have the energy for a lot of idle chit-chat.

No matter how successful you are, you sometimes have to wonder how long it will last. I did all the time. It was gratifying reading articles saying I was causing more excitement in the pop music field than anyone had in five years, that no one since the Beatles had drawn so many screaming fans to airports. But every front-runner has to worry about who might be gaining on him. I was filled with self-confidence one moment, touched by pangs of self-doubt the next. If a concert didn't go over quite as well as expected, I'd wonder if it was just a meaningless blip on the graph or possibly the first sign of trouble.

When I returned to the Wildwood, New Jersey Convention Hall in the summer of 1972, *Variety* noted with approval that I'd become 'a well-rehearsed and disciplined talent'. But they also noted that, 'Although the Wildwood area was jammed with over 400,000 tourists, Cassidy did not repeat last season's bonanza business when he had even the aisles crowded in the 3,800 seat hall. This time, he pulled only slightly over 2,000 to each of two shows on Sunday.' *Variety* thought the problem was due to some poor press. But was that it? Or were the concerts not promoted as well as they should have been? Or were the fans who'd been dying to see me last summer simply not so eager to see me a second or third time? Reporters always asked me, 'How long do you think your popularity can last?'

My concerts were selling out and my fees for appearances were still rising. But mass opinions can change unpredictably. Why? Who knows? In 1972, I was as 'in' as bell bottoms were. But I'd wonder how long it would be before bell bottoms were 'out'. Along with, perhaps, David Cassidy.

One 17-year-old fan from Long Island, Penny Bergman, told the *New York Times* she'd be hesitant about admitting to friends at school she was still a fervent David Cassidy fan. 'He's known as a teenage idol. I'm too old.'

One 13-year-old even insisted, 'Just about everybody in my class thinks he's gross. He's for those younger kids who read dopey fan magazines.'

But a lot of kids all across America were buying those 'dopey fan magazines' and avidly reading the articles relentlessly being ground out with headlines like, 'You Know Your Love for David Cassidy Is Deep and True', 'Why No Girl Can Make Him Happy' and (a classic) 'Would You Like to Know When I Was Born, How Old I Am, My Colouring – and All My Measurements?'

The people around me assured me I was just as popular as ever. They pointed out that, in 1972, we were conquering the British pop record market in a way no American had in years. In May 1972 a David Cassidy single with *Could It Be Forever?* on one side and *Cherish* on the other reached number two on the British charts. My career as an international pop star was still growing.

Dick Leahy: David Cassidy happened in England before *The Partridge Family* television show was shown. We released *I Think I Love You* without any television support and it took awhile but we promoted it and broke it. Television in England wasn't particularly into *The Partridge*

Family; they saw it as very American. David's success in England started purely through records and images. In those days, we had massive support from some huge-selling teen magazines like *Jackie*. We occasionally gave *Jackie* some exclusive pictures. Their circulation in a country this size topped a million, principally because of David.

The big challenge was to promote the records without the tool that made them huge in America, which was *The Partridge Family* television show. Here was a kid who was making very good pop records and using the tools available – the support of one or two disc jockeys and the teen media. That's how we broke David in the U.K.. Once everything else kicked in, as with any phenomenon, people tend to play things anyway. They'll just programme them because they know they'll get audience numbers.

The other great challenge was to start pushing David's talent, not just *The Partridge Family* phenomenon ... I was quite disappointed when *The Partridge Family* started to be shown in the U.K. because I thought it might inhibit his musical growth. By that time, David was doing solo albums as well. *The Partridge Family* helped build David's success but it also led to massive numbers of both David Cassidy and Partridge Family records being released. I always focused on his solo records. Of course, we did push The Partridge Family records but not with the same effort.

David Bridger: When we got the first solo album together, it shipped gold. We had half a million copies going out the door on the first Friday. I think it went platinum within ten days. They couldn't press the album fast enough. They kept the presses going 24/7 and still couldn't satisfy the demand.

I increasingly had contact only with the people I felt safe with, my inner circle: my head of security, Billy Francis, my personal photographer, Henry Diltz, and, of course, Sam.

Henry Diltz: I'd been living in England in Stephen Stills's manor for three or four months, working for him and taking photos. On the plane coming back to L.A., I was reading about this new TV show, *The Partridge Family*, and I was thinking to myself, Wow, that's kinda like *The Monkees*. And I'd become The Monkees' photographer through working for teeny bopper magazines like *Tiger Beat*. No sooner did I get home, the phone rang and it was *Tiger Beat* asking me if I would go down to the set and take photos of *The Partridge Family*.

I started taking a few pictures and was talking to David. I mentioned that I had just been shooting Stephen Stills and his eyes lit up and he said, 'Hey, come on back to my dressing room.' He was an aspiring rock and roll singer trapped in the body of this young actor. Then he found out that I'd done album covers for Crosby, Stills & Nash and The Doors and James Taylor. I was somebody that was kind of in the world that he was interested in, and so we got to be friends immediately.

I considered Elliot Mintz another close friend in the 70s. I was impressed that he was close to John Lennon and Yoko Ono. He started doing radio shows profiling rock celebrities. He seemed to know everybody. He came along on one of my European tours and did an audio documentary; he just kept the tape rolling the whole time. Eventually, I agreed to a lot of frank, in-depth, off-the-record interviews with him. He said he wanted background for a proposed biography of me, which he never wrote. He later attempted to sell those tapes to publishing companies without my authorisation, for which I can never forgive him. I finally concluded he was just another parasite, eager to find any way to make money out of knowing me.

I met so many people like that. For a while in 1972 I was seeing a girl named Lyn, who was into photography. I met her in New York at the Garden. Sweet Little Lynnie, she had every move. She went from rock star to rock star. When we were together, she took photos of me that she then sold to a magazine. That was it. I blew her off at that point. I just said, 'I really don't want to talk to you again. You broke a trust.' I heard she did the same thing to Bruce Springsteen. Somebody told me he punched her out on the stage. Every time I met someone like Lyn, the urge to withdraw grew greater. It seemed safer not getting too involved with anyone. Everyone ultimately disappointed me and sold our friendship out for the almighty dollar.

I'd occasionally find girls that I liked and had short romances with them. But my career affected every part of my life. I wasn't good at relationships. I couldn't let people get too close. I didn't feel I could trust anyone.

More and more, I felt resentful of the merchandising, the records, the television, the posters, the pictures, the magazines. I started to hate the David Cassidy the public saw. I thought, *Look what they've created, this crass pop-up, this transparent, shallow, sweet, innocent, goody-goody who's now selling cornflakes.* I began to lose perspective about my positive impact on other people and how much that meant.

I had been a very positive, happy person when I went into this. I always felt this was what the public responded to in me, more than my looks and voice, but now I was becoming embittered. I wanted people to know that I was very different. I looked so sweet and innocent. Yeah, right. I wanted to say, 'See! I am really a *bad boy*!'

18 The Naked Lunch Box Experience

Jann Wenner (publisher, *Rolling Stone*): There seemed to be a certain something about David that was more special than the rest of the teen idols. He was cuter. He was livelier. He could sing and he could act and he was obviously the star of *The Partridge Family*. There was just a little ring of authenticity there. He became the outstanding teen idol of his time. He didn't look manufactured. He was just a cut above the other teen idols. All of that went into the opportunity to do a cover story on him in *Rolling Stone*.

We don't usually out teen idols on the cover. There was a talent reason and there was a real sociological reason to examine the whole phenomena of that show and the level of popularity of a teen idol like David. Was it risky for David to appear on the cover of *Rolling Stone*? Some of your hard-rock readers may have said, 'Why are you doing that? That's plastic. That's selling out.' But there wasn't much of that. Everybody liked him. There's a real validity to the people that we put on the cover. We knew that the issue would do well.

I was happy I'd be given a chance to really speak, to let people see the real me. I liked the idea of being profiled in a serious, respected rock journal, rather than just another cheesy teenybopper fan magazine.

They put one of their writers, Robin Green, on it and she travelled around with me for a few days. I agreed to give her virtually unrestricted access to me. She recorded whatever she saw. If she came to my house to interview me and Sam was sunning himself naked, she noted that; I wasn't hiding anything. If she saw bimbos trying to put moves on me, she noted that. And I didn't stop her from talking to the women around me either, at least one of whom told her I was good in bed. If she saw a half-empty bottle of booze in my room or smelled pot in the air, she noted all that too. She said she wanted it to be an honest piece. The booze and the pot weren't mine. Just to keep it honest, I didn't smoke marijuana at that time. Not since 1968. I couldn't possibly do it; it made me stupid and paranoid. I'm stupid enough already and smoking weed makes me stupider. That was the only beef I had with it.

I spoke openly about who I was and what I wanted. I told her of my frustrations at being pigeonholed as this white-bread pop singer for pre-pubescent girls, that I was actually a direct contradiction to my public image. I acknowledged I didn't have any meaningful, committed, long-term relationship with a woman. I answered whatever she asked.

Maybe it was too real for the masses in 1972 America. I hadn't envisioned what the combined impact of the nude photos and the equally revealing interview would be. Nor had I envisioned the tone the writer would take. She wasn't greatly impressed by me.

Robin Green (writer, *Rolling Stone*, 'Naked Lunchbox'): Everyone else got to interview the Rolling Stones or John Lennon. The Bee

Gees weren't *Rolling Stone* type material but I got those kinds of stories. They knew my pieces were funny and ironic so they set me on David. The article was pitched to me by Jann Wenner, publisher of *Rolling Stone*. My impression was that David's people brought the idea to *Rolling Stone* in order to help him make the transition from teen idol to serious musician. This is how it was presented to me by the editors at *Rolling Stone*. He wanted to express his adult angst about being a teen idol.

I was vaguely aware of *The Partridge Family*. I had an idea right away what the editors expected from me. They knew I would do something tongue-in-cheek. It was that kind of set-up from the start or they wouldn't have assigned it to me. I was this Berkeley hippie with a cape and long hair. I went out on the road with David for five days. I remember going to the airport and sitting in first class next to David. That's when he said a lot of that stuff to me that made it into the article. I tape-recorded everything he said and in that way he kind of hung himself because he was very dramatic about his situation. He spoke about how he had been taken advantage of and how he had been led down this path into becoming a bubble gum guy. He said he was in a lot of pain from it. He was clearly very conflicted with his stardom.

The article touched on the whole teen idol business and I interviewed a lot of those people. I think David felt like a product. He felt that he was a product that the teen magazines were selling and I think he felt guilty that he had allowed himself to be sold in this way and used by them to make money.

I don't think the article did David any good. I felt bad about it. I think the article backfired. But I think it was gonna backfire from the beginning and that it was meant to backfire on him. I think that's what we expected the piece to be. It was tongue-in-cheek. Here's a guy who thinks *Rolling Stone* is gonna be the instrument by which he's going to be taken seriously. That it's really that easy, that you can almost manipulate the press to achieve your next goal.

The article had fun with him and I don't think that was his intention. Part of my problem with being a journalist is exactly that. What did Joan Didion say? 'Never trust a journalist.'

David Felton, one of the editors, came up with the cover headline 'Naked Lunchbox'. It was brilliant because we had a William Burroughs interview in the same issue and it was a play on the title of his book, *Naked Lunch*. So it was wonderful and funny. It hit on a lot of different levels.

As for the cover, I think it was a picture of someone who was misjudging a situation and bared himself. The picture freaked everybody out. He looked like a boy that wanted to position himself as a man. I understood what he was trying to do, which was to be taken seriously as an adult.

I was pleased with the writing and I was pleased with the reporting. I thought it was a very thorough exploration of the teen idol business, and that I'm proud of. But I do feel bad about the effect that the article had on David at the time. I felt the article and picture were hurtful towards David. It had a huge effect on his life. David's done some interviews on the subject of this article and he's forgiven me. It was a hard transitional time for him and the article that he sought was part of that painful transition.

I liked David very much as a person. I thought he was a really nice kid. He was from a show-business family and that's a different kind of animal. He and his family were very nice people and I certainly never wished him ill. But I think I caused him discomfort and trauma. I have to take responsibility for that. That was my job. I feel that ultimately his life worked out well and I am really glad that it did.

Robin's directive from the editor was to find anything that would be shocking or controversial. There was nothing about my life at the time that met their expectations, until Bangor, Maine, which is where we went directly after the Garden in New York. It was seven below with six feet of snow on the ground. We ran into the waiting limo, where the promoter had two women in their 30s wearing nothing but bikinis and lollipops all over their bodies waiting for me. I think there's a reference to it in the *Rolling Stone* article. And yes, I spent some time with those two girls. Robin discovered that I wasn't 16 and David Cassidy was not Keith Partridge.

After the show, I went to sleep. I would grab sleep whenever I could. I had a new tour manager at the time and he happened to be gay. I asked him to wake me, knowing that the girls were waiting in their room for me. Instead, I woke up and he was in the single bed next to mine with his arm was around me. I realised he had fallen in love with me. I said, 'Wait a minute. You didn't wake me up when I asked you to. There are two women waiting for me. Get out of my room!' And Robin Green was standing outside the room as I yelled, 'Make sure those two girls end up in my . . .' She couldn't have chosen a worse moment to show up.

After we'd finished with the interviews, *Rolling Stone* requested that I do a photo shoot with Annie Leibovitz, the best photographer in the world. She said, 'I'd like to photograph you naked in the field.' I said, 'Great idea. Let's do it. Let me just check with my manager.'

Ruth went insane and begged me not to do it, but I chose to go ahead with it. They'd be nude shots, but very tasteful, I was assured. Maybe they'd show a hint of pubic hair or something, but nothing really graphic. The photos would simply reinforce the idea that I had nothing to hide. I thought – and still think – that the photographs Annie took of me were great. Revealing and real.

We did the shoot inside my house in Encino and in a field. It took about an hour. I was totally nude. I'm not embarrassed by my body. The nudity was symbolic. It was artistic. It represented freedom. It was the real me.

Jann Wenner (publisher, *Rolling Stone*): As far as the photo shoot, Annie went to shoot him and David was extraordinarily cooperative. I didn't know about it until Annie got back and showed me the pictures. I mean, what a knockout. I was like, 'What? He did that?!' He was gonna get the cover, no matter what. From what Annie said it was his decision to take off all of his clothes. I knew we had a hot cover and I knew exactly which photo would make the cover. It was the one with his arms stretched out.

We said, 'We can't show everything, but we've got to really make it clear that he took all his clothes off so you see that little hint of pubic hair.' There were also pictures of him naked in the bathtub with bubble bath, on the rug and on the grass. And there's full frontal nudity. He went all the way with it.

After it came out, we got a letter from the actor Tony Perkins. He wrote a letter to one of the writers who he was friends with asking if he could have a copy of the picture. He was in love.

I got the rights to the photographs so no one could release anything inappropriate and Jann Wenner was as good as gold. I saw him last year at the '100 Greatest Covers of *Rolling Stone*' party that he threw in New York. Jann is a great businessman. He's a very savvy guy. He created the most socially and politically important music magazine in our culture's history. It was the apex and, at the time, being on the cover of *Rolling Stone* brought a tremendous amount of prestige and had a far greater impact than it does today.

It meant more to me than almost anything else. I didn't care about being on the cover of any of the teen magazines or any of the movie or celebrity magazines. *Rolling Stone* was the only credible music magazine and I'd been reading it since I was a teenager. Hendrix, Cream, Clapton, all the artists I cared about were in that magazine and on the cover. And my friends thought it was cool. Mine was the biggest-selling issue of *Rolling Stone* until John Lennon died. It was so controversial at the time; no one in my genre had ever been seen naked. No one had ever taken the risk and dared to do that. I did it because I think Annie's brilliant. I would work with her again in a minute because of the respect I have for her work.

The fallout from the article was so dramatic that I can't even describe it. I got the message from fan magazines when the editors wrote things like, 'Well, apparently David was kidnapped and they put a gun to his head.' I didn't think I'd done anything wrong then and I don't think so today. The article was 99 per cent truthful. Everybody reacted. The studio, the network and *The Partridge Family* brass hated it. Today, they'd look at me and think, *You're the coolest, most fabulous guy on the face of the earth.* They'd love the media attention. In those days, they looked at me and said, 'What kind of an idiot are you? Why would you do that?' People's values and openness were very different then.

Sam Hyman: I think he pulled the trigger on his career with the *Rolling Stone* article, which was kind of a professional suicide at that time. Subconsciously he wanted to end that part of his life. As for posing nude for the cover, somehow I would think it was Annie's suggestion and he said, 'Sure. I got nothin' to hide. Here I am. You want all of me, here's all of me.' To me, it was somebody crying out, 'I've had enough. I can't take it any more.'

Sandy Stert Benjamin (associate editor, *Tiger Beat*): I remember seeing the cover and thinking to myself that it was kind of racy for David, especially the way we had been portraying him. I could see that he was making an effort to break out of the mould. I saw it as a sign that he wanted to be more daring. That signalled to me that he wanted to move on from the teen audience and start showing that he was this 20-something guy in charge of his career and moving in a different direction. He wanted to declare his independence. I remember the general vibe around the office was, 'He's changed things and he's lost fans.'

Jann Wenner: With David posing nude on the cover of *Rolling Stone*, I got the impression that was how he was planning to escape the TV show. He was really taking a huge, and perhaps fatal, chance with his television career. I think his manager, Ruth Aarons, knew that and was very upset afterwards because she saw that he had just destroyed his career. His advisors said to him, 'If you do this naked, you're gonna become so controversial that the sponsors are gonna complain to the network and say, "We won't go on with this."'

I think it also had an adverse affect on his audience. David was androgynous and that was so powerful for his teen female audience. Androgynous means someone who's not sexually threatening. You fall in love with a boy who's really pretty like a girl, but the whole idea of having sex isn't there at 10 or 11 or 12. Once you put yourself out there naked, with your pubic hair showing, it's sexually threatening. It wasn't what teen girls or their parents wanted.

The cover is a pretty picture of a pretty boy in a classic, extremely sexually suggestive pose. It's a really nicely posed picture. You see tons of pictures like that now of male models, underwear ads. It's standard operating stuff now, it's everywhere you turn. In comparison to all this modern photography, that cover still stands out as better than most. It was special, with character and quality. The cover photo is beauty à la a great pre-Renaissance portrait of a young boy without the pornographic element or the Calvin Klein thing, which is such a cliché. It stands the test of time on that basis.

It was one of our big controversial issues at the time. Very high profile and high visibility. It did a lot for *Rolling Stone*. There we were dealing with the biggest and broadest level of American culture – television. Not our narrow world of Janis Joplin. Not our narrow world of Van Morrison. Not our small rock world. Here we're talking about the world of 50 million people watching TV. We were covering one of the American mainstream's most beloved people. The cover headline, 'Naked Lunchbox', is one of my two favourite cover lines of all time. I think it's just brilliant.

David could have gone on exploiting that teen thing and become some trashy David Hasselhoff type. But the devotion to what he really wanted to do in his life triumphed. I respect that. There's a residual love for him among his original audience, and for good reason.

In subsequent years, David and I met through mutual friends and got to be friends. We had some really nice nights together. He's a good guy and a rock and roller at heart.

There are people who still carry around that issue of *Rolling Stone* and think it's the coolest thing that's ever been done. It was the first time I spoke as me, which didn't happen for many, many years. It was real.

The article created tremendous controversy. I'm sure there were plenty of mothers who had never actually seen a copy of *Rolling Stone* in their lives telling each other over coffee or games of bridge or at PTA get-togethers that David Cassidy (scandal of scandals) had exposed himself, posing nude for a notorious *Rolling Stone* article, and had admitted to all kinds of debauchery.

The Partridge Family was just about the last gasp of real innocence on TV. There were no references to social problems of any kind on the show. Thirty-eight per cent of *The Partridge Family*'s viewers were children. Many people seemed to feel I'd violated the trust of young America by letting myself be photographed naked and associating myself with booze and pot. They thought I should be a role model for American youth.

I never asked to be a role model. But even so, I must say I was bothered by the writer's implication that I smoked pot. I've admitted that I tried *everything* as a teenager – from heroin, cocaine and LSD to the less hard stuff – but, as I've said, at the time of the *Rolling Stone* article I was not using any illegal drugs. And the writer *knew* that, but chose to take the low road. She violated my trust. The pot she'd smelled wasn't mine and she knew that.

I would hardly have thought that the article's suggestion that, at 22, I had a sex life would shock anybody. But, surprise, surprise, it did. The article was written in such a vague way that different readers drew different inferences about me. The writer Dennis Cooper, who I'm sure is no dummy (his book *The Tenderness of the Wolves* was nominated for a *Los Angeles Times* Book Prize) concluded that I 'as much as came out' as a homosexual in *Rolling Stone*. Of course I'd done nothing of the kind. But I can see how someone could have reached such a conclusion upon reading that I didn't have a meaningful, long-term relationship with any one woman, and that my roommate was sunning himself nude while I was being interviewed.

Other readers could (and did) just as easily draw another inference – that I was living some sort of hippie lifestyle, and that if I wasn't involved in any deep, lasting relationship with any *one* woman, I was presumably involved in casual relationships with many. After all, *Rolling Stone* even quoted one woman on my supposed sexual prowess. But heterosexual promiscuity was no more acceptable than homosexuality to the 'family values' crowd. The fundamental message was the same: David Cassidy is not at all who we've been led to believe. And the last thing a performer wants to do is lose his audience's trust.

Coca-Cola changed its mind about a David Cassidy TV special they had been planning to sponsor. Up until the *Rolling Stone* article, they'd felt I was as wholesome as Mom's apple pie. Now they no longer wanted to be associated with me. They said, 'We can't have somebody who's controversial like that representing our company.'

Bob Hope was committed to doing my TV special and he backed out.

General Mills threatened to stop using me.

And the new, serious rock fans I'd hoped to win by speaking frankly in the respected magazine never materialised. I wondered if I'd ever be able to get older, hard-core music fans to take me seriously.

I never regretted doing the article or the shoot. The only thing I said to anyone was, 'Don't fabricate stories and don't lie.' A gay magazine, for example, spliced someone else's body on to the *Rolling Stone* cover photo and it looked like I was holding my tool, only it wasn't mine. You know, don't show me as some gay porn star. If you're going to show me, then show *me*. They even sold posters of it. I was very weirded out by the whole thing.

Ruth cautioned me that I had to be very careful in the future. I couldn't afford any more blunders like the *Rolling Stone* story and photos. I felt totally spun out.

Shaun Cassidy: I ended up hiring the writer of the article, Robin Green, on my *American Gothic* TV series. She had a very successful career as a television writer. I remember re-reading the article and, this is coming from the adult perspective of a guy who'd gone through a similar experience, the whole thing felt like a cry for help to me. It was kind of, 'Get me out of this and leave me alone,' but also, 'Listen to me, hear me.' The reason why some actresses pose in *Playboy* magazine is that they think it will change their image. It always feels like a stunt and I don't think it's ever delivered on the promise for a lot of these people. And I would put David at the time in that category. It got a lot of attention, but I don't necessarily think it was the kind of attention he wanted.

Ruth, as always, had a solution for my problems. God, how I depended on that woman. She was, I thought, a lifesaver.

She introduced me to a special doctor. She assured me he could work miracles. His clientele included a lot of stars. He exuded confidence. Anxiety could be removed instantly, he said. He had pills for everything. He decided that, in my case, the drug of choice was Valium, which he prescribed like a vitamin. I remember him telling me, as I prepared for my 1973 overseas tour, 'Before you leave for Europe, make sure you have enough Valium. They're a necessity.' And he gave me plenty of it.

During the last year of *The Partridge Family* he had me taking first 20 and later 24 milligrams of Valium a day. It would help my acne, he said. I'd wake up in the morning, go to work and take a Valium. Then another after lunch. And perhaps another 'as needed'. I felt all right doing this, because the medication was being prescribed for me. And Ruth assured me he was a great doctor. So I didn't worry about it initially. After all, he was doing this sort of thing for a lot of big celebrities. It wasn't like I was addicted or anything, I told myself.

There I was, so proud that I was steering clear of all illegal drugs, yet I was seeing this doctor-to-the-stars who was the pill-pusher of all time. He wasn't doing anything illegal. But there seemed to be something wrong about the whole thing. He insisted we get our prescriptions filled by one particular pharmacist. We all did what we were told. My dad and Shirley, too.

I remember him giving me 100 Quaaludes, saying, 'Here, these will help you sleep.' Yeah, with 100 Quaaludes you could get a lot of sleep.

19 Come Fly with Me

On my 1973 European tour I had my own 99-passenger Caravelle jet. There's something satisfying about knowing you've achieved that level of success and power. For my guys, making the trip was like one big party. For me, the concerts were all the same. Everyone but me recognised that my workload was unsustainable.

Variety reported that, although my records were selling quite well throughout Europe, my planned concert appearances near Frankfurt had to be cancelled because of poor ticket sales. They pointed out that that was one region in which *The Partridge Family* was not televised, raising the question of how viable an attraction I'd be if I didn't have the TV show buoying me. Not that I worried much about that, with the screams ringing in my ears every night and my roadies having no trouble pulling chicks for me.

The British press made a big fuss over the fact that the Queen had invited me to lunch. I'd much rather have met Eric Clapton.

I figured it would have been the dullest and most strained lunch imaginable and I had no time for that. So I cancelled the Queen. No offense was intended, although the press could not understand that.

I have to tell you, I have no regrets about having stood the Queen up. Why? Because that was the day I met Sue Shifrin for lunch. She was a singer/songwriter on the same record label I was on. She was invited by David Bridger of Bell Records to one of my Wembley concerts and to hang out with me. The day I was supposed to be meeting the Queen, I was starting a little affair with Sue. At the time, neither of us had any idea about the significance of our getting together. Soon I would be back in America, while Sue would remain in England. Allthough she's an American, she lived in England for nine years. Eventually we both went on to other relationships and married other people, but we had a special connection from the start. And 13 years after our first meeting, Sue would become a very important part of my life.

Sue Shifrin Cassidy: David didn't come on my radar as a pop star. I was living in England in my own little isolated world as a new songwriter and was very preoccupied with myself, learning a craft and living in a different country. When he came into town I suddenly saw the fuss that was being made over this person. I was invited to go to Wembley Stadium in 1973 to see him perform because I recorded for the same label.

It was insane. I was brought in by the record company in one of their cars and there were thousands of people outside, lots of young girls. They started to attack the car I was in; it was really frightening. The noise in the stadium was deafening. The place was packed and it was vibrating! I was way back in the balcony and I was standing next to the actor Sal Mineo, who was a really good friend of David. I had seen him in *Exodus*, which was one of my favourites of all time as a kid. Sal was a sweet man and was genuinely thrilled to be there and see all this fuss going on for David. I was standing up there and I saw this guy run out on the stage and he was almost like a dot he was so little. I was so far away. He was wearing a white jumpsuit and he jumped in the air and did a split. He was electrifying, and I said, 'Oh my God.' With all the noise, you could hardly hear anything. He started to sing and work the audience and then he sat down at the piano and sang *I Am a Clown*, which is still my favourite song of his. I just love that song. And I just thought, *Wow, this guy's really talented. I get it.*

Afterwards, I was invited to the label party in the penthouse at the Wembley Hotel, right next to the stadium. It was absolutely jammed with people; you couldn't move. I was wearing this little jean jacket that my mother had embroidered for me, which had a jungle scene with giraffes on the back. I was introduced to a lot of people who worked for the record company. David walked towards me and I was introduced to him. I just thought he was beautiful. He had these thick, mink eyelashes and there was a very sweet quality about him. He was just a sweet young man in the middle of a hurricane, a monsoon, a typhoon and an earthquake all rolled into one.

I shook his hand and said, 'Thank you for a wonderful show,' and he walked away and I went to look for the bathroom. I came out about three minutes later and everybody was gone. Everyone had disappeared. Except for him. I said, 'Where did everybody go?' And he said, 'Oh, I told them all to leave.' I said, 'Why did you do that?' He said, 'I thought we should get to know each other.' And I said, 'No, I'm not that kind of girl,' because I really was a good Jewish girl from Miami.

We actually talked all night long. There was a piano in the suite and I played him a couple of songs that I had written. I remember being nervous, but it was OK. And he said, 'Gee, those are good.'

Then something happened. And he said to me, 'Please don't ever tell anybody that we've been together.' And I swore to him I would never tell anyone, and the only person I did tell was my mother. He and I had a total connection. It was as if we had known each other forever.

To make a long story short, I was seeing somebody else at the time, whom I later married, but whenever David would come to London, he would call me. One time he called me and I told him, 'I'm living with somebody now. We can't do this any more, but I want to come and say goodbye to you.' So I snuck out and went to Brown's Hotel, where he was staying, and told him that I could never see him again. And I didn't for a very long time.

I was on the front page of the papers every single day during this tour because I took a whole press corps with me on my plane. One journalist felt things had really gotten out of hand when even *The Times* considered it newsworthy that I'd caught a cold.

There were reports that I'd broken out in a 'rash', which was the recurring stress-related acne problem that Valium was supposed to alleviate. And that I balked at requests that I sing certain songs, saying I'd recorded them months before and didn't know the words any more.

Some reporters noted that both Sam and I visibly tensed when we saw groups of young fans approaching. One reporter quoted Sam as saying, 'People think we are strange when they see us get scared of little girls, but in a crowd, they get ferocious, particularly the young ones . . . I don't know what the answer is, but I *have* managed to find a way of dealing with them at concerts. I just run!'

Henry Diltz: I know from talking to David that he was afraid of being trapped in a crowd. I think one time he got trapped in a supermarket by adoring fans and it scared the heck out of him.

I was paranoid. You don't go through that experience and come out of it the same way. There were stalkers living in my air-conditioning units and following me all over the world. Some fans were doing ridiculous things like building shrines to me in their living rooms. It was madness.

The fans' intensity could get frightening, and some of my security people were really learning their business as we went along. My head of security had never been involved with anything of this magnitude before (he went on to handle tours for some of the biggest names in the business, but he was cutting his first teeth with me). Up to that point, none of the high-spirited young fans who filled our big concerts on this tour had been seriously injured, but at least one commentator felt that was due to luck more than anything else and raised a cautionary note for the future.

Dick Leahy: His live shows were a phenomenon. I remember we went to an old stadium in Manchester. It was very dangerous because people were standing on canopies over the aisles. The police were gonna close the show down. It was frightening. There were 40,000 people there. David was scared. We were all scared that somebody might get hurt. It was an old stadium and it wasn't equipped for all these thousands of people stamping their feet and climbing on to awnings. The screaming was intense. To his credit, David did manage to calm them down and tell them that he wanted to sing to them and to stop the screaming. It turned out to be a very, very successful concert.

Tony Palmer, pop music critic of the *Observer*, declared (25 March 1973), 'The disorder caused by the rampaging fanlets was often due indirectly to administrative bungling on the part of the tour's management. Both the road manager and Cassidy's personal assistant were California law students with little or no qualifications for organising such a quasi-military operation as a pop tour. The singer's manager, Miss Ruth Aarons, is an ex-ping-pong world champion. Her 22-year-old girl assistant was, until recently, a psychiatrist's assistant. The head of Cassidy's record company once worked in production control for a motor car firm until he decided that pop music was his true vocation . . . The English promoter who had spent six months setting up the tour did not receive a signed contract from Miss Aarons until half an hour before the first show at Wembley – already halfway through the English tour. Little wonder, therefore, that the whole fandango got out of hand.'

Perhaps we should have taken note of Palmer's concern. But by the time his words saw print, we were winging our way back to the States.

It became apparent in the fall of 1973 that in the U.S. (but not abroad) the David Cassidy/*Partridge Family* craze was over. The show's ratings, along with record sales for both David Cassidy and The Partridge Family, fell off precipitously as we went into our show's fourth and final season.

What happened? We were still a national favourite throughout our third season (1972–3). We were tied with *The Waltons* as the nineteenth most popular show on the air that season. But throughout the 1973–4 season, we were way down in the ratings. In January 1974 the esteemed television critic who went by the pseudonym of 'Cyclops' noted in the *New York Times* that there were only a couple of shows *less* popular than *The Partridge Family* and it was inevitable that the show would be cancelled, a fact, he added, that caused him genuine sorrow, since *The Partridge Family* was one of the few shows that a whole family, from children to parents to grandparents, could enjoy together. As our demise became inevitable, a number of critics confessed they'd found much to enjoy in our show.

We faced significantly tougher competition in our last season. ABC changed our time slot from 8.30 p.m. on Fridays to 8 p.m on Saturdays, putting us in direct competition with the most popular show on the air at the time, *All in the Family*. The network had pretty much given up on our show.

We did some episodes on location. On the show our manager Reuben got us a TV commercial for some chicken company. So we were on a cruise in Mexico in 120 degree heat and we had to wear chicken suits. The line that I will never forget was, 'Perfect. Here we are, six lunks in chicken suits.' That's when I knew it was time to leave *The Partridge Family*. I said, 'That's it. I don't want to do this any more. This is my sayonara.' It became kind of a mantra for me. *Here we are, six lunks in chicken suits*.

At 23, my face caked in three layers of make-up, I made a less convincing teenager than ever. The fan magazines made much less fuss over my twenty-third birthday in April 1973 than they had over my last two, but the space dedicated to me in the magazines was just a bit less than before and the headline one of them ran, 'Naturally You've Changed,' tacitly acknowledged that I was approaching the upper age limit for inclusion in magazines designed to fulfil the fantasies of young girls.

Many of those pre-pubescent girls who'd had crushes on me had outgrown me by our fourth year; they were now old enough to be going on dates themselves, rather than sitting at home on a Friday or Saturday night watching TV.

And I was burned out. The pills, I eventually came to realise, weren't helping me either. The doctor said they would help me sleep and would relieve my nerves, and they did help in those areas, but I became strung out on Valium. I was becoming lethargic. Without saying anything to anyone, I decided to stop taking the pills. I got into meditation for a while – the influence of Steve Ross – attempting to heal my worn-out nerves in a more natural way. Sam, Steve and I would also fast one day a week, which we felt was healthy for the mind and body. We'd listen to Indian music and try to glean wisdom from Eastern philosophies.

But kicking the Valium, I found, didn't make all that big a difference in my life. I'd simply had enough of everything – the show, the hysteria, the road, everything. The producers knew I had no interest any more. I just couldn't wait for the last year of the show to be over. I considered the whole manufactured Keith Partridge/David Cassidy image to be one enormous pain.

Don't get me wrong. It wasn't all bad. There are a couple of episodes of *The Partridge Family* that I've always liked. For me, the best episode we ever did was the Christmas show where I played Sheriff Swell with a lollypop stuck to my head. I love that episode.

I also like an episode that Louis Gossett, Jr and Richard Pryor guest starred in. I liked them both and got to know Richard pretty well. Richard was fantastic. I thought he was a wonderful actor and a really good human being and we got on great. That was just before his career took off.

Paul Junger Witt (producer/director): One of my favourite episodes that I directed was the one with Louis Gossett, Jr and Richard Pryor. That storyline was about a booking mix-up, which sent Smokey Robinson or one of the Motown groups to Salt Lake City and booked The Partridge Family in a primarily African-American inner-city club in Detroit. It was an interesting premise and the subtext was music is music. It brought home the message that there really was no more black music or white music. There was no more race music, as it was called in the 40s and 50s. We felt good music was gonna cross over and that's what we tried to make the episode about.

The Godfather was having such an impact at the time that the producers of our show decided that they would spoof it. (It's still one of the greatest motion pictures ever made, in my opinion. It's a masterpiece.) It gave them an opportunity to use me as the young Guido. The reactions, including my own, were pretty interesting to me and everyone else. The cast and crew had never seen me look like that. That's one of the episodes I like, because it's different.

But as an actor, I certainly no longer had the respect of my peers. Hell, I didn't even have the respect of my own father! In an interview he gave George Maksian of New York's *Daily News* (10 February 1974), headlined 'Cassidy Calls Son Bubble Gum Star,' Maksian asked my father if he'd object if any of his other sons followed in my footsteps. My father answered, 'Sure, some of the boys could follow David, the bubble gum star. But he can be used up and sucked up very fast in the business . . . The world is full of Xeroxes. But if they really have need for it, I wouldn't stop them. My main concern is that they're really decent people. I care about what they are, and how they deal with other people.'

I wasn't happy with my career myself. I knew it had really messed me up, changed me. You can't go through those things and come out the other side without being different. I hated the pressure of being an idol, of feeling I was expected to be a superstar on stage and a superhuman offstage. After four years of 'stardom', I just couldn't talk to people any more. *The Partridge Family*/teen idol trip had distorted people's perception of me and my perception of myself so much that I didn't like what I had become. I was a serious actor when I started, but I don't think anyone has ever taken me seriously as an actor in the years since *The Partridge Family*. I can't shake that albatross around my neck.

As we filmed the final season I'd sometimes deeply regret the direction I had chosen. I'd think, *I've got to get off this friggin' bus!*

The only way out that I could see was to simply quit show business entirely. Ruth certainly didn't want to hear such talk, not just for my sake, I'm sure. After all, I had become her major breadwinner. If I retired, she stood to lose a considerable amount of income. From her point of view, it was foolish of me to think of retirement. Demand for me on the concert circuit was strong and would likely remain strong for quite some time. Maybe years. Record companies and producers still had confidence in me. It was silly to talk of quitting.

The Partridge Family's first five albums, released within less than two years, had all gone gold. The first three had made it to the Top Ten on the *Billboard* charts. But the sixth album, *The Partridge Family Notebook*, showed signs of declining sales. I begged the record company to change the sound. And the seventh album, *Crossword Puzzle*, which made the charts for just five weeks in the summer of 1973, was only a mild success. It was the last Partridge Family album to make the charts at all, and none of the singles were hits. Throughout the 1973–4 television season *The Partridge Family*, for the first time in its history, was without a hit record. The producers just refused to change with the times. I lost a lot of sleep over it.

Deciding to quit was not a difficult decision for me. I told Ruth I'd fulfil my obligations – to finish the fourth season, make the records I was required to, do one last huge world tour and then quit while I could still say I was on top.

Finally, in the fourth year, I convinced the powers that be that Keith had to move out and get his own apartment. I said, 'What is this? How many years can I be in high school?'

Knowing that I was leaving the show, the studio brought in a young kid named Ricky Segall, who was very cute, to play Ricky Stevens. We all liked Ricky, but he wasn't a member of the Partridge family so the addition of this new character made no sense. They also brought in Andy Williams's twin nephews and that didn't work, either. And Danny Bonaduce as a teenager simply wasn't as cute as he'd been as a wise-cracking little kid. Things he said or did that seemed amusingly impish when he was 10 were irritating when he was 13 or 14.

I guess they assumed the show couldn't go on without me and I don't think that was correct. I think it could have gone on. The people they tried to introduce into the show just did not work. They weren't very talented. It was almost like nobody really cared any more.

As American newspapers reported that the David Cassidy/*Partridge Family* mania was receding into history, manufacturers quietly stopped renewing licensing agreements. They figured they'd marketed about as many units of *Partridge Family* bubble gum and David Cassidy beach towels as they were going to. Chuck Laufer changed the publication schedule of *The Partridge Family Magazine* from monthly to bimonthly to quarterly, then killed it.

When the last year wrapped, the editor and producer put together a blooper reel. My dad came in to help put it together. They used a shot of me and looped my father's voice over mine, which was really amazing. I thought it was fantastic. I wasn't prepared for it. I was looking at myself and there was my father's voice coming out of my mouth. Boy, was that weird. In addition to all the good reasons I had for quitting, I imagined that it might also bring my father and me closer together. He could be the undisputed star of the family.

I felt better once I'd made up my mind to get out. And it looked to me like the timing was just right. No one would outdraw my last concert tour. I would go out on top. My records were actually selling better than ever in England. I'd started later in England than the U.S. It was only logical, I suppose, that I would last later there. The British fans really took to me in a way that was gratifying.

Sam Hyman: The English revere their rock stars more than we do and put them on a higher plateau. From the Beatles on, the music industry was a great source of revenue for the country and a great source of national pride. Also, David's teeny bopper image was not as much of a turn-off in England as it was here. The Beatles were teeny boppers when they started. David was much bigger in England than he was in the U.S. It was Davidmania, and in some ways it was bigger than Beatlemania. When he did his concerts, he broke the records set by the Beatles and the Rolling Stones at Wembley Arena.

Musically, 1973 was a fantastic time for me. In October 1973 I topped the British charts for several weeks with a single combining *Daydreamer* and *The Puppy Song*, neither of which were hits in the U.S. And in December 1973 my album *Dreams Are Nuthin' More Than Wishes*, which I thought was the best of my first three solo albums, became the number one album in England.

After my second album, *Rock Me Baby*, came out and it was clear that Wes wanted me just to record songs by his writers, I called my manager and said, 'I want another record producer,' which became a point of tremendous contention. Unbeknownst to me, the president of Bell Records, Larry Uttal, had signed an agreement with Wes Farrell that said, 'You can produce The Partridge Family and any of its members for the remainder of our contract.' This was at a time when artists were totally controlled by the record companies.

Larry Uttal then had to pay Wes Farrell a sum of money to let me go. And, at that point, I became a bad boy. I became the unruly, undisciplined artist who was causing Bell Records a lot of problems. Larry Uttal said, 'How dare David elect to have another record producer?' It was insane. But understand, I was their puppet. I was nothing more to them than someone who would keep the change rattling in the register.

So I personally called Rick Jarrad. Rick had produced two or three of my favourite albums of all time: *Jefferson Airplane*'s first album and Harry Nilsson's *Aerial Ballet* and *Harry*, which were two masterpieces. I was a huge Nilsson fan and got to know him very well, eventually singing and writing with him a few years later. I had all Harry's demos because I was such a fan. *The Puppy Song*, which I recorded for *Dreams Are Nuthin' More Than Wishes*, was his song.

Rick Jarrad brought *Daydreamer* to me. A writer from South Africa named Terry Dempsey wrote it and it's a really good song. After Rick played it to me we looked at each other and I just high-fived him and said, 'That's a smash.' *Daydreamer* is just as good a pop song for the time as anything I've ever recorded, except for maybe *I Think I Love You.*

I'd been living in this bubble, cut off from most of the rest of the world. But finally I had the time and space to be creative. I called Tony Romeo and said, 'Tony, I'm gonna make an album without Wes. I want you to write a song for me. I want it to be kind of autobiographical, to reflect where I came from, who I am. So he wrote *Sing Me.* He sent me the demo with him playing this funky piano and singing. The lyrics go: 'I have some pictures of us, we're all at the shore. I must've been four then, I couldn't have been more. My father was holding me up just for show, my mother was posing like Marilyn Monroe.' It was like Tony had taken my life and written about it. We'd never talked about it. But I remembered being at the beach with my parents as a kid and I wept.

Tony wrote a song for *The Partridge Family* Christmas album, *My Christmas Card to You*. That is one of the greatest Christmas songs ever written, and I would love to re-record it. I re-recorded *Summer Days*, also written by Tony, because I wanted it to be mine!

Rick brought in a young guy named Michael McDonald, whom he had just signed to a publishing deal; he was working with Steely Dan. He came over to my house with Rick, sat down at the piano and played a little bit of *Hold On*, and I said, 'I love that. That's just a beautiful, beautiful melody.' Michael was very shy and extremely talented. When I first met Michael, he was living over a garage and I think I was the first person to record one of his songs. Michael played on every track on my *Dreams Are Nuthin' More Than Wishes* album.

Bali Hai is a tribute to my father, mother and stepmother for my musical upbringing.

Gary Montgomery wrote *Mae*. Kim Carnes, Dave Ellingson and I were over at a writer's house and Gary Montgomery was there. He said he thought the song was perfect for me and played it to me. The next thing I knew, I was singing it in the studio.

Peggy Lee's version of *Fever* was played a lot in my home when I was growing up and I always thought it was cool. I tried to put a different take on it. Ron Tutt, who was Elvis's drummer, played on that track.

I got some of the folky influences from Kim and Dave. They had come out of The New Christy Minstrels folk thing. Henry Diltz and the Modern Folk Quartet and all those guys were also friends of mine and they came out of that New York coffee shop, coffee vibe. Kim, Dave and I wrote a couple of songs together, *Can't Go Home Again* and *Preying on My Mind*. *Preying on My Mind* was more their creation. *Can't Go Home Again* was more mine. I brought the musical changes. At the time I wrote it, I was remembering when I was 18. It was 1968. I had just moved back to New York from L.A. I was on a bus from Port Authority to West Orange, New Jersey. I remember leaning against the window and looking out and remembering how many times my mom had driven me the same way. I hadn't lived there since I was 11. I saw a couple of guys I'd known who were now married. It was really odd. I felt so out of place.

Dave Ellingson: It goes back to the old Thomas Wolfe line, 'You can't go home again.' For me personally, as we wrote it, my input was I lived in an old town in Minnesota. I'd gone back to that town years later and it was very nostalgic. As we wrote the song it was very real to me.

Kim Carnes: Whenever we got together to write with David, there was an ease in it. We'd all become very close friends after touring around the world together, plus we had similar tastes in music. We laughed a lot together. Writing with David was the way it was supposed to be. It was a really neat experience. The songs came easily. He wanted so much to be proud of his music. He had great integrity and knew what he liked. He really wanted to show people more what he was about musically. He wanted to stretch out.

Can't Go Home Again came from a conversation we all had about what it would be like to go back to your hometown. Anyone who listened to the song who'd left their home and moved away could relate to it.

Our best times with David were when he'd come over to the house and just hang out until the wee hours of the morning, laughing and playing lots of music. Those were the times when nobody else was around and he could just be David.

In the summer of 1974 I had two hit singles on the British charts, *If I Didn't Care* (peaking at number nine) and a cover of the Beatles' *Please, Please Me* (peaking at 16), plus one hit album, *Cassidy Live!* (peaking at nine), none of which made a ripple in the U.S. I was more popular in England than I'd ever been but I wasn't going to overstay my welcome.

My routine continued pretty much as normal. I'd do the TV show weekdays. I'd record at night. On weekends I'd tour. And on Monday mornings I'd be back on the set, telling Susan how the security guards had had to hide me in the trunk of a car so I could escape my frenzied fans, how many chicks I'd had sex with, how frustrating it was for me that I couldn't form any kind of meaningful relationship with a woman. I moaned a lot to Susan, who seemed to understand so perfectly.

'You've got to be careful about Susan,' Shirley said to me one day.

I said, 'What are you talking about?'

'You've got to be careful how you talk to her about all of the other women in your life. You don't want to hurt her.'

I didn't get what Shirley was drivng at.

Susan knew me well. She was the sister I never had, my best female friend. I just couldn't imagine how my talking openly to her about anything could hurt her. I was so blind.

Shirley Jones: Susan had a giant crush on David. She was just mad about him. And David didn't see it coming. They were friends first. They worked together and confided in one another throughout the years. It was over a long period of time that her feelings for David developed. He wasn't aware of it at all. Susan would say things to me and make little hints about it.

Just after the final wrap party for *The Partridge Family* I took Susan out to dinner. We were now through with the show for good; the cast members were all moving off in different directions. I wanted to keep our friendship alive. I knew I'd be going on a world tour shortly and then retiring from the business for the foreseeable future. Susan didn't know where she'd be working next. Maybe that sense of things coming to an end helped draw us closer together.

After dinner, we drove by my old high school. We talked about the past years, from when we'd first met when she was a 15-year-old trying out for the show. We both started weeping. We must have spent three hours sitting there. She told me in great detail how she felt about me and how afraid she was of what was going to happen in the future.

I gave her all the help that she wanted with her career. I connected her with people who'd been guiding my career, whom I believed could help her get the work she wanted. And they did. Ruth became Susan's manager and saw to it that she was soon signed to another TV show. My agent at William Morris Agency, Lenny Hirshan, took a strong interest in Susan, both professionally and personally. Eventually, Lenny and Susan married. Susan actually went on to have the most successful post-*Partridge Family* acting career of all of us.

I took it for granted that Susan and I would always be very close friends; I knew her about as well as anyone did. And for some years afterwards, we did periodically get in touch. Don't ask me what's happened between us in more recent years, though, because I honestly don't know. We just don't talk any more. Communications were terminated from her end, not mine. I still love Susan in some special way. I can never let that go.

Perhaps the speculation that Susan and I had been lovers or boyfriend and girlfriend, which persists to this day and still appears in tabloids, made it too uncomfortable for her to communicate with me or any of our co-workers on the show.

It breaks my heart that someone I felt so close to is unreachable at this stage of our lives. Hollywood can be a wicked place. Relationships with co-workers go from intimate friendships to non-existent. Susan was one of the few people I thought I would know and see for ever. Sadly, it was not to be.

20 World Tour 1974

The last world tour turned out to be a circus. We were all partying hard – the band, the security people, everybody – just blowing off steam before we packed it all in for good. If you ask me what I remember from that tour, the hijinks and escapades come to mind before any of the concerts themselves.

That trip was a free-flying sexual playground. Three incredible Dutch stewardesses were provided with the private jet we chartered in Europe. Someone must have handpicked those girls for us. They partied with everyone. And when it was time for them to do their regular jobs on board the jet, they were thoroughly professional.

I remember hanging around Gina Lollobrigida over a period of several days in Australia. The Italian sex goddess was about twice my age, but very attractive. The first time she met me she said, 'I hear you're a monster. I want to meet the monster.' And she looked down at my crotch. She said she was doing a book of photographs – she'd gotten into photography after retiring from the screen – and asked me to pose for her. I'm glad she included me in her book, along with Henry Kissinger and other interesting men she'd known.

Henry Diltz: Gina Lollabrigida . . . became very enamored with David when we were in Melbourne. She came to the show and was there on stage with me, standing in the wings, shooting as David was out in the middle of this screaming crowd of girls at a soccer field. And then she wanted to do a private shooting with David, with David lying in bed surrounded by, as she said, 'fruits'. She ordered hundreds of dollars worth of grapes, bananas and other fruit, asked David to take his clothes off and drape a sheet around himself. We didn't get it, but she thought, *Here he is, all the girls are outside screaming. They want to see him and where is he? He's in bed with fruits*. She just thought the image of that was kind of interesting.

Gina Lollobrigida introduced me to the audience of 65,000 people when I played the Melbourne Cricket Ground. I really got a kick out of that, even though I'm sure my younger fans probably didn't know who she was. I was the last performer to play there until Paul McCartney in 1993, 19 years later.

Sam Hyman: We kicked off the Australasian leg of the tour in New Zealand. From there, it was Australia and then up to Asia. Elton John had toured the opposite route. He started in Asia and worked his way down, ending up in New Zealand. Elton and David were in Auckland on the same day, although their concerts were on different days. Elton came to David's show. And when David came off stage before his encore, Elton's back there going, 'Oh, great show, mate.' David said, 'Do you want to come out?' And Elton said, 'Sure. What are you going to play?' David told him the song and gave Elton the key, and Elton said, 'Got it.' David ran back out. 'I want to bring on a good friend of mine. Somebody you may have heard of. Anybody know of Elton John?' The crowd screamed, 'Yeah!' Elton went over to the piano player and said, 'Would you give up your seat, just for this song?' Elton took his place at the piano and played with the band and performed the song with David. The place was rocking and the fans were going nuts. It was great.

Dave Ellingson: Elton was at his absolute peak. He was red hot. He jammed with David at our show and that was a real big deal. For Elton to jam with him gave David more credibility as an artist. After the show, the hotel we were staying in had a bar and a big lounge. Elton came along and there was a piano and a stage and he took over. David and some of the players in the band got up and jammed and it went on and on.

I took maybe 25 of my own people with me as we toured, plus around 25 members of the press. I played for audiences of 20,000, 40,000, 60,000 people. Although by the last concerts of the tour I felt totally burned out, totally exhausted, when I'd hit the stage, the crowd would give me instant energy. There's a certain sense of power, too, communicating with tens of thousands of people. If you shout out, 'I think I love you,' you'll get countless shouts of 'I love you' back. If you reach out, as if trying to make contact, tens of thousands of fans will move, as if drawn toward you.

After a few hundred fans were hurt at one of my Australian shows, a government official declared me a hazard to public health. I was thinking, *Hey, listen up. We're just trying to give everybody a little entertainment.* It wasn't as if mine were the first rock concerts at which anyone had ever been injured. But to a significant portion of the press, I became this villain who brought mayhem to tranquil Australia. The press called it pandemonium. And that started to get to me, seeing the way the press could manipulate public sentiment to make me look bad. The way the press could turn on you, that was another reason I was glad I'd be getting out of the game soon.

The final stops on my tour were in the U.K. I played three huge stadiums in Scotland and England, the type of places the Beatles had played, but that no one else was playing. So that in itself guaranteed massive press attention. I arrived like a conquering hero. Approaching Glasgow, my first stop, the fans lined the road from the airport for miles, giving me the kind of reception they'd give to royalty.

Sam Hyman: David was embraced by the British rock royalty. Elton John would say, 'Hey, come on over.' David and I had dinner at Elton's house with Elton, his manager John Reid and Rod Stewart. At that point, Rod hadn't had a hit in a while. I remember Rod complaining about it and joking with Elton that he should give him some help. After dinner, we went into the living room. Elton played the piano and Rod and David sang. That was one of the highlights of my personal experiences. It was awesome that we were sitting there drinking brandy with Elton John and Rod Stewart.

Then I played White City Stadium in London. There were 40,000 fans inside in the bleachers and packed standing in the field, and perhaps as many outside. They went wild when I came on stage and every time I opened my mouth to sing or speak to them. I kept saying, 'Get back, get back, you've got to stop pushing! They're going to stop the show. You've got to cool it!' But when you tell people who are that worked up, 'Stop going berserk!' they only go further overboard. They were so loud, I didn't even know if they could hear me. The promoter and the managers even came out in the middle of songs shouting for the crowds to back up.

Richard Delvy (tour music director): That night was just crazy. We stopped the show about six times. The fans kept pushing forward,

> crushing the people in front of them. They were out of control. There were 30 to 40 security guys passing injured people over their heads and then putting them on stretchers and taking them backstage. It was awful. There were hundreds of people lying in the hallway on stretchers. It was very depressing. I actually cried more than once that night. It took us about two hours to get out of the building because the crowd had crushed the doors inwards. It was very frightening.

There was gridlock outside the stadium. Cars were parked six deep. I never had a harder time making a getaway. My security guys told me a lot of girls had fainted and some had been taken to the hospital, but I had no idea how severe the situation was. We always anticipated some fans would faint, due to all the excitement. We had first-aid people standing by. But I could already anticipate the press making me out to be the heavy, as they had in Australia, because the crowd at my White City Stadium concert had gotten so out of control.

One of my fans, unfortunately, did not come through alive. Bernadette Whelan, a 14-year-old British schoolgirl, was fatally injured at that concert. She was among those taken from the stadium by ambulance to a nearby hospital, where she managed to hold on for four days before dying. I had no idea the night I gave my concert that one of my fans had been carried out in a coma.

Her death received extensive coverage. The press, which would otherwise have focused attention on my retirement, understandably focused instead on her, casting a pall over my whole concert career. At the time, I was very unhappy and upset over the coverage, feeling I was being unfairly blamed for a young girl's death. I couldn't even bring myself to read all the things that were written, they were so painful. My people assured me repeatedly that we had in no way been responsible for

Bernadette's death. They told me that she had known heart problems and that she suffered a heart attack during the chaos of the concert. But when I was reviewing newspaper coverage of the event in preparation for writing this book, I realised that what I was told about her death – what I've always found comforting to believe – was simply not true.

For one thing, the government held a formal inquest into her death, which would not have happened had her doctor reported that she had died from a routine heart attack. *The Times* reported on 18 June 1979 that, at the inquest into Bernadette Whelan's death, 'Dr Rufus Compton, a pathologist, said the girl died of traumatic asphyxia. Obstruction of respiration was mainly a result of compression of the body. Her brain had been damaged by cardiac arrest.' In layman's terms, she had been crushed to death by the crowd. Her father, *The Times* reported, testified that the girl had gone to the concert 'in perfectly good health'. He received word some time later that she'd been taken by ambulance to Hammersmith Hospital. According to *The Times*, 'St John Ambulance workers dealt with 500 casualties, and 30 people were taken to the hospital.'

Hammersmith coroner Dr John Burton testified that 10,000 young fans had been 'crowded up against a barrier in the centre of the arena, with no means of getting out', in a highly charged situation, with hysteria spreading through the crowd. Burton cautioned those attending the inquest that he was going to play a tape-recording of a 20-minute portion of the concert which was so disturbing that some people might want to leave. On the tape, girls could be heard shouting, 'Please get me out,' while loudspeaker appeals were made in vain for the crowd to stop pressing forwards.

Disc jockey Tony Blackburn, who had served as an emcee at the concert, testified that he had never before seen so many people removed from a concert on stretchers, nor had he ever been at a concert at which seating had not been provided for everybody.

> **Sam Hyman:** David was very shook up about it. He didn't say that he felt responsible, but how could he feel otherwise? He knew it wasn't his fault, but it reinforced his feeling, 'That's it. I've got to stop this.'

> **David Bridger:** The White City show was a tragedy. There should have been more security. The crowd rushed forward and Bernadette got crushed. All it takes is for one person to fall over and of course it's the domino effect. On the day that Bernadette Whelan was buried, they closed the cemetery because they didn't want kids going up there and there were rumours that David was gonna visit the grave. I clambered over and laid flowers on her grave on behalf of David. He so badly wanted to be there.

I certainly did not want to believe that I could in any way have been responsible for the death of one of my fans. Although I was devastated, I still to this day believe that my security and I did everything we could to keep my fans safe. However, had you seen the thousands of fans pushing hysterically toward the stage that night, you would have concluded, as I did, that you simply can't contain teenage girls who are out of control. We did everything we could, but failed.

A few nights later, I gave my very last concert, in Manchester. The crowd, knowing it was my absolute farewell show, made more noise than any I'd ever heard. I had to stuff cotton in my ears. I had a Marshall amp turned all the way up to ten to try to project over all the screaming. I could barely hear anything I was doing. That was an amazing night. The crowd gave me so much energy. I remember running off the stage. Then I came back and said, 'I love you, it's been incredible. You're not going to see me for a while, but someday I'll be back. I just want you to know how much it's meant to me.' Then I sang *It's All Over Now, Baby Blue* for the final encore.

I ran the whole length of the field into a waiting car, while 40,000 people were screaming and crying. I left happy, but with a sense of disbelief that, after four years, I was leaving a stadium with fans still screaming for me, knowing I was never going to do this again.

The *Cassidy Live!* album was recorded at the White City Stadium show, and it was done on the fly. The most difficult part was keeping the screaming and shouting from the audience out of the recordings. We had to edit out all the times that I was saying, 'Push back! Push back! People are getting crushed.' That album depicts the madness of touring.

The world tour lasted nine months. It became nothing more than a love letter to everyone and everything I had experienced: the fans, the people who had supported me and the music. I could walk away from it at that point. And I'm glad that recording exists so that if I ever forget, I can go back and listen to it.

It was time, I felt, definitely time. I breathed a giant sigh of relief, *Thank God I made it.*

21 Alone Again . . . Naturally

Sam Hyman: He needed a break. He needed a vacation. He needed to live and enjoy some of the fruits of his labour. There was just too much work and too much responsibility. He was responsible for the livelihoods of a lot of people, the machinery behind him. And that's a huge load for a 20-something-year-old. It finally got to him and he said, 'I've had enough. Everyone go on their own way.'

The years from my retirement in May 1974, at the age of 24, up to about 1980 were the darkest I've ever known.

I walked away from the unnatural success I'd had. I don't think I could have stood it if it had walked away from me. That would have felt, again, like abandonment, and that is why I chose to leave while I was still at the top. I needed to find a way to be happy that had nothing to do with gold records and breaking attendance records. I was emotionally stunted.

When I retired, I suffered a breakdown. Or several successive breakdowns, it felt like, because each time I thought I'd fallen as low as I could go, the bottom would drop out from under me again.

For the first six months I locked myself in my room. I sat alone, talking to myself, trying to figure out what had happened. I can't remember a whole lot about that period. I just remember feeling bleak. Empty. I increasingly found solace in drinking. I wanted to anaesthetise myself. I was so lost.

The pain I was trying to numb was rooted in the reality that I didn't have the kind of career I'd wanted. And the career I'd had, I never wanted. Sure, I still had plenty of fans. But did they love *me* or just the image of me, which had been totally manufactured and marketed? I thought I'd like to sing songs that truly expressed who I was. But who was I? I hadn't a clue. And would the fans have any interest in the real me, anyway?

I regretted having ever climbed aboard *The Partridge Family* bus. Sure, I'd become a star. But I was also trapped, cut off from everyone else, unable to go anywhere, unable to interact with others in a normal way. I'd lost the ability to really relate to people.

I had no idea how to start rebuilding the real me, not the pop star. The easiest course to take was to just shut down. To withdraw into my cocoon and hope that time would help me heal.

I was an insomniac to begin with and I now found the problem was getting worse. I was staying up later and later. I couldn't sleep and there was no joy in being awake, so I tried to dull my existence one way or another. The clean-living, hard-working vegetarian turned into this guy who was willing to try anything to take him outside of himself. I didn't care.

My mother saw me spinning out, drowning in my sorrows, and made a couple of attempts to intervene. I didn't want to hear it. Like a teenage brat, I'd tell her, 'Leave me alone, Ma.' My mother actually moved in with me for a couple of months, but that was a mistake. When you're an adult, you can't live with your mother. If I wanted to play drums at five in the morning, I wanted to be able to do that without my mother saying, 'Go to sleep.' And I often liked to play music all through the night. I had a few musician friends I felt comfortable with who would stay up all night with me, partying and playing. I told my mom, 'This is my house. You can't tell me what to do.'

I'd replay in my mind the events leading up to me quitting the business, trying to analyse what I'd done. I thought, *I don't know what I want to do, or if I want to do anything at all.* I became very undisciplined.

After I retired, my father was in the spotlight a bit more, which I hope brought him some happiness. He got some of the best roles of his career, including recurring guest-starring appearances on *Columbo* and he particularly delighted in portraying his idol, John Barrymore, in the film *W. C. Fields and Me* (1976).

He said he wanted to become closer to me. Maybe he was worried about what was happening to me; I don't know. Instead of starting slow, maybe suggesting we have dinner together, he brought my brother Ryan out to my house in Encino and spent the weekend with me. As we talked, I realised that I had nothing in common with him, except for the fact that we'd both become pretty heavy drinkers. But I didn't want to drink with my father. Or do much of anything else with him. I couldn't wait for our weekend together to be over.

And yet, I found myself unexpectedly feeling sorry for him. There was something frighteningly desperate in the way he was trying to hang on to a relationship with me that really wasn't there. You could never talk about what he did wrong. He could never admit his mistakes. If you disagreed with my father, he basically cut you out of his life. If you didn't see the world the way he saw it, he couldn't have a relationship with you. He did that to one of his brothers in the end, to his sister, to my mother and eventually to Shirley. And to me.

I think reality was so painful for my father that he preferred to create his own. My father would look at a white wall and tell you that it was black and you'd have to say, 'OK, you're right, Dad.' If you didn't he would go insane, totally out of control, throwing tantrums and breaking furniture. Few knew there was a very dark side to my father. Most of his showbiz pals never saw it, or pretended not to see it. Those of us who dealt with him intimately – my mother, Shirley, my brothers and I – instinctively tried hard to keep him happy, always tried to agree with him as much as possible, to keep that dark side from rearing its ugly head.

It was sometimes hard for me to reconcile the often difficult, mercurial man I knew with the popular, hardy fellow who everybody in Hollywood used to tell me he was.

Jack Klugman, of *Odd Couple* fame, told me how one day in 1974 he found himself riding with my father in a crowded elevator in the executive office building referred to as the Black Tower, at Universal Studios. When the elevator reached my dad's floor, he kissed Klugman on the mouth and said, 'You know, I'll always love you,' and gaily walked out, letting the elevator doors close on a startled, chagrined Klugman who was babbling to the studio executives all around him, 'I had nothing to do with that; I don't even know that person!' Klugman had never been put in a spot like that in his life, but he took it as a typical Jack Cassidy gag. My dad would mess with people all the time and they would say, 'That Jack! What a guy! What a character!'

My dad had a wonderful relationship with James Cagney. He worshipped Cagney. He spent time at his home and even called him 'Dad'. They established this real bond, based on their shared Irish roots and showbiz interests. But my dad would spin too far out. And eventually, not long before my father died, Cagney had to tell him, 'I can't see you any more. You're out of your mind.' He burned up people like he burned up money.

Late that year, I got a call, quite unexpectedly, from David Bowie. He was already doing pretty well as a performer; his career, it appeared, was on the verge of exploding in a big way. I liked his work, particularly his album *The Rise and Fall of Ziggy Stardust and the Spiders from Mars.* I was intrigued that he appreciated my work. People had often said I had an androgynous look, but Bowie took the concept of androgyny to a whole other level.

He told me he wanted to produce an album – me singing songs that he and others would write. He said he envisioned an album that would give me a far more adult image. I was intrigued enough by what he said to fly to New York, where he and his entourage were encamped at the Sherry Netherland Hotel, and meet with him.

I found that he lived in a very subterranean New York, an avant-garde world of transsexuals and transvestites. It was like a carnival at his place. There were people in his rooms doing mime. He surrounded himself with people who, I guess, made life interesting for him, including some whom I couldn't tell the gender of – and perhaps they weren't sure either. Bowie just enjoyed feeling part of this very hip, artistic, New York scene. To me it held no fascination at all. It felt false and posed.

We were at different ends of the spectrum – one guy whose success in the pop music field was largely behind him, the other whose success was still growing. He was very enthusiastic about the next album he had coming out and all the touring he'd be doing to promote it. The album was *Diamond Dogs*. The thought of touring again was almost repulsive to me. Even if I did make the album he had in mind, there was no way I was going to go out and do concerts to promote it, something you really need to do if you want to make an album a big hit. He really craved all of the mass adulation that I'd had enough of. My take was, *I don't want to be where you're headed. Been there. Done it. Thanks.*

He played me a couple of songs he had in mind for the album – one that he'd written, the other written by Lou Reed. I didn't think they were interesting enough or right for me. One was called, as I recall, *I'm All Grown Up Now* – too obvious, I thought. I said, 'I like the idea. I just don't know about these songs.' The proposed album never came to be. We couldn't even decide on *where* to record it.

Instead, I wound up signing a contract with RCA Records. I agreed to record again, but only if I could do material I believed in. I'd had enough compromises in my career and wanted to feature mostly my own material from now on, and I agreed to the contract only if I would not have to tour to promote my albums. If I toured, I knew the fans would expect me to perform the old songs from *The Partridge Family* days. I couldn't stomach that thought.

Variety had the right take when they wrote that I was dropping my 'manufactured image' to offer the real me. A lot of people who bought those albums have come up to me and said, 'They were the best you ever made,' which I really like hearing. I was particularly proud of the first RCA album I did, a tongue-in-cheek, satirical, semi-autobiographical thing called *The Higher They Climb, the Harder They Fall*, which was about the rise and fall of a rock and roll star. Through the songs, I tried to tell the story of this all-American kid – me, of course – who lives the American dream that goes wrong. People were shocked. They didn't think I could make fun of myself like that. It was the most honest artistic statement I'd ever made.

Massacre at Park Bench was a piece that I came up with with Phil Austin, of the comedy group The Firesign Theatre. Phil, who was one of the great improvisational comedians, was a friend of Henry Diltz. The Firesign Theatre had made an album which was so smart and satirical, it was just wild. I laid down on a bench in the studio and we basically improvised *Massacre at Park Bench.* I had a beginning and an end written and we just riffed through the rest of it. It took three minutes. We recorded it and listened to it and we knew it worked. I did a lot of the effects and the fading and editing myself because I wanted to make sure the story flowed.

I was into developing ideas and songs and working with a lot of people I respected in Los Angeles, people like MFQ (the Modern Folk Quartet), Gerry Beckley and Dewey Bunnell from the band America, Harry Nilsson, Mark Volman and Howard Kaylan from The Turtles, who were all great singers. They all sang on various tracks on the album. Bruce Johnston, of the Beach Boys, arranged all the background parts; he's magnificent in that regard.

In America, RCA said, 'There are no hits on this album.' I told them I disagreed. I thought *Darlin'* could be a hit and that *I Write the Songs*, written by Bruce Johnston, was a classic. I was the first person to record that song, which became a million-seller for Barry Manilow. But RCA thought the album wasn't commercial enough.

The plan was to launch *The Higher They Climb* in the U.K. and Europe, where it did extraordinarily well. Right after it started breaking all over the world, RCA said it wouldn't play on American radio, so they released *Get It Up for Love* as a single instead and it was banned (it was banned by the BBC as well) because, they said, it had sexual connotations. Can you imagine? 'Get it up, get it up for love.' I mean, come on. It's a great song.

All of the albums I recorded for RCA were in the black financially, but they didn't get played much on the radio in

America or make the charts. A couple of the singles made the British charts that year, including *I Write the Songs*. It was released first in the U.K. and when it became an instant hit a record exec from another label, who was on a trip to England, heard it, brought it back to the U.S. and had Barry Manilow record his cover version. Not only was it million-seller for him, it was the 'Record of the Year'. My recording of the song went Top Five in probably 25 countries.

Bruce Johnston: I would not have picked *I Write the Songs* for David to record. I'm not putting my song down, it's a cool song for the right artist, but I think it was too gooey for the direction he was going, not unlike The Partridge Family stuff. He extracted it from me. I happened to be writing the song at the time he was recording the album and he liked it. I was taken aback that he wanted to do it, but I didn't fight him on it.

I was fascinated by David's song selection for *The Higher They Climb, the Harder They Fall*. Artistically I prefer *Home Is Where the Heart Is*, but *The Higher They Climb, the Harder They Fall* was more balanced. When you're a producer, you're often a musical artist yourself and you have to be very objective so you don't send someone down the wrong path. I'm a good listener and sounding-board and I thought what David wanted to bring to the table was really cool. He was very hands-on in the studio, which I really liked. It wasn't about the money, it was about making music that mattered. He'd sit down and play guitar in sessions with the best players in the world. David would sing live. He was as good as any major artist I ever heard or worked with. With those albums, David was taking the next step.

Working with David was good news and bad news. The good news was that he was red-hot from his days on *The Partridge Family* and that was also the bad news. He had to live down the image of him as this cute, long-haired teen idol. His fans were expecting

Partridge Family sounding music, but that didn't happen. It was the same with Brian Wilson – they kept waiting for more surf music and he came up with *Pet Sounds* instead. Some people weren't ready to accept that David had a lot of depth in his artistry. He was convicted by some fans for his desire to grow as an artist.

Shaun Cassidy: I think the albums David did with Bruce Johnston are the best records he ever made. I'm a huge Beach Boys fan and there's a lot of echoes of that group in those records. Those albums feel true to him, which is something that he didn't have much of an opportunity to do on *The Partridge Family*. For the first time, he was allowed to push the boundaries and do what he wanted without having to try to figure out what the public was going to buy. It felt like he was doing exactly what he wanted to do.

People don't know how good a singer David is. He's a really good singer. He has incredible range. He has incredible pitch and I know this because Patrick and I have sung with him and we've tried to do three-part harmony, and he's always the most solid.

When it came to photographing the front cover of *The Higher They Climb*, we spent a lot a time trying to figure out how to make it look like I was reaching for a star. Henry Diltz was a genius at that kind of thing.

Henry Diltz: For the cover, it looks like David's shooting up into the air with his guitar in one hand and one hand out kind of like Superman. We did that in a studio in L.A., where David held on to a rope and I got up on a ladder so it actually looked like he was climbing and reaching for a star.

We shot the back cover in an alley in Venice, California. There was an abandoned purple 1960 Eldorado convertible that had probably been there for years. The alleyway was awful. I bought an old tattered suit at the Salvation Army, I let my beard grow for a few days, greased up my hair, and smeared dirt on my face. I looked like a bum. I lay on the ground, propped up against the licence plate, with a bottle of Jack Daniels and a couple of my personal artifacts and copies of *Life* and *Rolling Stone* (with me on the cover) next to me. It looked great.

RCA saw it and said, 'No, we can't have you like that.' So Gary Burton, the art director, came up with the idea of showing some smouldering saddle shoes and bobbysocks, like I had combusted and disappeared. It was good, but the original artwork was so shocking and dramatic.

The record company wanted hits. They were also in a transitional period; they didn't really know what they were as a label in America. On the other hand, I'd had so many hits that at the time I was really just into satisfying myself. Some of what I did was misguided and some was on the money. What *was* on the money was my vision for the album.

My RCA recordings were successful enough worldwide that if I'd wanted to carry on making records I could have, but making records wasn't doing it for me then either. I wasn't finding satisfaction in life. I was just looking for various means of escape. I even got into gambling somewhat, which had never been my thing before (my dad was the one who'd sometimes get into trouble for gambling too much). A lot of the time, I'd simply stay in my room. I wasn't sure I wanted to record any more, yet I kept composing songs the public never got to hear. I felt like the square peg unable to fit in that round hole. I've found myself feeling that way many times in my life: that I don't quite fit.

22 Life Is Just a Bowl of Pits (Without the Cherries)

In late 1974, I got a call from my dad. He and Shirley, and a few supporting singers and dancers, were touring the northeast with their show *The Wedding Band*. He wanted Shaun, Patrick, Ryan and me to fly out and spend some time with them in Massachusetts.

Although Dad and Shirley were separated throughout 1973, they got back together again the next year. Shirley may have been the one drawing the crowds, but Dad was the one who put together the acts. *The Wedding Band: The Jack Cassidy and Shirley Jones Show* was, according to the credits, 'conceived, written, produced and directed by Jack Cassidy'. It was inspired by their courtship, marriage, separation and reconciliation. My dad had a good eye for what worked and what didn't.

And he had exquisite taste. Do you know, late in his life, he decorated friends' storefront windows just for fun? I was always impressed that he had so many talents. It was actually intimidating. He could draw, sculpt and create just about anything artistic. If Hollywood ever turned its back on him, friends would joke, he could start a new career as a set decorator.

Interestingly enough, my brother Ryan inherited that gift and is a successful set designer, working in television and film in Hollywood. So he isn't on the stage, but he creates it. And he's great at it. We got to work together when VH1 and Sony partnered to further exploit *The Partridge Family* with a reality-based show in 2005.

Flying to see our parents was the first time all of my brothers and I had been together without either my dad or Shirley. I was the only real adult. Well, sort of. I was 24, Shaun was 16, Patrick around 14 and Ryan 12. We checked into a hotel in the middle of Nowhere, Massachusetts.

My dad was in the restaurant with Shirley, James Cagney and Cagney's wife, Bill. He stood up and ran across the room to us. Ignoring my brothers, he put his hands around my face, grabbed me, kissed me on the lips and started to cry, saying, 'Oh thank God you cut your hair. You reminded me so much of your mother before.'

I mean, 'Hi, Dad! Great to see you!'

My brothers' mouths just fell open. It was like my dad didn't even see them there.

He said, 'Oh God, David, I'm glad to see you again.' He hugged me, standing in the middle of the room weeping.

In the last years of his life, lots of things were going askew emotionally with my dad. Anytime you tried to get my father to deal with reality, it was, 'You either see it my way or else you're off the show.' Lately, I'd been hearing some weird things about his behaviour. Word would filter back to me. But hearing things is one thing, seeing them for yourself is another.

On the way to the theatre where he and Shirley were to perform that night, Dad pulled out a hip flask, took a swig and said, 'Let's forget about the show and go get drunk.' And then, after a beat, he laughed like he was kidding. He did the show, but I knew he was close to the edge.

What I remember most about that weekend, though, is that I had an instant rapport with one of the girls in the show. We had dinner, went back to my room for drinks and I did what I used to do best. In the afterglow we talked. She went on and on about what a wonderful man my father was and how she thought so highly of him, and a light went on in my head. *Oh, no, she's been sleeping with my father.* She confirmed that that was the case and that my father had told her that, although he and Shirley made a good team professionally, they no longer enjoyed marital relations.

In the meantime, who should come knocking at my door but my father? It was five in the morning. I was lying in bed with this girl, and my father – who'd been up all night drinking (and perhaps had gone looking for the girl) – decided to pay me a visit. He was in his robe, smoking and holding a snifter of brandy. We chatted and he said it would be a nice night for us all to go out for a walk. A walk? Dad, it's 5 a.m.! I tried to get rid of him, saying, 'What about Shirley?' His attitude was, *Who wants to talk to Shirley?* 'She needs her beauty sleep.'

I couldn't get rid of him, so the three of us awkwardly talked in my room. When he finally left, around eight in the morning, the girl left with him. He was pretty blatant about what he was up to. I really felt sorry for him. The girl told him she'd had sex with me, which probably sent him further over the edge.

Ruth was as concerned as I was – and, in fact, had been for quite some time. She said that sometimes he'd say things that simply didn't make sense and he was losing his professionalism, which wasn't at all like him. There were nights when he would start winging it on-stage, ad-libbing monologues, putting Shirley in an untenable position. We didn't know what to do. He was a ticking time bomb.

Things reached a head one weekend in Las Vegas. He'd been having terrible vocal problems, which weren't helped by his smoking several packs of cigarettes a day. He was drinking to excess and had been gambling heavily and losing a lot of money. The pressures were too much. He went mad. After the show, he locked Shirley in her room, perhaps so he could pursue his activities with the girl he was fooling around with, without risk of interference.

He appeared to suffer a complete breakdown, singing things that had nothing to do with anything. He was filming *The Eiger Sanction* simultaneously and the schedule was too much for him. He began taking pills to wake up and pills to sleep. He lost his voice and began missing shows. Shirley found him curled up in the corner of his room – nude – unable to carry on.

Ruth sent an associate, Howard Boris, our business manager, to Las Vegas to deal with the situation and bring my father back home. The hotel removed my father's name from the marquee. For the rest of the week it would simply be *The Shirley Jones Show*, which wasn't easy for Shirley to deal with, since my father had created the show based around the two of them and their marriage.

What happened next, I didn't witness. Boris had hired a small plane and got my father on to it. They were in the air for 20 minutes without my father acting in the least bit peculiar. Then suddenly he unstrapped his seat belt, leapt over the seats, grabbed the controls from the pilot and started screaming, 'I'm going to see my father!'

Howard Boris went white and was yelling, 'Jack! Jack! You're going to kill us!' He and the pilot wrestled my father away from the controls and strapped him back in his seat.

The next day he was sighted watering the lawn in the middle

of the afternoon – stark naked, sharing himself with his presumably admiring public.

Ruth flew to the house. She found him standing atop a coffee table, pounding on a Bible, saying, 'J.C. – don't you get it? Jack Cassidy, Jesus Christ. They're both J.C. Don't you see? I'm me, J.C.' He'd never been interested in the Bible before. He told my brother Shaun to read the Bible to him, which Shaun did. He had lit every fireplace in the house and refused to put on any clothes.

Ruth sent for the doctor, the one who had prescribed Valium for me. He was ready to sedate my father. When the doctor approached him, my father picked him up and threw him down so forcefully that the doctor dislocated his shoulder. The doctor called the men in white coats who sedated him, put him in a straitjacket and carried him off. This was grist for the tabloids. *The National Tattler*, giving him more attention than he'd ever received during his career, screamed (22 December 1974): 'Jack Cassidy Cracks Up, Enters Mental Hospital, Wife Shirley Jones Forced to Commit Him.'

They held him in the hospital for 48 hours, which was, I was told, as long as he could legally be held against his will for observation, since once he had calmed down he was lucid, rational and appeared to pose no threat to anyone.

A week or so afterwards, acting as if nothing untoward had happened, he called me up and asked me to have lunch with him. That turned out to be horrible; the most uncomfortable lunch I'd ever endured. He'd been drinking. He was bloated. He started doing the song-and-dance charm routine I'd seen him try so many times on so many people. But there was no way I was going to let him charm me any more. His timing was way off. He tried to act like he was my father and we had this unbreakable father–son bond. He couldn't manipulate me into helping him. I didn't really want to be around him any more.

He said, 'Shirley and I have been having problems.'

I suppose he expected me to feel sympathy for him. I knew something was coming.

'I need to borrow $10,000 from you.'

I looked at him and said, 'Dad, I'd love to help you but I don't have any money,' which was a lie. I knew that giving it to him would contribute to him spinning further out. That was the last time I saw him alive. He never called me again. I knew him so well.

Ryan Cassidy: Near the end of his life, my dad wasn't coming round just to see David, he was coming round because he needed something and I think that really made David very bitter. He wasn't on good terms with David at the end and David had a really hard time with that.

I was able to have quality time with my dad because I was so young and I was the most available. I did things with him that were very bonding. I think David feels that I got the best of him. Patrick was involved with school and sports and Shaun was starting his career as a singer.

I stopped seeing my father because I felt I'd taken just about enough abuse from him for one lifetime, although deep down I still held on to the hope that he would change and one day we could have the relationship I used to long for. It was less painful for me to simply avoid him.

New York Post columnist Earl Wilson interviewed my father on 12 November 1975, as he prepared to open in a new Broadway play. He asked him if he saw much of me.

'No. His crowd doesn't even know me. I don't talk about him because the interviews with me turn out to be about him. I have another son, Shaun, 16. He's a singer and composer, and he has a hell of a chance to take off,' my father said.

Early in 1975, my father and Shirley got divorced on grounds of 'irreconcilable differences', although my father continued to insist to interviewers that he still loved Shirley. Shirley began dating – and soon married– comedian Marty Ingels. I stopped seeing her at the time because I didn't get along with her new husband.

The funny thing is, I thought I was just making up an excuse when I told my father I didn't have any money. But, surprise, surprise. I was just about to have to swallow a big bad reality pill.

I had never worried about how much money I had. Why would I? I was making a lot and just kept making more. My business managers always spoke glowingly of the wise investment moves they were making on my behalf. That was the only thing that compensated for the hell I'd gone through in the last five years – at least I'd made a lot of money and it was being invested wisely. I believed I was set for life and could stay 'retired' for as long as I chose. As far as I knew, I was worth millions. I was so damn trusting and naïve.

I had never kept tabs on how much money was coming in and going out. The bills went to my business manager. I didn't write cheques. I figured that was what business managers were for. I had no business or accounting education whatsoever. Nobody in my family had any sophistication when it came to investments; they came from working-class backgrounds. We were all busily making money and putting it in the till, until one day we looked and discovered that the till had been raided.

I really can't blame Ruth. She came from a wealthy family and, like most women of her generation and socio-economic class, she simply had not been raised to worry about money. After the death of her brother, who had handled the business side of her operation, she'd hired business managers. Unwittingly, she went from one thief or incompetent to the next. That ended up costing my dad, Shirley and me a fortune.

One guy simply ran off with millions of dollars of our money. Another was investing wherever he could get the biggest kickbacks, after apparently skimming off the top. We also didn't have any money in tax shelters, which meant we needlessly had to pay a fortune to the IRS. I was in the 70 per cent tax bracket in 1971. In one year I paid the IRS more than $400,000. A good business manager could have legally avoided most of that tax obligation.

A light should have gone on in my head that I didn't have the best business management in the world the day one of the managers showed me I had $1 million in a checking account. If only I'd known then that there was no reason I should have had that much money in an account that didn't even earn interest.

For three years I invested in heavy oil, or so I thought. I was certain to make a fortune, right? Wrong. Do you remember the Home Stake Oil deal? That was one of the biggest scams in the history of the United States. Even some members of Congress were among the victims. It resulted in the largest class-action suit in history. It was an operation so fraudulent that at one point the perpetrators were actually painting water pipes orange to convince gullible investors the pipes were filled with oil. In the Home Stake Oil deal I was one of the top ten biggest money-losers in the country. I got burned really badly, losing hundreds of thousands of dollars. My father and Shirley also got burned, but not like I did.

All told, millions of dollars of our money were squandered and lost and invested poorly. It's a shame that my family and I never had proper guidance. Even Ruth got suckered out of a lot of her money. We all got taken to the cleaners. It's a sad and too familiar story about Hollywood business managers and their wealthy celebrity clients. Fortunately, I wasn't cheated out of *all* of my money.

We sued the one business manager who admitted taking kickbacks. He could have gone to prison, but he was an old man and we settled out of court in exchange for his paying back the money he'd taken. We let him off way too easily.

The people who wronged me, taking advantage of a naïve young guy, I can never forgive. The opportunity to earn that kind of money again will almost certainly never present itself. And that harsh reality further fuelled my depression.

With the arrival of disco in 1976, I was considered old news, my music dated. My highly successful former record producer Wes Farrell was also passé. He didn't understand it; he couldn't change with the times. And this man, who had been mega-successful throughout the late 60s and early 70s (his stream of big hits with me and The Partridge Family had earned him the Producer of the Year award) suddenly found that nobody seemed to want him any more. When he had been making the big bucks he had spent lavishly. He bought the house on Sunset Boulevard and put two Rolls Royces in the driveway. He wound up deeply in debt. He married Tina Sinatra, Frank's daughter, and I heard he somehow managed to fall out with Frank, which was in itself a big mistake. He left town. Broken.

Meanwhile, I was staying home, trying to keep the harsh realities of life outside at bay. But news from outside, too often not good, had a way of invading my sanctuary.

Late on the night of 12 February 1976, a male assailant plunged a knife into the chest of Sal Mineo near his apartment at 8563 Holloway Drive. Mineo was heard by neighbours screaming, 'Help! Help! Oh my God,' before he died and his attacker fled. He was 37. Elliot Mintz handled the press, striving to ensure that Mineo's privacy was respected as much as possible.

The police, knowing of Mineo's lifestyle, originally speculated that the crime had been sex-related, but when the assailant was finally apprehended more than a year later, it turned out that he was merely a common thief and hadn't even known who Mineo was when he killed him with a five-dollar knife.

I blotted out reality by immersing myself deeper in drugs, alcohol and music.

Sam Hyman: You've got to reach your bottom. It's got to get real dark before the light can come in. It was a very painful period for David as well as me; I couldn't be around him. He was spinning out of control and starting to experiment with drugs, getting high to escape and kill the pain. The unresolved father issue has always been the underlying motivating factor with David. And he'd reached the apex of his career. You know, when you're at the top of the mountain, you want to step down gracefully, but to get to the top of the mountain you have to have an ego. And your ego is very fearful: 'Oh my gosh, I'm losing it. I'm not going to be the most popular guy in the school. I'm not going to be at the top of the game. And will I ever work again?'

Every performer in between jobs has a tremendous amount of insecurity and fear that they'll never work again. And that even included people like Henry Fonda and Jimmy Stewart. I think that being at a young age and not having the tools to handle these serious matters drove him to look for the magic pill again. I remember going to David and saying, 'Hey, David, I can't be around this. It's killing me to watch you kill yourself.' And I remember him saying, 'I understand.' And that's when I moved to Colorado, in 1976. I had to get away from it. And that's when his father died.

23 Breakin' Down Again

The night of Saturday 11 December 1976 started out like any other for me. Some musician friends dropped over to party and jam with Steve and me. We stayed up most of the night playing music. Because that was such an unhappy period of my life, I spent as much time as I could outside of myself – being in the zone, I used to call it. We were all pretty wiped out, emotionally and physically, by the end of the night. Numb. I always wanted to keep the party going so I didn't have to go to sleep, so I didn't have to be alone, so I didn't have to deal with real life.

Around five in the morning, after we'd stopped playing, I still felt too wired to call it a night. We had the radio on in the background. I was just sitting around talking to Steve, half listening to the news on the radio, when the newsman announced it had just come over the wire that actor Jack Cassidy had apparently died in a fire that had swept through his apartment. His body had been so badly charred, however, that it had not yet been possible to make a positive identification. Silence. Was I dreaming this? I looked at Steve. He looked at me and said, 'Oh, shit.'

I picked up the phone and called my brother Shaun. No answer. Then I called Shirley. No answer. I called her service and waited for a call back. It must have been nine or ten o'clock, a long time, before anyone called me back. It was Shaun. They had been out trying to identify the body, which had been so thoroughly burned that an absolute identification was only possible through dental records. I just listened in silence. I couldn't believe this was happening.

I drove to Shirley's house. It wasn't until I opened the door and saw my brothers that I suddenly realised that there was no one left except us. We were the only ones who could relate to each other's loss. At that point it felt as if someone thrust me down to the ground. I completely collapsed, dropped to my knees and wailed, weeping like a child, which is just how I felt.

My brothers and I held each other. I remember saying things like, 'It's just us now. His job here is over. We just have each other.' I felt so much stronger because my brothers were there. And it's been like that with us ever since. We have a bond.

Shaun Cassidy: I remember hugging David, Patrick and Ryan in a circle at our father's wake and it felt mythic, like we were forging some kind of a bond that was stronger than anything we might have had otherwise. Nothing was spoken, it was just something we felt. I think the subconscious realisation was, *We're not gonna have our father any more, the only connection we're going to have to him is through each other*. David's older than my father was when he died; I'm getting close. The truth is I've discovered aspects of my father in all my brothers over the years. In that sense, he hasn't died. We have sons and we see our father in our sons and that's the cycle.

Patrick Cassidy: The fact that he disappeared on us so early in our lives, when boys really need a father, created a void that can never be filled. We've all had to deal with it in our own different ways. I think David has come to terms with a lot of it, but certainly not all of it. I think it will be with him for the rest of his days. I believe that the power and strength and ghost of Jack Cassidy is that strong in all of us. We each in our own way battle with the demons and the angels of this man who was our father.

Ryan Cassidy: There are times when I've felt that my dad was around watching over our shoulders. David has said that he's felt that way, too. What my father left behind was so strong that there remains so much of him, in different ways, in David, Shaun, Patrick and myself. It's as if he lives on through us.

We didn't know much about his death at first. There seemed to be some uncertainties connected with it, and that bothered me. The police asked an awful lot of questions in an attempt to reconstruct his final night. He had had dinner with actress Nanette Fabray and her husband. After he'd called it a night with them, it was believed that he had gone to meet some guys for drinks. It appeared that he got drunk with them that night. Although he'd told interviewers shortly before his death that he'd quit smoking and drinking, that did not seem to be the case. Later, back in his apartment, he lit a cigarette but apparently fell asleep, or passed out, on the couch, which then caught fire. His body was found on the floor, as if he'd been trying to crawl to the apartment's sliding glass door, where it seems he died due to smoke inhalation.

But some believed there was more to his death than met the eye. Syndicated columnist Liz Smith, for example, reported (2 March 1977): 'The Los Angeles police have not closed the book on the tragic death by fire of that wonderful actor Jack

Cassidy . . . The dapper Jack loved to gamble and there are those who believe he was heavily in debt to the mob. To add to the mystery, two unsavoury type guys were seen at his apartment earlier and a young woman who had been visiting the actor contends that he was safely tucked in bed when she left him. So why did Jack get up and move to the couch? And was his death an accident or wasn't it?'

I believe it was.

What some of the columnists and police investigators knew, but the public did not, was that my father was bisexual. The police concluded that on his last night my father had gone out drinking with some of his homosexual friends. However, they never found out who was the last person who saw him alive.

Though I'd heard some rumours, I didn't really know about my father's bisexuality until after he died. Now I can see it; it fits with the man I knew. Certainly he never discussed it with me, although he could have been open with me had he chosen to. But I guess, in some ways, he was very private. I can understand that.

Cole Porter had an extended sexual relationship with my father, according to information he shared with his friend Truman Capote. In Gerald Clarke's bestseller *Capote: a Biography*, Capote is quoted as saying how Porter described 'his long affair with that actor Jack Cassidy'.

Of course, my father, an aspiring singer and actor at the time, revered Cole Porter and Cole knew it, which I'm sure made the keep-it-cool psychological power-playing possible. Being close to Cole Porter, one of America's most important writers of Broadway and Hollywood scores, could only have helped my father's career.

In Boze Hadleigh's book *The Vinyl Closet*, *Dance* magazine editor William Como confessed that when Jack Cassidy – in his eyes, I guess, an unapproachable star – made a pass at him, he initially thought 'it had to be a joke'. But it soon led to a 'scorching affair'. Como said of my father (whom he found quite vain), 'He loved the showbiz whirl, and he loved seducing VIPs of both sexes, even if he had no intention of bedding them.'

I was sorry I didn't see my father for the last nine months of his life. If I had one more chance to speak to my father again, I'd say, 'I forgive you.' I couldn't do that at 25, which is how old I was when he died.

As it turned out, my father left me the big goose egg. I was cut out of his will, which placed his estate at $100,000. It made the news that he had excluded both Shirley and me. Maybe my father decided we were rich and could take care of ourselves. Or maybe he wanted to pay us back for how he felt we'd treated him. In the end, though, the lawyers' fees and the taxes and everything else ate up most of the estate. They had an auction of his clothes. I didn't go. I bought my father's pocket watch for $1,000 before the auction, just to have it to remember him by. He had had it engraved to himself. That was my father. It was later stolen by someone close enough to me to have access to my home. I can't prove who did it, but I have some strong suspicions. I really would like to have kept that watch. My son would have had something of his grandfather's.

The only other thing I had from him was a ring that I had always wanted. He gave it to me for my twenty-first birthday. He went back into our family history, and found our family crest and had it made for me as a ring. That ring was my connection to him. I've been all around the world and managed to hold on to it for years until it was stolen in Las Vegas when I was starring in a show I wrote, *At the Copa.* It could have been stolen by anyone who came through the backstage area. I offered a $50,000 reward for it, even though the ring itself wasn't worth anywhere near that. It wasn't returned. Someone has it who doesn't know what they have, or they had it melted down for the gold. It's very sad that it's never been recovered.

The desire to anaesthetise myself was already pretty strong, but when my dad died my desire to make the pain go away doubled. That was such a horrible time in my life. I just retreated further into myself.

My father's death was also a terrible blow to Ruth Aarons. They had been close for more than a quarter of a century. She began noticeably deteriorating, both psychologically and physically. I don't know that she had many friends, other than her small (and dwindling) pool of clients, now my father was dead and I was retired. I resisted her periodic attempts to get me to go back to work, which she felt would have been good for me – and, of course, good for her. I didn't mind visiting her when I could, to try to buck her up (although I was bothered by the hundreds of pills she had at her home), but I rebuffed her suggestions that I go back to work, even when she tried to get me to do a proposed TV show called *The Hardy Boys*. I turned it down, but it ended up launching Shaun's career. Ruth received a further blow when Shirley decided to leave her. Who did she have left? Her world was shrinking.

Shaun's career, which kicked off in 1977, was Ruth's last hurrah as a personal manager. She wasn't sure if they could get lightning to strike twice, but they did. His career trajectory followed much the same path as mine. Although it didn't last long, for a couple of years, 1977–9, he had enormous success on TV, with his records and in concert. It would have been a trip if we could have worked together. As it turned out, we had to wait 15 years before performing together, which we did in the Broadway production *Blood Brothers*.

Shaun had three platinum albums in 1977 and 1978 and five

hit singles. He donned the tight white jumpsuits and shook his backside at screaming young girls, just as I had. His face appeared on posters, magazine covers and lunchboxes. *Rolling Stone* even profiled him before the fever ran its course. He retired from recording four years after he began.

> **Shaun Cassidy:** I learned by David's example. Very, very few people go through the experience he went through and certainly having two people in the same family go through it is incredibly rare. Having been able to watch him and see what was thrown at him, and see how he managed some things and couldn't manage other things, was probably the best education I could have had. I think the consequence of that was I never expected it to last very long and didn't take it seriously at all. It was like a novelty. The greatest challenge I had was trying to figure out what I wanted to do with the rest of my life when at 21 I was married and kind of retired. I didn't have bitterness about it and didn't feel that I'd been used up, all of the things that I know David experienced. Unfortunately, when I was going through it, he was in that bitter place. He hadn't embraced it or come around to seeing the good in it yet. It wasn't something that I could really talk to him about much.

For a while, when Shaun's career first began happening, it must have seemed like old times for Ruth, having another Cassidy become a teen idol. This time, she vowed, we won't make the mistakes we made the last time; we'll keep a careful eye on marketing and all the rest. She meant well, but the drugs had taken too great a toll on her. Shaun needed a manager he could feel confident in. He saw her failing, due to her drug addiction. He felt she was losing her mind and he bailed out.

All Ruth's clients left her in the end. I'd visit her a couple of afternoons a week. She wouldn't leave her bed. She didn't have the energy. She was so drugged from all the Seconals she took, she was just out of it. She'd tell me things like, 'I *have* to take the pills; I have a terrible backache' – the rationalisations of an addict. Her muscles atrophied. It was such a shame, seeing this once vibrant person becoming so weak.

Then one day I got a call from Lloyd Brown, a man who worked for her. Apparently she'd slipped in the shower, hit her head and died. It was perhaps almost inevitable something tragic would happen. When she died, there were thousands of pills in her home.

With Shirley, with my father, with me, Ruth Aarons had the world on a string. She played all 88 keys of the piano, and the piano was the agents, the PR people, and the rest of the people she had to deal with. I have met millions of people in my lifetime. I have never met anyone who had the intellect, the humour, the passion, the business savvy, the boldness to do what she was doing at a time when women weren't expected to do that. They weren't invited to the party. She could be as tough and as ball-busting as any man. She was strong and competitive, but also sensitive, bright, instinctive, cutting-edge and wickedly funny. I'm convinced my father and she had a love affair without ever physically touching.

When she died, I realised I had been so protected and kept away from the business that I had no professional relationships or connections. And really, at that point, I did not know what to do without her. I was completely lost, because I had known nothing but her guidance.

She and I would sit for hours at a time talking about what we should do next and how to do it. And she would go and make it happen. For a long time, I didn't know how to function without her. I was crippled by her death. Had she lived, my career would not have had such a large hole in it. I would have found my way a lot sooner, figured out what I wanted and at least moved towards accomplishing whatever that was. We had started to set a lot of my goals in motion – as an actor, as a recording artist, as a writer, a producer and all the rest of it. Then she died and it all died with her.

24 Sorry, I Don't Do Disco

RCA wanted me to record more because my first solo album and single did so well. I think it sold two million copies outside the U.S.. But because of what was happening in my life, I didn't have any idea of what I wanted to do musically. I was just searching on the *Home Is Where the Heart Is* album.

I started writing more songs with Gerry Beckley, from the group America. And it was really just wild. Every night we'd get to the studio at seven, have some food sent over and stay until four or five in the morning. We'd go home when it was getting light, sleep almost all day, then go back to the studio. It was perfect for me. I've never been someone who can function in the mornings. I was too distracted during the day. Nighttime, when everybody else was asleep, is when I would play and write. I loved the vibe of what we were doing on that album. There were a number of different people who would drop by the studio – Sly Stone, Buddy Miles, Tommy Boyce, Bobby Hart – brilliant musicians all.

Bill House (session musician/songwriter): That was a good record. It was more like a band record than the previous one. It's better than *The Higher They Climb, the Harder They Fall* because we had that same rhythm section and David was more in control of what he was trying to do. It's so rare that you get a band together that really wants to play with each other. It was a great band and we had so much fun making the record. We'd stay at the studio until late into the night – the same routine for weeks on end. David and I were spending a lot of time together by then. When I first met David, it was almost like we'd known each other for a long time. I think it was inevitable that we were going to write together.

For *Home Is Where the Heart Is*, David and I got on a plane to Hawaii. We were there for two weeks and . . . we were gonna write religiously every day. We did a lot of stuff together. I went on a ginseng fast for seven days. David took me to dinner and we broke the ginseng fast with a bottle of tequila. David was driving this big jeep and we ended up out in this cane field filled with huge spiders. The next day, David woke up filled with energy. We hadn't really written anything for most of the trip. He said, 'OK, let's write songs!' We wrote them all that day. There was such good compatibility between us that we'd write line after line. We were tuned into each other as writers. We wrote most of that stuff on the piano. David's a great guitar player. He was every bit as good as I was.

We shot the album cover in an apartment that was a museum of art deco and art nouveau, off Melrose Avenue in Los Angeles. It was magnificent. They showed me two locations and when I saw that one, I said, 'Stop. This is where we'll do it.' It was just like a womb, and the title of the album, *Home Is Where the Heart Is,* signified the safety of home.

I had my friends around me, people I felt really comfortable working with. They were working with me as contributors, not just as musicians for hire. We were developing the stuff together

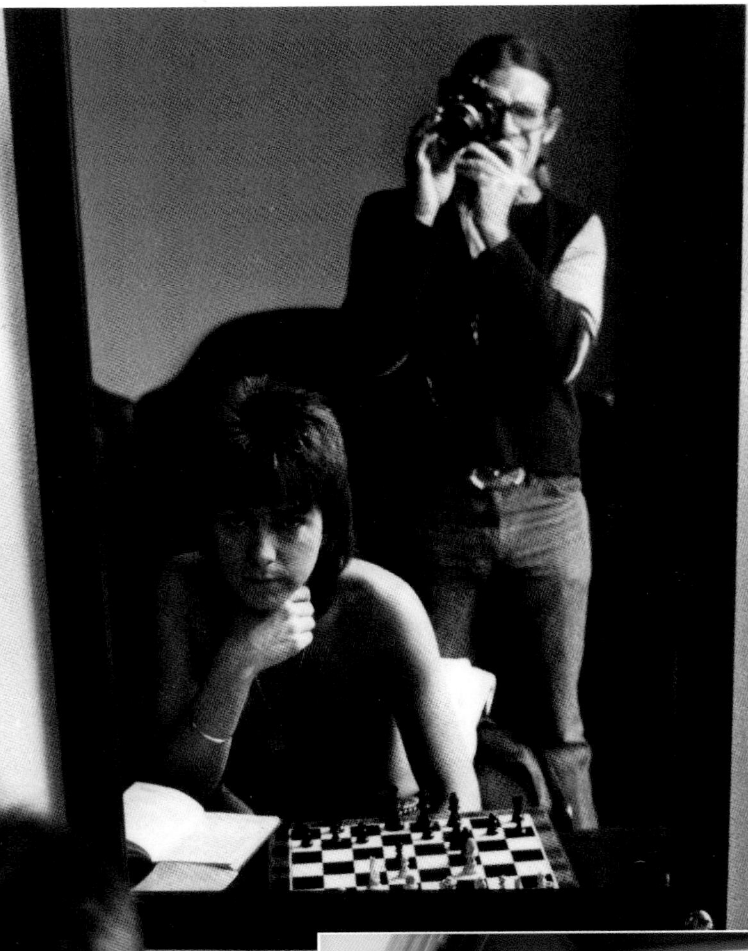

PHOTOGRAPHS BY HENRY DILTZ

K. Henry, no more
this one-on-one
trip Chess!

I think I lived
in a Blanket for
half of the 70s!

Above: Taken for *The Higher They Climb, the Harder They Fall*, 1975.

The 1st time around... The Beautiful Kay and I.

Beautiful Wife
and Bad sweater...

PHOTOGRAPH BY SHARON JULL

Sharon says this is one of her favourite photos from 1985. It was taken while I was promoting *Romance* at the BBC in Manchester.

1990: With Sue in Moscow, where I was performing at the May Day celebrations.

Sue and me with baby Beau in 1991.

This is Your Life, 1999. I'm the short brother on the left
God I love these boys...

This is Your Life, again. My beautiful mom, while she was
still dyeing her hair!

With a Special Olympics team member, at one of my charity golf tournaments.

Me with a very special friend at my golf tourney... What a doll!

My beautiful kids, Beau and Kate, in 2000.

Singing at the World Series, 2003.

PHOTOGRAPHS BY JO-ANN GEFFEN

Touring the U.K. with The Osmonds in 2004.

Singing with Beau for the first time publicly at Wembley Stadium, London, 2004.

Below: Out amongst the crowd at a live performance, 2004.

PHOTOGRAPHS BY JO-ANN GEFFEN

Performing live.

PHOTOGRAPHS BY JO-ANN GEFFEN

Above: In Scotland, indulging my passion for horses.

Below: With Sam Hyma

Sam and I in the
last couple of years...
he's still like my brothe

and it was a really creative time for me. I was trying to escape the difficulties of losing my dad. It was a time when I was trying to become a human being again, to find my place in society, after having basically lived in a vacuum for six years. It was an undisciplined life; I could go to bed when I wanted, wake up when I wanted and had no responsibilities except to work when I wanted to work.

On *Home Is Where the Heart Is*, I covered the McCartney song *Tomorrow*, which was on Wings' *Wild Life* album. I loved the song. There were three or four songs that he wrote after he left the Beatles that I thought could be embellished upon. Paul told me, 'It was pretty cool.' I played an old piano live on the track. I hated playing piano with a band because I'm not a trained pianist, and when you have to play your part with a band it's much tougher than when you play on your own. But I played it because I had arranged the piano part. Bruce Johnston arranged the background parts in the middle of the track. It's beautifully done. Bruce had just done *Don't Let the Sun Go Down on Me* and other great tracks for Elton.

Gerry Beckley: I co-wrote *Take This Heart* with David for the *Home Is Where the Heart Is* album. I think I started *Take This Heart* at home and I remember driving over to the studio and saying, 'I think I've got something.' I played it for David and he said, 'That's great, I'll add a bridge to it.' It was just a natural progression from adding harmonies to actually writing together.

I also co-wrote *Bedtime* with David for that album. That was a good ballad. I really enjoyed writing with David. They say everyone has one novel in them, but to make a career out of it is a far different thing. David is across the board; he's capable of doing lyrics and music. He's a great piano player, a good guitar player, a nice lyricist and he's got a great voice.

Bill House: *Breakin' Down Again* is an interesting song. I came up with the title. To me, the lyrics represented what David was going through in his life at that point. It had an autobiographical bent. David's a really good writer. He wrote songs that I would have been proud to have written. I loved his vocal on *Breakin' Down Again*. I think that was a really different kind of thing for him.

For the next album for RCA, we went to Caribou Ranch in Colorado, where Elton had made the *Rock of the Westies* album. I had worked with his bass player, Kenny Passarelli, and I knew a couple of the guys in the band a little bit. I had heard some of Elton's tracks, I'd seen him live and even played with him, and thought there was some magic to going to the studio together. I rented a Lear jet and brought my dog Bullseye with me. He wouldn't go in a regular plane; he couldn't handle it.

We spent a month there recording *Gettin' It in the Street.* Bruce Johnston was getting more and more involved in producing and working with the Beach Boys again, so he wasn't very available. Because I had started working and writing with Gerry Beckley, I asked him if he wanted to co-produce the album.

Gerry Beckley: I ended up producing *Gettin' It in the Street* with David. That album was a natural progression. I was trying to keep the America schedule ongoing, so I ended up doing three albums and a world tour in one year and it was all a little bit chaotic in my mind. We went to Caribou Ranch to get out of town and focus on this thing. By that time, David's relationship with RCA was starting to fracture a little bit. I don't think the previous two albums had done that well.

I had never been to Colorado and found that I couldn't sing up there because of the altitude and because it was so dry. I lost the top few notes of my vocal range. But we had a lot of fun there. We went horseback riding every day and there was plenty of frivolity – lots of very pretty girls worked there. I invited guitarist Mick Ronson up. He'd done a lot of work with Bowie and I loved the *Ziggy Stardust* album. I flew Mick up and he stayed for a couple of days. We jammed and we'd get all worked up about songs and ideas. He was one of the most unusual guitar players I ever worked with. His style was so different. There was nothing conventional about what he did; which is why it was so interesting. I think he was very flattered that I wanted him to play, but I think he was worried that the fan base that he had established in that avant garde, Velvet Underground kind of world was going to elude him if he went too mainstream – from being David Bowie's sideman to David Cassidy's sideman. And I don't think he was wrong. But we had great fun together.

Gerry Beckley: David and I were such big Mick Ronson fans. David had been a megastar around the world, but particularly in England. Mick had quite a bit to say during those sessions. I remember that there was a song we were going back and forth on for this album that was written by Tandyn Almer, who had written Along Comes Mary. David was fond of this song and I think we'd cut the track and Mick came in and said, 'What is that crap?' Immediately it was off the album because David held Mick in such high esteem. Everybody had a voice and this was a circle of people that David highly respected.

On *Gettin' It in the Street* I was trying to experiment with different genres and ideas. I wrote a song called *Junked Heart Blues* and that one has always stuck with me. People sometimes come up to me and tell me how cool they think it was.

I tried to stretch myself musically during that period. Those three RCA albums were the most interesting for me because I didn't do them for commercial purposes. That's not why I ever went into the recording studio. Record companies want you to make commercial records. They don't want you to change. RCA was not terribly behind the idea of me exploring my creative side, my dreams. I wanted to see how far we could take this. But the way RCA looked at it was, 'Well, we've made money with him, but we don't get it. We don't hear a hit here.' There wasn't a hit on that third album like *Rock the Boat*, RCA's big single for the year. And there were personnel changes at the label, so suddenly there were new people there who hadn't been involved in signing me.

I wasn't making disco music, nor was that the direction I would ever go in and that's what RCA wanted. The label was completely unsupportive about *Gettin' It in the Street*. They thought the album was too hard, too edgy and not commercial enough. I had made the decision not to tour, but I now think that if I had toured and really cultivated the relationship with RCA, the record would have done much better.

From a business standpoint, RCA was probably right. I've learned to be a good businessman from the mistakes that were made on my behalf and the mistakes that I personally have made. But I don't regret any of my mistakes. Honestly. I wouldn't have traded the experience of doing what I love to do and having it on vinyl forever.

The Higher They Climb, the Harder They Fall, *Home Is Where the Heart Is* and *Gettin' It in the Street* are much more 'me' in terms of the music. I played on all the tracks, I wrote a lot of them, I explored my musical vision with other great writers, singers and musicians. My fans love those albums. It was a very dark period for me in a lot of ways, as I've said, so I've tended to disconnect myself from that material, although I still do one or two of those songs live, like *Common Thief*, because it represents that period of time for me. I love to surprise people and I wanted to expose a lot about myself through those albums. I think I achieved that.

Gerry Beckley: It's an irony that sometimes just as an artist is reaching his stride and starting to find his voice and craft, maybe the wave of the following has moved on. How do you hold on to all those millions of kids who've followed you? Now those kids are starting to grow in age and they're not all gonna hang around, they're starting to go off to college, they're developing other tastes in music.

25 One Wedding and a Funeral

In 1977, I married Kay Lenz, a sweet, bright, beautiful actress whom I'd known for all of six weeks. We instantly hit it off and became great friends. She was funny, she was smart, she was talented. What did we have in common? We'd both just recently lost our fathers, we were both feeling lost and lonely and we were both actors, with all the insecurities and self-absorption that seems to go with the occupation. We were two lost souls who made each other laugh. That seemed good enough to me.

By the time Kay and I met, she had already done more than 20 different TV shows, including the acclaimed mini-series *Rich Man, Poor Man*. She'd won an Emmy and had been nominated for another, not to mention a couple of other awards. When we married, I had not been working at all for the last couple of years, so I'd stay home and she'd go off each day to work. It's funny how life works out. I was now in much the same situation my father had been in years before – married to a much-in-demand actress who was the household's principal money-earner.

Unfortunately, we had married for the wrong reasons. We were both immature and we really weren't compatible as a couple. It became apparent almost immediately after we married that Kay wanted much less emotional involvement than I did. I felt I gave up a lot the day I married her. I gave up being old 'Jack the lad' with countless women and the freedom to do anything I wanted. And Kay, I discovered to my dismay, was actually not that interested in me. Her career, I soon realised, definitely came first. I thought, *What irony! I marry the one woman who doesn't want me.*

The truth is, we should have just remained friends; we would have been the greatest of friends. We should have just lived together for a while to see how things worked out before making such a commitment. The problem was neither of us had any guidance. No one said, 'This is a mistake. Don't do it.'

She is a great person. She's got a lot of good qualities. And I identified with that; she was a lot like my mom, people I grew up around, my family. I still have nothing but great, great feelings for her. I don't know how she feels about me. The marriage got in the way of the bond we shared as friends. We didn't know enough about each other to know what wasn't right about the relationship.

I loved her independence. I wanted her to do all the things she wanted to do, to do well in her career, but unfortunately things didn't happen for her when she wanted them to. And at the time I didn't give a damn, really, about doing anything productive, because I had already achieved about as much as anyone could achieve professionally. It had already been three and a half years since I'd worked. No television show, no job, no place where I had to be. I could do anything I wanted and was just sort of trucking through life.

But it started to seem wrong, staying home all the time while Kay went to work. I remember Kay would get scripts sent over by her agent. Ding dong. There'd be a messenger with a script at the door, and I'd think, *Gee, I used to get scripts*, and sometimes I'd miss that. She'd get up and go to work and I'd call my friend who lived downstairs, a great guitar player, and go hang out with him for a while and jam. But after a while that got boring.

Sue Shifrin Cassidy: I read that he'd married Kay; I was already married to my first husband. My husband and I moved to Los Angeles and lived in Tarzana, on Van Alden Avenue, close to Encino. I remembered that David lived on White Oak Avenue in Encino. My husband and I had a horrible, horrible fight on New Year's Eve and I ran out to the car in tears and roared down the street. By now, years had gone by since I'd seen David. I had never given him another thought because I was committed to my husband. That night, it was pouring rain and I started driving and the windshield wipers were going and I saw White Oak Avenue and thought, David. I got off the freeway and I went looking for him. I didn't know where he lived; I had never been to his house. But I went looking for him anyway – unsuccessfully. I found out much later that he had sold that house years before. I went home and made up with my husband, but not that long after we divorced.

A couple of months after we got married, after such a long hiatus from working, I let it be known in the business that I was available as an actor again. And there were old friends who remembered me. Former *Partridge Family* producer/director Mel Swope was, by this point, producing a dramatic series, *Police Story*, and he offered me a role guest starring in 'A Chance to Live', a two-hour movie that aired on 28 May 1979 on NBC. That *Police Story* episode was directed by Corey Allen and was a really nice piece of work. To me, it was different, something that was more challenging. People hadn't seen me do that kind of work before. I had a chance to work with really good actors, a good script and a good director.

I did some press to promote my work. The headline above James Brown's piece in the *New York Post* was typical. It read, 'Cassidy: Time Ripe for Comeback'. Another line promised 'A Look at a Teen Heartthrob's Return'. I explained to Brown that by the end of *The Partridge Family* I was emotionally and physically drained. 'I was all used up, and for several years thereafter I wasn't sure I ever wanted to work again. But there's something to be said about getting up in the morning and having something to do.'

I received an Emmy nomination for Best Dramatic Actor for my performance in what was the highest rated *Police Story* ever. That was enough to convince NBC and Screen Gems that I might be worth gambling on for another series.

The head of the network at the time, Fred Silverman, called and said, 'I want you to do a television series.'

And I said, 'Oh, great. What?'

He said, 'What do you mean, "What?" You've just given us the highest-rated show we've ever had. We're gonna do a television series based on that character.'

I wrote the main title song, *Hard Times*, with Jay Gruska and it was really good. Originally, either that title or *A Chance to Live*, like the episode, was going to be the name of the series. At the last minute, the head of the network decided the series would be *David Cassidy – Man Undercover*.

I said, 'No, wait. I'm playing a character named Dan Shay here. This is not The Loretta Young Theatre, is it?'

It was a good two-hour movie that was not intended to be, nor should it have been, a series. That was the same season they did *Supertrain*. They had some bad ideas back in those days.

That job destroyed me, emotionally and physically. We'd work 18 hours a day and do lots of night shooting in the gutters of downtown L.A. We made ten episodes and they were horrible. It was the middle of the season and all the good writers and directors were already booked, so we got cast-offs, guys that couldn't cut it. And they didn't have any original scripts, so they took old scripts from *Police Woman* and just revamped them a little bit. It was awful.

And there was a single released. They wanted me to perform it in *David Cassidy – Man Undercover*, and I was appalled. 'Wait a minute. I'm playing a policeman now. I'm not playing a musician. It doesn't make any sense.'

I managed to pick up a few other television movies over the next few years (all, incidentally, on my old *Partridge Family* network, ABC). But Kay got far more work than I did. In the 70s and 80s she made 60-odd TV appearances, guest-starring in one top series after another and some great made-for-TV movies. So – thanks in no small part to Kay – we continued to make a pretty good living. With her money and mine, we began speculating in southern California real estate. The problem was, we got in when the market was just about reaching its peak. When the bottom fell out, around 1980, we lost a fortune. How much? Our mortgage payments alone were over $15,000 a month. It would take me all of the 80s to pay off the bank loans. I would have to say that the boom and crash in the real estate market wiped us out almost completely.

Our marriage became full of heartache and disappointment. I knew early on that we were in trouble and the strains of our mounting financial worries certainly didn't help matters.

I must also note that Kay was not prepared for my old fans, some of whom kept coming on to me, sometimes right in front of her. That situation still occurs, with women hitting on me right in front of my current wife, Sue. It's embarrassing.

Between 1970 and 1974, I had made about $8 million, virtually all of which was gone by 1980. Don't forget, in the early 70s a house on Beverly Drive that today would cost $6 million was selling for $125,000. By 1980 my net worth was less than $100,000. That, to me, was dead broke.

More than that, my career was in the toilet. I had trouble getting anyone at my agency, which had been handling me since the early 70s, even to return my phone calls. If you're not a big moneymaker any more, they don't want to know you, and no one in Hollywood seemed eager to hire David Cassidy any longer.

OK, so I had retired from the business. But now I was back and I really needed work. Yet nobody at William Morris seemed to feel they had any kind of moral obligation or loyalty to me. No one said that, because I'd been such a huge money earner for them in the early 70s, they'd make sure I'd get work now that I needed it. I felt they didn't give a damn about me or my career, but maybe there was nothing they could do.

I went in to see the head of the agency, Sam Weisbord. He bullshitted me about what a champion I was and how I had the blood of champions; he had a great respect for my whole family. He pointed over to the new wing of the agency, saying, 'It's because of you and your family that we were able to build that wing.' I thought, *That's great. That's really wonderful. Our family made a lot of money for you. Now what are you going to do to help me?* I needed work, not just for financial reasons but for my mental wellbeing.

In 1981, Kay and I separated, leading to the divorce, which we knew was inevitable the following year. If my personal life was not gratifying, it was essential to me that my professional one was.

My agency got me one final decent job before our relationship came to an end. They figured Broadway would be the place for me to make a comeback. So in 1981, I went out on the road for a pre-Broadway tour of a new production of George M. Cohan's *Little Johnny Jones*. Believe me that was one tough role – singing and dancing to classic Cohan songs that we've all seen James Cagney perform superbly when he portrayed Cohan on screen in *Yankee Doodle Dandy*. However, the critics didn't think I was ready to step into Cagney or Cohan's shoes. Let's face it, no one was. Before the show made it to Broadway, where it quickly died, the producers replaced me with Donny Osmond. In the months of our pre-Broadway tour, we did boffo business. I was paid well, but by the year's end I had nothing to show for it. God, what I wouldn't have done, over the years, for some good financial advisors.

I picked up whatever work I could in regional theatre, including a production of *Tribute*, written by *The Partridge Family* creator Bernard Slade, a loyal friend from the old days.

In 1983, I finally did get back to Broadway, but I can't say I made any great waves. I replaced Andy Gibb in the leading role of Andrew Lloyd Webber and Tim Rice's hit show *Joseph and the Amazing Technicolor Dreamcoat*, which had opened the year before. The show was going to close until I joined it, but my fans came in droves and I stayed for the entire six-month run. Ironically, my brother Patrick has been starring in the same show in the same role, touring the U.S. on and off for several years. He is arguably as good a Joseph as anyone who has ever played that role. And, by the way, he undoubtedly has the best six-pack of anyone who has ever worn that skirt.

In 1984 I moved to England and started writing new songs and recording for MLM/Arista Records. I had a Top Five single, *The Last Kiss*, in the British charts in March 1985. On *The Last Kiss* I got to work with George Michael when he was just starting to break with Wham! He was a big fan of my work.

Alan Tarney and I had written *The Last Kiss* and I had just sung the lead vocal that afternoon. I went out to dinner with George and said, 'Come back to the studio. I want to play you something.' And he listened and said, 'Wow!'

I said, 'Would you sing the answer part?'

He said, 'Yeah, I'd love to.'

So I said, 'Go out and riff, man, I love your voice.' And he sang fabulously. He's a tremendous talent.

Alan Tarney (producer/songwriter): *The Last Kiss* was an unfinished song idea that I had; I loved the melody, mood and chord sequences. I didn't know what to do with it. It was David who came up with the title and lyrics. It was such a fabulous idea.

I was working with the Norwegian group A-ha, who were signed to Warner Brothers in Burbank. Some representatives from the Burbank office came to my studio to meet me. After that they went to see Def Leppard's producer Mutt Lange and when they got to his studio there was a huge poster of David Cassidy on his wall. When *The Last Kiss* was released in the U.K., the single came with a huge poster of David. And that's the poster that was hanging on his studio wall.

They asked Mutt, 'Why do you have a picture of David Cassidy hanging here?'

And he said, '*The Last Kiss* has just been released and that's my favourite record.'

Mutt is one of the best record-makers; that was a fantastic compliment.

We did the *Romance* album at RG Jones Studios. I was living with Dick Leahy and his wife, Tinca, at The Wick on Richmond Hill and I was making the album with Alan Tarney, who lived around the corner. There have been so many hits recorded at RG Jones over the years. It's this little studio in Wimbledon, this little hole-in-the-wall kind of place that has been there for so long that at one point or another most artists had recorded there, the Rolling Stones, Iggy Pop, Average White Band, A-ha.

> **Alan Tarney:** *Romance* was just a groove and David started singing over it. It's a great mood all the way through. Basia sang background vocals on *Romance*. She later found success as a big star on her own.

The single *Romance (Let Your Heart Go)* made it to number 54 in May 1985. That same month, the album reached number 20 on the British album charts. I believed in the *Romance* album and the record company believed in it and it worked. I got a platinum album and a platinum single. I changed my look by tinting my hair. They thought I needed to get away from the look I'd had in the 70s.

I had a sold-out British concert tour, including two nights at the legendary Royal Albert Hall. The audiences were incredibly receptive and enthusiastic. What was really amazing was that a lot of the fans brought their kids! Had that much time gone by?

In the U.K., I gained a lot of people's respect for what I was doing as a writer and a singer. In America people still saw me as Keith from *The Partridge Family*. The *Romance* album was never released in America. I was frustrated that no matter what I tried, a really successful comeback never seemed to materialise for me in my own country. Sometimes I felt I was truly close. It was clear as I toured that I had a loyal audience, I'd made a hit record, but I just didn't have the support I needed from others. I had no management to speak of any more. I went through several managers, none of whom were committed to me the way Ruth had been, and they certainly didn't work towards long-term career building. They just wanted to make some quick money off me, which, of course, they did.

My record companies kept disintegrating under me. In 1985, the very week that *Romance*, on Arista Records, made the Top 20 in England, BMG acquired Arista and fired the whole staff, so there was nobody there to promote the album. I dropped off the charts immediately. My relationships with record companies have always been, at best, frustrating.

26 Below Zero

Many years ago, I made a promise to myself that I wasn't going to spend any time focusing on revenge or re-experiencing the painful moments when people intentionally went out of their way to cause me pain and to try to impose their wills on me. I also made a promise never to mention my second wife's name in public and have made a concerted effort not to think about her in private. I don't really want to regurgitate what was undoubtedly the deepest, darkest place I have ever been. But as this book lays bare the most intimate parts of my journey through life, I would be remiss if I left her out of the equation, as dark and grim as this particular part of my life was.

I have a deep passion for horse racing and breeding racehorses, thoroughbreds, and it has taken me all over the globe. I have spent a lot of time throughout the past 30 years in Kentucky. In the late 70s, in the early days of my dealings in the horse business, I met a couple named Mark and Meryl

Tanz. He was Canadian, she was from South Africa. She was a strikingly attractive woman with a very strong personality.

My very first recollection of the two of them is that he seemed much older than her. I learned later that he was a very kind, very generous and very tolerant individual. I also learned that she was psychologically totally unbalanced. She hid it very well, particularly when you first met her. She could be charming and laugh and be jovial and gave a good impression. But what she was hiding was really very dark. I'm talkin' black. All of us have insecurities. All of us have flaws. I accept them. I have my own.

I happened to be doing some business with some very dear friends of mine who live in Kentucky who, in turn, were doing business with Mark and Meryl, which is how we met. And we became acquaintances. They were having quite a lot of success in the racing world, and I was having a fair amount of success breeding horses. They purchased a couple of horses from me that I had bred, who went on to become, I believe, fairly successful on the racetrack.

This led to a casual friendship over the next few years. At one point, I found myself in Kentucky, staying with my friends, who had a wonderful farm there and were almost like my adopted family. And, lo and behold, Meryl Tanz was also staying there. She had divorced, re-married and divorced again, all since the last time I had seen her. And she was lookin' for love. As for me, I was rather lost, feeling quite depressed over the divorce from Kay and the loss of my friendship with her.

There was something in Meryl that I felt I connected with. Certainly the horses were one thing we had in common, but mostly I think it was that she was damaged. And I have always felt, from the time I was a little boy, that I could make everybody OK. I believed I could fix her.

But after 18 months of fighting, raging, brooding, screaming, crying, I packed what I could fit into two suitcases and walked out the door, never to return. I knew this was the first step for me to find happiness. So, as I had preached so many years before, it was time for me to come on, get happy.

I left that marriage with less than a thousand dollars in my bank account. My only possessions were the things I could carry out of the house. I didn't have a car. I didn't have a job. And I didn't have anywhere to live. Yeah, I did a good job of wrecking my life, didn't I? Emotionally I bottomed out. I had two failed marriages and a failed career. I knew I was smoking and drinking way too much. I even began to black out on a number of occasions.

When I was going through that divorce, I rented a room across from my best friend, Sam's. Then, for about six months, I lived in the guest bedroom of his sister's two-bedroom apartment. I believe it cost me $350 a month. I bought a bed. I bought a clock. I bought a set of sheets and a pillow. And that's about all I had. I was broke, but I was whole. I had huge debts, no job, no agent, no money, no prospects for a job, but I had myself.

Sam Hyman: David had a failed second marriage and it was not a pretty divorce. It was costly and it pretty much wiped him out. David always knew that as long as I had a roof over my head he had a place to stay, and vice versa. It was a scary time because now we were in our 30s and didn't know what we wanted to do when we grew up. It was especially difficult for David. If he couldn't make a living acting or singing, what could he do? He couldn't bus a table. 'Aren't you David Cassidy?' 'Yeah.' Boy.

My brothers were busy with their own lives. Although they were sympathetic to what was going on in mine, they could offer nothing more than an occasional 'Let's go have lunch', or 'C'mon, you've got to get rid of this anger and get out of this funk.'

So by the mid 80s, I was broke and almost everything in my life was negative. I was depressed and withdrawn. My debts only kept growing larger. My attorneys kept sending me bills. At the time, I got hit with a paternity suit, which made the *New York Post*'s notorious 'Page Six'.

While the *Post* was printing the news of the paternity suit, halfway around the world a sleazy little newspaper in Germany was printing an 'exclusive interview' I'd supposedly given them, in which I allegedly came out as a homosexual. Incredibly, the story got picked up by a paper in England, then another. You try to deny something like that and you only wind up drawing more attention to it. More recently, it's even found its way into a book, which reported that I had revealed my homosexuality while in Germany. Yeah, right. I hadn't even been to Germany at the time of the supposed interview. I was in L.A., struggling like hell to come up with another rabbit to pull out of my hat. But it always amused me when people assumed I was gay. It still does.

But I couldn't worry much about what newspapers were or were not writing about me. That was the least of my concerns. In almost every way imaginable, my life was just not working.

When I suffered these severe financial problems, no one in my family was in any position to help me out. None of my brothers had made that kind of money. They were all struggling to take care of themselves. By then, my brother Shaun had a wife and three kids to support. His career was not exactly going very well at the time I was hitting bottom; he had his own problems to deal with. Shaun didn't make as much money from his handful of hit records as some might imagine. It's pretty much a myth that recording artists make a fortune from records. Most of the time, the record companies make the money, not the artists. My brother Patrick was an actor trying to make a living himself. So there was really no money around. I had no one to turn to for help. I did borrow some money a couple of times, just so I could make my child support payments.

Taking the money and running is not something that has ever enticed me. Doing crap for a big cheque is not something I've ever done or ever want to do. Having to work just for the money is something I had to do a couple of times in my life and I always regretted it. I did it only to survive, not because I wanted to buy a car or live on a yacht.

I turned down a small fortune to work in South Africa when apartheid was still in effect. My conscience wouldn't allow me to do it, even though I desperately needed the money. But I couldn't have lived with myself if I hadn't respected the sanctions. I was offered a million dollars for me, along with another half a million in cash and half a million to the government of Sun City, but I had to turn it down.

People still knew my name, they knew I had been a teen heartthrob many years before. But all that was ancient history. Professionally, nobody really cared about me any more.

Most people, at this point, might have contemplated suicide. Not I. I always believed that I had the strength and the talent to make it through this darkness. I've always seen suicide as the ultimate sign of weakness and failure.

Meanwhile, I received an invitation to go Aspen, Colorado, for a couple of days. Get out of L.A. and ski? Sounded too good to be true. While I was there, I ran into an old friend who said

Don Johnson, who had by now made it big, was in town and was throwing a party with Bruce Willis. This friend said, 'David, Bruce knows you're in town and wants you to come to the party. Your name will be on the list. All of Hollywood is going to be at this party.'

So I decided to go to the party. When I arrived, there were only a dozen or so people there; I was one of the first to arrive. Don was holding court, wearing a ridiculous mohair suit that must have cost two grand! I walked up to him. This was a guy who'd known me from the beginning, who'd been to my home – an old, old friend. I feel close to people I go way back with. The last time I'd seen him, he'd driven up to my house in his beat-up old Volkswagen. I was thinking, *This is going to be great; I can tell him how happy I am for all his success.*

I said, 'Don, how are you, man? Great to see you,' thinking how glad this old friend would be to see me.

He just looked at me, smiled tightly for just a beat, and then went back to his conversation with somebody else. He absolutely iced me.

I laughed to try to break the tension, and said, 'Don, you're kidding. Right?'

When he didn't turn around, I said, 'Don't do this, Don.'

No response.

'I don't fucking believe it,' I said, and walked away, wondering, *Are you a human being any more, Don? Are you for real?*

Was this what being a star had done to him? Did he think that he could now snub people he felt he'd risen above? Maybe, in his mind, that was his way of paying me back for getting jobs he'd wanted when we were both starting out. Maybe he didn't want this reminder of his early years hanging around. I've witnessed how fame corrupts people. He was gone.

I was feeling a lot of pain because of my divorce, and so many other things. I just felt like I'd failed at everything. I'd done a lot in England, but nothing in America, where it really counted, my home. I'd felt lost many times in my life, but this time more than ever. I was hypersensitive, kind of like an outsider coming back, trying to start my life and career over again. And to have Don snub me . . . I felt as if he was saying, *Hey, I never really rated you anyway* or *I don't need you losers any longer.* At the time, it hurt.

It seemed like a thousand people walked through the door of the party, a veritable who's who of showbiz. I walked out quietly. Alone. Nobody noticed I'd left, I'm sure.

Maybe most people in the business no longer cared about me. One did, however. That same year, I found someone to represent me as an agent who eventually became my manager, Melanie Green. She was a real fan of mine and, even though I told her I was fundamentally a mess, she offered to represent me. And that, I think, marked the beginning of my professional recovery.

I realised that I needed to get myself healthy and try to rebuild my life. I began searching for the tools I needed to make that happen. I began searching for the keys. It was one step at a time. Then two steps. Then three steps. Suddenly I was walking again. Suddenly I was beginning to feel like my life was my own again.

The only difference between a happy man and an unhappy man is how he feels within himself. It has nothing to do with what he has in his bank account, nothing to do with his creature comforts. It was an internal search that I began. Trying not to make the same mistakes I had made in the past. Trying to learn from those mistakes. Trying to rebuild my life from the bottom up, from the very basics of waking up in the morning to taking care of my body. I knew I had to take baby steps. And so it began.

27 Light at the End of the Tunnel

Sue Shifrin Cassidy: I was on the phone with a friend of mine who had been my roommate in London, and we were talking about the guys we dated. She said, 'Who was the nicest guy you ever dated?' And I said, 'David Cassidy.' She said, 'When did you date him?' I said, 'When I lived with you.' And she said, 'Wow, I wonder what's happened to him?' I said, 'God, I don't know, but I want to find out.'

When I was in London around 1984, I stayed for something like a month and a half with my friend Terry Britten. Terry and his wife took care of me while I was in a lot of pain after my divorce. David was staying about 30 seconds away. He was friends with Terry and his wife, as well, but we never talked about him – I kept my word and never said anything to anybody about our fling. So we found out later that we had all these mutual acquaintances, all these mutual friends, all this stuff in common. We had been like ships passing in the night.

I wrote a letter to an assistant at my music publisher, Warner

Chappell, who was a huge *Partridge Family* fan. She said, 'Let me find him.' And she found his agent and lawyer's numbers. I wrote a letter to one of them and I called the other.

I received a call from my attorney who said that an old friend of mine, Sue Shifrin, had called and that she was back in Los Angeles and that she wanted to speak with me. I wrote down her number and immediately called her and invited her to dinner. We had dinner a few nights later and then the next night, and the next, and, well, you know how that goes.

Sue: About five days after I had sent the letter, I was out in the yard gardening and the phone rang. It was him. I said, 'I can't believe that it's you,' and he said, 'Yeah, I got your letter. I've just come back from England and I was going to call you. I was told that I needed to start writing songs with you.' This was on a Wednesday that he called me, and on the Saturday, which was 6 September 1986, I saw him for the first time in 13 years.

It was really wild. He drove up in his car and his hair was blond. It was like I'd just seen him yesterday, but a lot of life had happened to him. He had been going through a really ugly divorce. We talked over dinner about how life had treated both of us. After he told me everything he'd been through, he said, 'I'm not crazy, am I?' I said, 'No, you're not crazy.' He was actually doubting his own sanity because he'd been so devastated by this last marriage and his retirement.

We've been together ever since.

On our second or third date he came over to my house and said, 'You know, I remember what you were wearing the first time I ever saw you.'

I said, 'Just a minute, I'll be right back.' And, hanging in my closet, I still had this little jacket that my mother had embroidered for me. And it still fit me. I put it on and I walked out and we were both in shock. He'd met so many people, millions. I mean, people walk up to him all the time, 'Oh, hi. Don't you remember I met you at such and such?' How could he be expected to? But he remembered everything about our meeting. Everything about me.

Sam Hyman: I remember coming home and sitting on the couch with him and he goes, 'Hey, guess who I called?' He was calling everybody. He was reaching out.

He said, 'Do you remember Sue Shifrin?'

I said, 'Do I remember? I was just pissed off that she hadn't fallen in love with me. I mean, my God, what a gorgeous woman. And talented.'

He said, 'Yeah. Wasn't she? I want to get together with her.'

And that was the beginning of the spark and of his turn-around. She was the light at the end of the tunnel. I can remember a change in his attitude after he'd heard from her. And then the rest is history. She gave him hope and encouragement.

Once I re-connected with Sue, I really began to shift my life from the dark side into the light. Just being around her made me feel better – she was so positive, so supportive, so caring, so loving. Her whole attitude was *I don't care that you're a drunk, David; I don't care that you're a mess. And I don't care that you have no money.* When someone embraces you at your lowest point, it really means something. It carried a lot of weight with me.

With Sue's support, I made the decision to go into analysis. Emotionally and professionally, I had pretty much bottomed out. I found my analyst through Sue, who had benefited greatly from analysis herself. Even though the process is painful, it's not anywhere near as painful as living with the kind of misery I was experiencing. I just couldn't stand it any longer. I knew I must find a way to change, to be happy with myself again.

So I began to concentrate on healing myself. I had to feel whole as a person. My hope was that, through analysis, I could rebuild my life. I didn't hold out any hopes for my career, which seemed, to all intents and purposes, dead. I really didn't begin changing as a person until the late 80s, when I began analysis more intensely. What a difference it made for me. Three and a half years, three times a week. Every week, a little more light.

I was standing at a crossroads. I tried to keep Sue away from my life at that point; I didn't want to involve her in the difficult journey that was facing me. How do you bail yourself out of a million dollars of debt? How do you try to reconstruct an image that was so vividly ingrained in everyone's mind and change people's false perception and see the real you? And how do you become humble enough to start over after having had that level of professional success? It was humiliating in many ways. I don't believe that experience builds character. I believe you have to have the strength of character in the first place.

Sue continued to pursue me in a loving, caring way and we still saw each other. She wanted the relationship to evolve and I told her that I was incapable of that at that time. 'Why would you want a broken-down piece of junk like me when you can go out and get a shiny, new machine?'

I knew that the only way for me to heal and wake up in the morning and feel good about myself was to continue on my path alone. So I ran – literally and figuratively. Every day. Everywhere. I would drive to Mulholland Drive, Santa Monica, Venice Beach and run for miles. All I could think was, *Run, boy, run*. I ran past the homeless and thought, *I'm one step away from that*. Ran past mansions on Sunset Boulevard and thought, *I'm one step away from that. Just keep runnin', boy.* And so I did.

I guess that thinking that we can choose just one perfect mate to spend our lives with is innately flawed. There's no person that's going to fit you like a glove, who's going to share all your likes and dislikes, who's going to be 100 per cent compatible in every way. The bottom line is, would you climb a mountain with them? Do they love and care for you and your needs? Do they put themselves second sometimes? Do they accept your flaws? Can you embrace the things that you don't like about them?

Sue is so talented and so naïve, which is something that's still endearing about her to this day. Her naïvety is so innocent and so pure She's the most solid, kindest best friend one could ever have. We have an incredible bond that has lasted for 20 years now. We're partners, friends, business associates and co-writers, yet we have our own friends, our own lives, our own interests, and that's very healthy.

It wasn't long after Sue came back into my life, maybe a couple of months, when I received a call regarding an offer for me to replace Cliff Richard in a musical in London's West End, at the Dominion Theatre, entitled *Time*. I listened to the music, they sent me the book. The music was pretty good. The book? Oh God, dreadful. Not just poor, absolutely dreadful. And I thought, *Hmm, let's see – go back to theatre, move to London. I don't know.* They increased the offer. I still wasn't sure. They increased the offer again. I sat and waited.

Even though I had less than a thousand dollars to my name, I turned down the first three offers the producer of *Time* made to me. I really played this poker hand well. As if I was still rich. And that's the only way that I've ever negotiated. I've always been willing to walk away from a deal if I didn't get what I felt I deserved. I began to regain a sense of power, once I had someone to support me, someone who loved me – Sue.

Finally they said, 'This is our final offer.' I looked at the money that they were offering me – a lot of money. I looked at the opportunity that it would present and thought, *Can I make something out of this?* I took a deep breath, signed the contract and I was on the next plane to London to do *Time*.

I must say that, even though it was successful, I thought *Time* was a bad play – no real story, no substance. It was just a poorly written star vehicle for anybody who could sing and had a little charisma. But it had incredible sets, lights and special effects. And it was promoted extremely well. So, even though the play was really a piece of fluff, I had great success with it. My fans came in droves. Business was terrific. It was the first step of a real comeback. I was finally being treated as an adult.

About three weeks after I arrived in London, I was in rehearsal when I met one of the great theatrical actors of all time. Yes, it was me and Sir Laurence Olivier's head. What a fine, fine predicament this was.

So what was it like working with Laurence Olivier, David?

It was absolutely marvellous.

We met, Sir Laurence and I. I found him to be kind and very funny. He was very respectful; very complimentary. And very old, with gout. Were we going to look at his career and think that the man has no credibility because he appeared as just a head in Dave Clark's *Time*? I think not.

So I thought, *I can make the best of working with his head every night.*

I found myself working 15, 16 hours a day in rehearsals. As always when you're preparing for an opening, the rehearsal period is the most difficult time. You have no time for anything else, it's all encompassing. So, it was a bit of a shock when, about three weeks into rehearsals, there was a knock on my front door. I had a little apartment in Knightsbridge, near Montpelier Square. Two bedrooms, a little balcony; a nice little place.

I opened the door and there stood Sue, with a big smile on her face – and 15 pieces of luggage.

'Oh,' said I, 'Coming to stay for a few days, are we?'

'No. Actually, David, I'm moving here. Isn't that a fantastic coincidence? I'm joining Emerson, Sue and Palmer.'

'Emerson, Sue and Palmer?'

'Yeah. Carl Palmer, Keith Emerson and I are working on material. We're putting a band together.'

'No kidding? Well, come on in. The bedroom's upstairs. I guess you'll need a little help with those bags.'

Need I say any more?

The seven months I spent performing in *Time* were very good months for me and Sue. We got a place together a couple of months later, a little mews house in South Kensington. I would go to work. She would go to work. I'd finish the show and have my driver take me back to our little house. She'd make a late dinner. We got on well. We had no connection with the real world. I was dealing with a lot of my problems, so it seemed. I was repaying banks and some of my other debts every week. I had very little money but we had a great time.

It was, arguably, the time that we were able to do the most healing and bonding because we had no distractions. We had a single telephone line. There were no cell phones at that time. We didn't have an answering machine. So I was virtually cut off from the rest of the world. I was working and enjoying life. We began writing songs together and we proved to be quite a goldmine of creativity.

Thanks to analysis, I stopped drinking during the run of *Time*. I stopped smoking cigarettes shortly afterwards. I woke up one day and realised none of my vices were working for me; I realised how much I loved myself and my life. How blessed I was.

I can't drink any more. I certainly can't do drugs. I hate the thought of them. I guess the only things left for me are cookies and milk. But I feel better now than I did before I gave up those old habits. I mean, I look at what I am: pretty clean, pretty light – and pretty lucky.

I've been a chronic insomniac for as long as I can remember. It comes and goes, is more or less intense depending on what's going on in my life. I lie awake in bed at night and think about choices I have to make. But if that's the worst of my problems these days, all right, I can live with that. I'm doing meditation at night now.

I eat healthy foods, though I'm not completely vegetarian any more – I eat fish and fowl. I feel good. I really believe I owe it to myself to wake up every morning and feel good. And I'll do whatever it takes to get me there.

When my contract for *Time* was up, they asked me to stay on, but I knew that I had to go back to America and face the realities I had left behind. I didn't want to perpetuate the mid-80s success I had in the U.K. and I didn't want to continue to try to be a rock star. I wanted to find my way. I'm an American, after all. I wanted to move back home and spend time with my brothers, my mom. I wanted to rebuild my life there.

Sue and I came back from the U.K. together at the end of 1987 and realised that I had nothing. I no longer owned a home in Los Angeles. Sue had a house there and invited me to stay with her. I moved into her lovely little house in Studio City. Small but very quiet. She had a pool and a Jacuzzi. Sounded pretty good to me. I thought, *Hmm, I guess that means we're living together now.*

The weather was as we remembered it. The city was as we remembered it. And the baggage was still there. It was time for me to face the music. And face it I did.

The first thing I did was call my brothers, then I called my two other best friends. And I found an analyst. At that point I resumed self-exploration through intense work, three times a week. The ensuing two years were financially a struggle, but creatively quite fertile. I started writing a lot, alone and with Sue, and I received an offer for a music publishing deal for my material. *Just do the work, kid. The rest will follow.*

One day, shortly after that, I heard about these guys on the radio, Mark and Brian on KLOS. They had what was becoming the most popular morning show in Los Angeles. Apparently, they had been talking about me for a couple of days, saying that they were fans of mine. So I called them and they invited me on the show. They asked me what I'd been doing. I told them I had been writing some material and making some demos and some artists had cut songs of mine. The following week, I accepted their offer to come back to the studio and was on air all morning with them. By the end of the show, I had played three or four demos and had three offers of recording contracts. Ah, Los Angeles, how sweet it is.

I went with an offer from Enigma, a small, credible record company, almost the antithesis of a mainstream pop label, which is what I felt I needed. Do the things that people don't expect. Don't be predictable. There was great enthusiasm for me and my material at the label. They were a young, upstart label but were seemingly carving out their own little niche. I believe they had quite a bit of success with a band called Poison. Who's on our label? David Cassidy and Poison. Yeah, that sounds right.

It was an experience that, in retrospect, was a good one for me. I began recording with a very, very good engineer–producer named 'ET' Thorngren, who produced and engineered a couple of Robert Palmer's great records. We worked on a new album, *David Cassidy*, for six or seven months in 1990 and spent a lot of time promoting it. The single that Sue and I wrote, *Lyin' to Myself*, was released to radio and it was the number one added single on AC (adult contemporary) and pop radio the first week. People in the business were shocked; I guess they thought I was dead. It looked like I had a real hit in the making. But by the time the single was a bona fide hit on the *Billboard* AC charts, the record company had unexpectedly closed its doors. It went belly up. And without a strong company behind you, pushing your record, stores aren't going to stock it and disc jockeys aren't going to play it. It was devastating.

> **Sue Shifrin Cassidy:** One night, in the little rented house in South Kensington. I had a little keyboard and when David was at the theatre performing in *Time*, I came up with this idea, 'So I'll never feel your touch again I'll get used to it. Hearts don't break they just bend.' I played it for David when he got home and he said, 'I love that,' and we started writing it together. We had a completely different chorus to it. We took it to Dick Leahy and played it for him and he said, 'This song is fantastic, but you need to rework the chorus.' We changed it and Dick said, 'This is a number one record.' I'm just so proud of *Lyin' to Myself*. It would've been a big, big hit had the record company not gone under. That was heartbreaking.

Ah, show business. You gotta love it. So now what do I do? I've just invested a year and a half of my life with a record company that doesn't exist any more.

I really wanted to get back to playing live. I knew that I could control things when on the stage, something I couldn't do in the record business. I called a couple of friends to see if they wanted to join me on what I called the 'credibility tour'. I wanted to give my fans and the people who cared about me and my music an opportunity to see me again.

So I began a three month bus tour. Trust me, folks, this wasn't exactly like having my own plane and 15 security guards. It was me, the four guys in the band, the bus driver and a drunken Danny Bonaduce, my old buddy from *Partridge Family* days. Oh yeah. Let's get back on the bus, Danny.

I was glad that I was in a position – sort of – where I could do somebody else some good. Danny had been arrested while working for a radio station called The Eagle in Philadelphia. He had gone to Florida on a weekend when, ironically, they were doing remote broadcasts for the anti-drug organisation DARE. In the course of the weekend, he was arrested for buying crack on a street corner at two in the morning. He was on parole after that, so I had to call his parole officer to get permission for him to come along with me, since we would be crossing state lines for the tour.

Danny got into trouble again in 1991 for beating and robbing a transvestite prostitute in Phoenix, Arizona, which really messed up the career he was trying to make for himself as a disc jockey. I've tried to stand by him. I believed in him, as a person and as a talent.

I'm still like Danny's big brother. I've tried to help him to get his life together; he'd been almost out of control at the time of the arrests. His self-esteem was very low. He has been very self-destructive. I really do like him and feel for him. I think he's a good person underneath all that. He deserves forgiveness and support.

I think he sees me as something of a pain, this voice of reason, you know. When I call him, he probably thinks, *Oh no, here comes the medicine again.* But I'm one of the only people who gives a damn and will say anything to him about it. When he got arrested for the drug deal and he was in jail, I was the only person who called and asked, 'What can I do to help? If you need something, I just want you to know I'm here.'

He was blown away. He never felt worthy enough for anybody to care. I think he's still amazed that I take the time to call him. I call him every few months, just to find out how he's doing. He's worth saving. He's got a lot to give. I think he's genuinely gifted and very funny.

I really don't mean to be patting myself on the back here.

Whatever I've done for Danny, I've done for myself too. I simply like talking with him. He's about the only one left who I can really reminisce with about the old days. Danny and I are friends, peers. I've taken him out on the road a few times. He's a terrific opening act for me. He's hysterical.

I don't remember many details from the 'credibility tour' except how incredibly uncomfortable it was, how humbling. I think at the end of the three months, I netted around $800, maybe even less. No lie. It was less than $1,000, I know that. But at least everybody got paid. Except me. I don't regret doing it.

There were moments that I will never forget, particularly at The Bottom Line, the New York club, when I invited Tony Romeo and Wes Farrell, both of whom I hadn't seen in many years. I dedicated some of the material I hadn't sung in so many years to them. All in all, it was good for me because I got back up and stood on my own two feet and started playing again. At least some of my fans had been able to see me again and I got to share some of my memories with them. Something I wouldn't do for another ten years.

28 All You Need Is Love

What I have been able to do from 1987 until now – I'm talking about rebuilding my life, from the bottom up – I could not have done without Sue, the woman I stood up the Queen of England for back in 1973. Little did I dream when I first met her that 13 years later, after we'd both had unsuccessful marriages, we'd end up together and ultimately get married and have a family.

Getting married? I don't think either one of us ever had any plans to do that. But Sue came into my office one day, shortly after my tour, and said, 'I'm pregnant.'

I stared at her for a moment and said, 'No, you're not. You're kidding.'

'I'm not kidding. I know I've always been told that I can't get pregnant, but guess what? I am.'

Me? A parent? Oh, Lord.

Sue and I got married shortly before Beau was born. We wanted to do things in the right order. I have to say, five o'clock in the morning, on the eighth of February 1991, watching the birth of my son, was arguably the most joyous moment of my life. I remember seeing him screaming and taking his first breath. Cutting the umbilical cord. Crying with joy, thinking this is what my life is all about now. Thank you, God. Thank you.

So I skip ahead to changing diapers, thousands of them, mind you, over the first nine months to a year. Living my life every day with my wife and my newborn son. Experiencing something that I never thought I would. Bringing another life into this world. Protecting him. Loving him. Caring for him. And, oh yes, being financially responsible for my family. Now there's a concept.

I had bailed myself out of $800,000 worth of debt. I no longer had banks calling me. No lawyers harassing me. I got a call from Hal Prince about the possibility of appearing in *The Phantom of the Opera*. I told him that, as much as I appreciated his interest in me, I had just had a child, a baby boy named Beau, and at this time I wanted to spend every day with him, at least for the first six months of his life. Sue and I had been hunkering down together in a home we bought. Playing house was fun.

Sue Shifrin Cassidy: I had been told I could never have kids. When we were living in London, I was in the kitchen, washing dishes, and David said to me, 'I have the weirdest feeling that I'm looking at the mother of my children.' And I said to him, 'I can't have children.' I mean, what do you say when a man says that to you? It was like, wow.

About four years later, the doctor confirmed that I could not have children, that I couldn't hold a fertilised egg, I was allergic to sperm, I was too old, you name it.

In 1990, David and I went to Russia and performed. I had been there before, on the first Songwriters Summit, with superstar songwriters including Cyndi Lauper, Michael Bolton, Brenda Russell and Diane Warren. I was invited back to perform and I took David with me. We sang *Lyin' to Myself* and a song that I wrote with Jon Lind, *All Because of You*. We came back in May and in June my mother had a devastating stroke. I was 40 or 41 years old. My mother was lying there paralysed, and I thought I was having a nervous breakdown.

David said to me, 'You need to call the doctor.' I was a wreck; I just didn't feel right. I went and saw my gynaecologist and he said, 'We should just do a pregnancy test. Even though it's impossible for you to carry a child, you could have an ectopic pregnancy.'

So they did a blood test and I got a call saying, 'You're positive.'

And I said, 'Oh, I'm positively sick. There's something wrong with me.'

'No, you're positive.'

And I said, 'What do you mean I'm positive? Positive what?'

They said, 'You're pregnant. Your test was positive.'

I said, 'That's impossible. I can't be.'

And they said, 'Those are the results. We have them right here.'

I ran downstairs and David saw the look on my face and said, 'What's the matter?'

'David, they're on the phone, they told me that I'm positive.'

He said, 'What do you mean positive?'

I said, 'I'm pregnant.'

He said, 'That's impossible. You can't be. Let me talk to them.'

And he told them, 'My girlfriend can't be pregnant.'

They said, 'We've never made a mistake.'

We both started to shake and we drove to the doctor. George Weinberger, my gynaecologist, gave me an ultrasound. David, who'd seen so many ultrasounds of his horses, knew exactly what he was looking at when the blip, blip, blip was there, right where it was supposed to be. And we burst into tears.

I had never even wanted children. I had never held a baby. And it was at a time in my life when it was least likely I would get pregnant, after a stressful thing like my mother having a devastating stroke.

I had an uncomplicated pregnancy and David was right there, even though he had to travel through most of it. He was on tour with the Beach Boys then. That was very hard, but he was there for the birth. He cut the umbilical cord. He changed the first diaper. He gave him his bath. That was the highlight of our lives and that was the turning point, I think, in David's life. More than being with me, more than anything, being a parent changed him.

He became really committed. His attitude became, *Now I really have to get my act together*, because he hadn't worked in a long time. He'd done the tour with the Beach Boys, but he really wasn't serious then. And he was dabbling in horses, but he was kind of lost. It all changed when we became a family.

Like Sue, I had never had a desire to have a child, I had never imagined that happening. So it was such a shock to both of us. But it has added such an incredible dimension to our lives. If you've never had a child, you can't ever imagine what it's like until it happens. And when it does happen, you can never be the same again.

Sue Shifrin Cassidy: David has a great sense of humour and we laugh a lot together. We're very much alike; we're both Aries. We're both very opinionated, very controlling and very high-strung. So we have some dynamics that have not been easy. But, in general, we're just supposed to be together. We're still standing after 20 years and I can't believe it. It's gone so fast. I just love his spirit. I love the fact that he's a survivor. I love the fact that no matter how hard he gets kicked, he gets up. And he's been kicked really hard. I've been around it and I've seen it and my heart has bled for him. But he always manages to get back up. I tell him all the time, 'You remind me of the Terminator. You're like the steel skeleton.' He has miraculously survived a life that has been a huge rollercoaster.

The way that Sue and I evaluate someone is, *Would you climb a mountain with them? And, if you were slipping, would they reach down and say, Come on, I got you?* The more willing you are to care for your family and make sacrifices for the people you love, the better you become as a human being. You become a more well-rounded person and look at life from different perspectives. I had gotten myself out of debt. I had rebuilt my soul and spirit and physical and mental health. I started on a journey as a parent that's been an unexpected gift and joy and I now find that my family is the most important element in my life. And that includes my brothers, my nephews, my nieces, my sister-in-laws, my cousins and my mother.

My mother, sadly, is now suffering from a horrible disease that none of us is immune to – dementia. I support her, take care of her, see her as often as possible. I know how important she has been in my life. My heart breaks daily for her and for others who have endured this painful disease.

My cousin Charlie, who's my dear friend, helped me along the road to becoming financially solvent, protected and free of the pain and the choking fear. Things that are monetary are not the most valuable things in my life. The most important thing is intangible – love.

I've been able to heal a lot of my wounds through becoming a parent. My father was a role model for me, both positively and negatively. Everything he never gave to me, I give to my son. Everything he didn't do for me that I wanted and needed, I do for my son.

Shaun Cassidy: Becoming a father has made David a much better person. You can't be completely self-involved when you have children. David has been a terrific father to Beau and takes great pride in Beau's accomplishments. He doesn't seem to have any of the issues that our father had with him. He wants Beau to succeed and to do whatever he wants to do. He's very helpful and supportive.

Recently, David sang the National Anthem at a Chicago Cubs game and he brought Beau with him to sing. For Beau I know that was like the Triple Crown. He's a huge baseball fan and he got to be in the middle of Wrigley Field. So that was a dream come true. He loves to sing, and is terrific at it, and has eyes for being a performer. The icing on the cake was that he got to do it with his dad, whom he reveres. That's a moment that I'm sure David would have loved to have shared with our father and couldn't. He spoke to me about it with such pride, that he was able to do this with Beau and how proud he was of Beau and how beautifully he sang.

Sue Cassidy: I've said to Beau, 'I really apologise to you for your parents.' We're basically great parents, great people. We love him unconditionally, but we have certain expectations. I said, 'The thing is you have parents who had parents who were very hard on them.' My dad, no matter how well I did something, would find one little thing to fault.

What's really wonderful for Beau is that he's got the best of both of us. When David wakes up in the morning, no matter what's happened to him, he's a very happy person. He's got a smile on his face, he's loving and he's sweet. He's, you know, smiling Sam, that's what they called him when he was a little boy. Beau got that. David wants very much to protect Beau and he can't.

I'm not the sunnier disposition of the two of us. David is basically a very positive person. The events in his life have scarred him. David has a tendency to feel very put upon and because of his fragile and sensitive nature, he gets easily overwhelmed. He can't just have simplicity, and he wants peace.

29 Work It, Baby, Work It

In 1993, some time around June or July, I got a call from a very successful producer in the United Kingdom, Bill Kenwright. He told me he had a show on Broadway called *Blood Brothers* and asked me if I would fly to New York to see it. He told me he was interested in me for the role of the narrator. To go back to where I had been born and raised, to be back on Broadway in the theatre, seemed like the perfect next step.

In New York, I met with the general manager, Stuart Thompson. I saw the show and was amazed. I thought it was such a powerful, magnificent piece of work. I went back to my hotel room, called Bill Kenwright and told him that I couldn't possibly play the narrator. If he wanted me to do the show, the only role that I would be willing to play, that I was right for, that I knew I could win with, was the role of Mickey Johnston. He argued with me for an hour. I argued back. I told him to sleep on it and call me in the morning. He called me the next day and said, 'OK. You got it.' OK, Broadway. Third time around, here I come.

Appearing with my brother Shaun in *Blood Brothers* gave me about nine of the ten jolts anyone could possibly get from a creative project. It was a terrific opportunity for both of us. It was the first and only time we ever worked together. We played twin brothers who'd been raised apart. My character had grown up in a poorer home and had experienced far more problems with his marriage, he loses his job, and his life falls apart. As you can imagine, I could relate.

I'd never felt as close to Shaun as I did then. From time to time we would have dinner together after the show. We would contemplate having our grandchildren on our laps, telling them about the time that we did *Blood Brothers* together on Broadway. Ironically, we had come back to the place where our father had built his reputation, where he'd lived and breathed.

Shaun Cassidy: The *Blood Brothers* experience was perfect, and I hadn't wanted to do it initially. I had gotten a foothold as a writer/producer, with an office at Universal. I was on a different career track and David called and said, 'They want me to do this show in New York called *Blood Brothers* and I think it would be great for us to do it together.'

I said, 'Thanks but no thanks, I'm doing something else now.'

He said, 'Well, just come and see the show.'

I said, 'David, I really don't want to do it.'

He said, 'Just come and see the show.'

I said, 'When do you want me to come?'

He said, 'Next week.'

And I said, 'I can't, I have a date.' This was when I was single and dating.

I only went to New York because I got the girl to go with me. I ended up having a terrible weekend with her, but loved the show and I called my studio and said, 'Look, how would you feel if I went to New York for a few months to do a show?' I told them I'd keep writing because I was working on a movie for television at the time. Thankfully they said OK.

I got a little apartment in New York and David and I went off on this *Blood Brothers* adventure, which ended up being amazing in every way. It was great living in New York. It was great working with him. I think the reason it was so successful was the fact that we were actually brothers. That resonated for the audience and it imbued the show with a layer of reality. The characters were as different as David and I are, although neither of us are like those characters.

Petula Clark: Bill Kenwright, the producer of *Blood Brothers*, had this brilliant idea of casting David and Shaun in the show and asked me to do it with them. I thought that was great, but I didn't quite know what to expect. David surprised me very much with his talent.

The whole play takes place in Liverpool and we're all supposed to be Liverpudlians. I've always found the accent to be a little bit difficult. In walks David and goes through his lines in a perfect Liverpool accent and I was totally blown away by that. In fact, his accent was almost too good. Taking the play to America, from London, I think the accent might have been too much for the Americans, so we all had to water down our Liverpool accents.

From the beginning to the end it was a sheer joy working with David. It was not an easy role for him. In his first scene he had to play this rough little boy from Liverpool in short trousers. It was not what people might have expected to see. They'd come to see David Cassidy. But he carried it off so well. When he's an adolescent, he comes on in his blue jeans – then the audience can start relating to him. He was extremely funny and in the later scenes his acting was absolutely superb. I've worked with some pretty good people through the years and I thought he was brilliant throughout, and consistent.

The audiences adored him. It was definitely a triumph for David. I have to say he and Shaun together were amazing, just incredible.

We all know David is a great pop singer. But the music in this play was not particularly poppy. It's poppy here and there. But the great thing about playing a role is you can put your own stamp on it. I had heard these songs sung several times before by other performers – *Blood Brothers* had been performed for many years in London before we took it to New York and then on tour. But suddenly they sounded totally fresh and wonderful because it was David. Every night he used to listen to me sing and I was listening to him. There was a mutual admiration. I got to know him quite well. We worked together for two years. That's a long time. We had fun together. We had a lot of laughs. We also went through difficulties doing the show because it's not always easy on tour. We had a different band every week and sometimes it wasn't always up to scratch.

I would work with David again any time. He is a perfectionist and so am I. Perfectionists are those who are a bit tortured because they can never quite reach that point where they think they've got it right. It's a difficult way to be. He's constantly trying to be better and that's what drives him. That's also what drives me and what drives a lot of the great performers in this business.

I loved being on the road with Petula Clark. What a wonderful human being. We became very close, Petula and I, during that time. We were always together, either on stage or travelling. I think, out of all the great people that I have had the privilege of working with, I've never met anyone with more talent, who was kinder, more genuine, more deserving of success. She has style and class. She was and is a great friend and I think of her all the time now and miss her. She was a great foil. I will forever be grateful for her friendship, for her support, for her love and for her gifts to me and my family. Sue, Shaun, Beau and I will always have a spot in our hearts for her.

Patrick Cassidy: I went to New York to see *Blood Brothers* and I was completely knocked out by David and Shaun. This was an example of David's talent as an actor and singer. There wasn't a horde of screaming girls, so you could hear the music and dialogue, you could see him doing what he does best. I think if my father had seen David in *Blood Brothers* he would have been so proud of him and said, 'Yes, that was the way to go.'

The following three years – the first year on Broadway with my brother and Petula Clark, a year of touring with Petula in the national company, three months in the West End and three months in Toronto – were arguably the most creatively and emotionally satisfying, physically debilitating, financially rewarding years of my life. I did make a lot of money but what my body suffered playing that role I can't describe.

A week or two into our rehearsal period, I tore both my hamstrings. I had to find a way to get through it. I began taking Advil. Daily. Many, many Advil a day, to ease the pain. I didn't want anyone to know I was suffering. It took me 10 to 15 minutes, bent over, just to get out of bed in the morning. I suffered from terrible back and neck aches. My whole body was in agony. I stretched 40 minutes in the morning. I stretched 40 minutes before each performance. I was doing eight shows a week and I think I only missed two or three days during the entire year we were on Broadway.

A few blocks away, many years before, my father had starred in a production of *She Loves Me*, during which he had become a theatrical master. It was the most powerful performance I ever saw. Period. *She Loves Me* opened to rave reviews on Broadway.

The casting director of *She Loves Me* called me towards the end of our run in *Blood Brothers*, knowing my contract was nearly up, and asked if I would take over the role my father had created. I wanted so badly to play the role of Kodaly, as a tribute to my father, to repay him for all the great things that he gave me – the talent, the work ethic, the self-absorption and creativity, the love of theatre. But alas, I had another path to take. I had to move forward. And forward I moved.

We bought a house in Connecticut, Sue, Beau and I. We loved it there. We had four and a half acres. It looked like a picture postcard. Sue was never happier. Beau began going to school.

When I was on Broadway, I would spend 45 minutes with my son before I went to the theatre. We'd play the piano, I'd read him a story and work on a puzzle with him. It really was quality time. He has always known that I'm there for him and that's the most important thing. Even if I work a ten-hour day.

As an actor and singer, sometimes I have to protect my voice. I have to remain silent for major portions of the day, so I don't overtax my vocal cords. My son learned at a young age to understand that there are times I have to be silent. He knew it was nothing personal. Sometimes I whisper to him, rather than speak aloud. He whispers right back to me. Sign language with him is a ball.

During this period, I spent a lot of my time writing songs on the guitar. I wrote and recorded the theme song for *The John Larroquette Show* on NBC. It's a bluesy little song; whenever I pick up the guitar, instinctively I always end up playing the blues. That's where my heart continues to be. Incidentally, although *The John Larroquette Show* is written and produced by a friend of mine, I wanted my work to speak for itself, so I submitted the demo tape that I'd recorded under a pseudonym,

Blind Lemon Jackson. The people who made the decision listened to the tape without knowing they were actually listening to David Cassidy.

For the last production of *Blood Brothers* that I did, I moved to Toronto and came home to Connecticut on the weekends. This was in 1996 and I'd done 800 or so performances by this time. I never once walked through it. I never once disrespected the responsibility of playing that role. That opportunity that Bill Kenwright gave me changed my life forever. He gave me the platform and I sold the tickets and we did great business. Words can't describe the profound impact that role had on my life. I think of it often. I wish I could go back and do it just once more. Shaun, Petula and I. Ah, well.

During the last month in Toronto, in August 1996, I began receiving phone calls from my attorney, John Frankenheimer at Loeb & Loeb in Los Angeles, who said the MGM Grand in Las Vegas was interested in me taking over the lead in *EFX*, a $60-million production that was failing miserably. Michael Crawford had injured himself and had had to pull out. I told him I would consider it, however I would need to make some creative changes to the show.

We were in negotiations for about a month. Richard Sturm, the head of entertainment for the MGM Grand, and Alex Yemenidijian, the chief operating officer, flew the corporate jet to Toronto to see my final performance in *Blood Brothers*. They took me out to dinner afterwards and said, 'We want to do this deal with you. We'd like you to move to Las Vegas with your family.'

I said, 'OK, when?'

'Tomorrow.'

'Tomorrow?!' I started laughing, it was so crazy. 'I'm on *Live with Regis and Kathie Lee* tomorrow.'

'OK, we'll keep the jet here an extra day. We'll come pick you up the day after tomorrow. Bring everything you've got.'

One day. Pack your bags, move to Vegas. What a concept.

Sue, Beau and I arrived in Vegas and it was a 100 degrees at six in the evening. This was in early September. My wife looked at me and said, 'Are you sure about this?'

And I answered, 'Yeah, I think I can make this work.'

We flew there with the chief executive officer, Terry Lanni, a very bright, fantastic guy. He was in the thoroughbred business as well. We had a long talk about living in Las Vegas, working in Las Vegas and the changes that I wanted to make to create a show that would work with me as the star. He seemed very supportive. He was straightforward, sincere, extremely well-polished, arguably one of the best minds in the gaming and hotel business. He proved his value in the ensuing decade.

I will never forget the opportunity that Terry Lanni, Alex Yemenidijian and Richard Strum gave me to perform, create and execute the transformation of *EFX* – in three and a half weeks! I called Shaun and Don Reo, my good friend who is an Emmy Award-winning television writer and producer, and we put together a creative team and worked around the clock.

The rehearsal process was a nightmare because of the number of individuals who had to be there while we were still making changes. There were at least 75 people backstage because of all of the special effects. All of the music or any other creative aspect of the show had to be entered into computers that ran the special effects, so it was a complicated and time-consuming process.

We created a whole new story and it was an overnight sensation. *EFX* became the most successful show in Las Vegas for the 27 months I was there. Within six months, the show went from one to two performances a night, and they were selling out.

It was a dangerous show to perform. Once I fell through one of the trapdoors in the floor, which had not been secured, and nearly plummeted five stories down. Fortunately, someone was there to pull me off one of the traps. I was injured a few times.

After two years of starring in the show, ten shows a week, 50 weeks a year, I began having foot problems. The stage was made of steel in order to support sets weighing nine tons. That caused nerve damage in my left foot. Towards the end of the run, after about 1,500 performances, I injured my foot so badly that the doctor began giving me cortisone shots between my toes, which was excruciating. And I was told that I needed surgery to remove the nerves in my foot. As time went on, I was getting more and more shots.

When I recorded my album *Old Trick, New Dog* I was working ten shows a week. We recorded a lot of it, and then started overlaying. I was also starting a record company, Slamajama Records, and creating and producing a television series for Fox, *Ask Harriet*. I'd actually written and originally copyrighted the show for myself. Had I played the role, like I wanted to and should have, I think it would've been a successful series. It's a tough thing to pull off, having people believe you're both a woman and a cigar-smoking, Scotch-drinking sports writer, but I think I could have done it because of my physical appearance.

I was 48 and working seven days a week. And there's a big difference between what you can do when you're 21 and what you can do when you're 48. I was close to a nervous breakdown and my wife and I were as close to splitting up as we have ever been.

The photographs on the cover and inner sleeve of *Old Trick, New Dog* were taken by Henry Diltz, with Gary Burton as art director, the same team who had done many of my earlier album covers. I can't remember the last time I cried before that day, but I was weeping intensely for an hour prior to taking the cover photograph. We went out into a canyon outside of Vegas and I stopped by the side of the road and Henry took that shot. The photo is completely untouched. I wanted it to be like that.

I think *Old Trick, New Dog* is a good record. This album is not overproduced like the previous album. When your life is in chaos, you try to find a way to simplify.

No Bridge You Didn't Cross is a really good song. That song came through my friend, publisher Linda Blum-Huntington. She put me together with a couple of different writers. I was trying to get away from writing almost exclusively with Sue, which is what I did for the previous two albums.

Tony Romeo sent me a demo of *You Are the One*. He passed away prior to making this album, had a heart attack and died instantly. I took the song and reworked it, added a bridge and made a completely different record out of it. His heir discovered that I had taken the song and worked on it and said, 'I can't allow you to use this song.'

And I said, 'Well, then you're going to have to sue me because Tony was my friend for many years. And it was the only song that he and I ever collaborated on together. I know if Tony were alive this conversation would never take place.' And nothing more was ever said.

I went back and looked at some of the songs that had been very influential in my career. I redid a few Partridge Family songs, *I Can Feel Your Heartbeat* – I love that song – *I Woke Up in Love This Morning,* and *I Think I Love You*. Old trick, new dog. I also re-recorded *Ricky's Tune*, taking a different approach to the tune.

Whatever Happened to Peace, Love and Happiness is a track that really reflected where I came from. I'm proud to wear it like a badge of my political and social attitudes.

During this period, I was totally overwhelmed. My personal life and my relationship with my wife were also suffering. I worked all day. I worked all night. For two and a half years, I didn't get home until one or two in the morning. Sue had to get up with Beau and take him to school. Neither Sue nor Beau enjoyed Las Vegas at all. In fact, they often complained to me about how much they disliked it. This was, of course, very difficult for me because I was making a fortune and I was in what was arguably the most fertile, creative time of my life.

I went to see a shrink and lost it in his office. He sent me to a doctor who gave me a prescription for an anti-depressant, anti-stress pill. Within a matter of two weeks, it was like a different world for me. I was able to get a grip on all of it and put things into perspective.

I had a conversation with the MGM about leaving the show to have the operation on my foot and try to heal. I would need to be out for at least three months. They didn't want to put an understudy in for that long, so I completed the term of my contract. By the last week of performances, however, I couldn't walk. I was on crutches. My brother Patrick was kind enough to perform in my place.

The day after my contract at the MGM ended, I went in for foot surgery. While in my hospital bed, I called my friend Don Reo once again and said, 'I've got this great idea. I want to do a show about the old Vegas, about what made Las Vegas, Las Vegas.' The first time I went to Las Vegas was with my dad and Shirley in 1961. They took me to see Frank and it was pretty fantastic. I loved it.

Don and I began discussing and brainstorming and started writing *The Rat Pack Is Back!* Don Reo and I co-created, co-wrote, co-produced and I directed the original production. The play takes place on 12 December 1961, Frank Sinatra's birthday, and Frank is performing in Vegas, with Joey Bishop opening for him. Don came up with the idea of using that date so there would be a reason for Dean and Sammy Davis, Jr to come to see Frank. As a device it works, but in reality they never performed as The Rat Pack.

I took the idea to the people at the Desert Inn, who didn't have a show, despite the fact that it was one of the original places where Frank Sinatra, Sammy Davis, Jr and Dean Martin had performed. It was a beautiful property and had the perfect intimate room for the show.

Sure enough, after about four or five days, we made a deal. We opened not long after, and within two weeks it was selling out. I own the U.S. trademark for *The Rat Pack Is Back!*, which has become a business all over the world.

I gave myself a little cameo role as Bobby Darin and I got to sing while I was recovering from my foot surgery over the next months. I still make guest appearances as Bobby at different venues when I'm available. The only artist my father and I could agree on was Bobby Darin. I thought Bobby Darin was the most talented of all those guys. I thought he was a really good actor, a very good songwriter and singer, an incredible entertainer and a great producer.

The show played at the Desert Inn for a year, and then for two years at the Sahara. I still produce it all over the U.S.. The music is second to none. I called Quincy Jones and asked him for the original music chart for *Seven O'Clock Jump*, which we used. It's as authentic as you can get. He came and saw the show and loved it.

About this time, my wife got very involved with children's and humanitarian causes around the world. First, we used our song *Message to the World* to attract attention to the situation in Bosnia and then she formed an online charity called KidsCharities.org, which helped kids all over the world.

Using my 'celebrity', our music and connections to help others was nothing new to us.

David Bridger: While he was touring the U.K. in the early 70s, David got very involved in the Keep Britain Tidy campaign, which was based on the Keep America Beautiful campaign. Nobody in the rock and roll business had done anything that really leaned towards helping other people, except George Harrison who did the Concert for Bangladesh a few years prior. This is something that was so environmentally important to England. There were great big double billboards all over Great Britain with an enormous photo of David and the slogan, 'David Cassidy says you must Keep Britain Tidy.'

It was a time when it wasn't fashionable in the rock and roll world to lend your name to anything that was establishment. David was the first person who made a commitment and said, 'I'd like for everybody to please make sure when you leave the concert not to throw your trash down.' This was one of many charitable commitments David made. Eunice Shriver asked David to be the first Junior Chairman of Special Olympics that she founded in America. I don't know how he found the time for everything.

In 1992, Sue and I organised an all-star recording of a song we wrote, *Stand and Be Proud*, immediately following the Los Angeles riots. The number of stars who came out was amazing, and people told us that the song helped to rebuild people's strength and unity.

Sue Shifrin Cassidy: *Message to the World* was a song we wrote to help to make people aware of the horrors of the war in Kosovo. The lyric is about a person who is in a war, in a place where they were being forgotten. 'Send a message to the world, everybody say yes, send an SOS.' We donated the song to War Child USA to sell online to raise money to help kids who were victims of the heinous treatment of the civilians of Kosovo.

The John Lennon Educational Tour Bus, a mobile recording studio, was coming to Las Vegas so I called and asked, 'On your way out from New York to Las Vegas, if I get you a track of a song, can you stop at gas stations and record voices for the record?' 'Yeah, we can do that.' And they did.

David went up to the studio of Narada Michael Walden (who produced Whitney Houston and a lot of other big stars), who agreed to produce the track. David recorded a 'guide' vocal, in other words, the lead vocal that would guide the other thousands of voices of celebrities and ordinary Americans across the country that we wanted on the record. The bus made its way all around the United States.

At the Woodstock revival festival, we had almost 100,000 people singing on this song. It's one of the first songs to be made available for download on the internet, for charity. We raised a lot of money and I'm really proud of that.

While I was producing, directing, and performing every night as Bobby Darin in *The Rat Pack Is Back!* the president of the Rio contacted me about putting a show on at that hotel. We signed a two-year contract for a production that I would star in eight shows a week. Don Reo and I partnered again as producers and writers. I created the story for *At the Copa*, which took my character from his 20s to his 80s, singing music from each era. It gave me a chance to perform some of my favourite songs.

I realised I needed a female who could carry some of the weight for me while I wasn't on the stage. I went to the hotel folks and said, 'How do you feel about Sheena Easton?' And they raised a couple of eyebrows and said, 'Well, if you think she's what you need, OK.'

Originally, I had gone to Paula Abdul. I flew to Los Angeles and had lunch with her, but in the end she didn't want to move to Vegas. So I went to Sheena. She wasn't working, so she agreed to come and do the show with me.

When we opened, the show was panned. I had to replace my director. So I rewrote the show while we were performing it. After about four or five months, it was completely different and by that time it was really great.

I had 77 employees for *At the Copa*. I was basically producing it from my office at home. I was working seven days a week, seven nights a week and I began to feel like a workaholic. I had been performing non-stop every night for nine straight years.

My schedule and the stress I was under put insurmountable pressure on my marriage and, for about six months, Sue and I were separated. This was extraordinarily painful for her. For both of us. It was virtually impossible for me to work. I had to find the balance, which was lacking in my life. I think I was going through an enormous change. Let's call it your standard, good old-fashioned mid-40s, mid-madness, mid-life crisis. Thank God for Paxil, that's all I can say. I knew I had to find another way to live or I would lose my family.

When I realised that my family was more important to me than the fame, the work, the attention, the money, I made what I consider to be the best decision I have ever made – move back home, create an exit strategy and do it with dignity.

I sat down with the Chief Financial Officer of Harrah's, which owned the Rio, and the president of the Rio. I told them that I wanted to end my contact with them a year early. My suggestion was that I go out and do concerts at various properties they had all over North America. And they agreed. We came to a beautiful settlement that worked for them and worked for me.

I had an offer from Universal Music while I was doing *At the*

Copa. They wanted me to re-record my hits and some of the songs I was performing at the time. It seemed like a great idea. I recorded some of the songs I loved that I'd never recorded before. It became a platinum album.

30 So . . . You *Can* Go Home Again

NBC wanted to do the David Cassidy story and I made a deal with them. Knowing network television as well as I do, I wanted to have a little bit of creative control. I was able to have some influence in the casting. I asked Malcolm McDowell if he would consider playing my father. The network loved the idea, as did Malcolm and he agreed to do it. I think he was brilliant. He completely captured my father, the madness as well as the humour. My father was up there, I'm sure, smiling.

When you're seeing other actors recreate your life, it's very odd and it's hard to be objective. I tried as much as possible. Because I was in Las Vegas during the week, I was only on the Los Angeles set four or five times. All I did was observe and try to give Malcolm a little bit of insight into my father. I tried to stay away completely from the actor playing me. Andrew Kavovit did a very fine job.

The network asked me if I would be willing to go back and

re-record some of my old hits for the film and I told them I would. I strongly suggested that if they wanted the original feel of those Partridge Family songs, we should record in the original studio, with as many of the original musicians as we could find. Mike Melvoin and I got hold of all of the original players and they did a fantastic job. It was amazing that I got to work with those people again, that I got to celebrate, for lack of a better word, the emotional experience again.

Mike Melvoin: Working with David was like resuming an old friendship. We started up where we'd left off – two really good friends working together. The people who owned The Partridge Family recordings wanted a prohibitive amount of money for them to be used in David's TV movie. So we said, 'Let's reproduce the records. Let's do it again – live.'

What a wonderful stroke of luck when the bad news turned out to be good news. We had the opportunity to call the original band and work in the original studio, Western Two at Capitol Records. From the very first tune, it was apparent that we had hit a home run. We went into the control booth to hear the music and it was instantly a party. David was thrilled. It couldn't have been better. Everybody was playing great. It was like everybody put themselves back in time and relived that moment. Those songs sounded so good that they were included on David's *Then & Now* album.

John Bahler: I had one of the vocal charts open and I was standing there in the booth and David walked up to me and said, 'What would you give to know where the original charts are?'

I said, 'This *is* the original.'

And he said, 'Get out of here!'

I said, 'My wife found them in the garage in a box.' So I have all the original vocal arrangement parts for The Partridge Family records.

Entertainment Tonight showed up at Capitol Studios. They wanted to know what it was like being back there together. Hal Blaine had a great line. He said, 'Oh, it's just like it used to be except we have to nap a lot now.'

The lyrics had more weight for me now that I was much older. I sing them from a different perspective now because I'm a different guy. It was really thrilling to know that there were certain aspects of my voice and personality that I couldn't recreate because I wasn't 20 years old any more. In certain aspects, I had so much more to offer because I had lived so much and had worked so much and experienced so much since the original recordings. Emotionally, I was singing from a different place. Just for that experience alone it was worth doing. Trust me. You *can* go home again. It's just that you ache a little more 25 years later.

When the film was edited, it was difficult for me to watch some of it. But it's a biopic. You can't cover somebody's whole life in a biopic; you can only depict the highlights, or lowlights, and that's what we accomplished.

In 1993, Nick at Nite asked me to help them promote *The Partridge Family*, which they were planning to air on their network in the summer. I told them I wanted very much to help them because I had come full circle with it. It's no longer an obstacle for me. It's an asset. It is a classic sitcom and for me it now represents all the good times, not the artistic frustrations. I finally got over the hump. I wanted people to hear me and see that I was OK with it. That I, too, loved it for what it was. I do. I've embraced it now.

Devoting as much time as I had over the previous ten years or more to work had made me a wealthy man again, but I had cheated myself and my family; my personal relationships had suffered. The people I loved and cared about – my brothers, my few friends, my wife and my son and my estranged daughter –

had suffered. So, I stood at the crossroads again in 2000. The exit strategy that I created for myself was a fairly complex one. I needed to find a place where I felt Beau, Sue and I could flourish, but where I could also feed my hunger to create as a writer, a songwriter, an actor, a director, a producer and a performer.

I met with Mike Pick, who owns the booking agency MPI. He told me he felt there was a lot of work out there for me and he wanted to represent me. He began booking concerts for me. I told him that I wanted to work part-time, on weekends. I was no longer willing to devote seven days a week to my profession. I told him I was leaving Las Vegas. Leaving Las Vegas. It sounds like a great title for a film, doesn't it?

Sue and Beau and I began seeking refuge. We decided on a quiet little waterway, just off the Atlantic Ocean in south Florida, called Fort Lauderdale. We built a home. We packed our bags and left Las Vegas. Ah, sweet Jesus. What a refuge. Arguably, the most beautiful, peaceful, tranquil and lush little spot we have ever lived in.

Although I was living in Florida, I recorded the *Touch of Blue* album in Hollywood. It is one of my two or three favourite recordings of mine because it was recorded live and in the studio at Capitol. It was as organic as I could possibly make it – live vocals and singing with a live band and different rhythm sections put together for different tracks. I wanted to record the way Sinatra did and at the same studio where all those fabulous Big Band recordings were done for so many years. Nat King Cole. Sinatra. Bobby Darin. Sammy Davis, Jr.

I hadn't toured for well over ten years. Since 2000 it has been the most satisfying and enjoyable experience for me. I got to go back to Australia, where I hadn't been for 25 years. I got to go back to the U.K. and I have performed throughout the United States and Canada. I put together a great band and we used the musical arrangements for all those great songs that I hadn't looked at in well over a decade. Instead of doing eight to ten shows a week, I do five or six shows a month and I get to be home at least half the month. It's provided me with the balance that I've been seeking all these years.

Most of my life, I either worked all the time or I didn't work at all. And now, for the first time, my home life is actually normal, although I still travel a lot. It's so much better every time I hit the stage now. It feels fresh and new. It doesn't feel like something I've been doing for 37 years.

This has been my life for the past several years now. I'm a very fortunate man. I work when I choose, where I choose and I do exactly as I choose. I take none of this for granted. I realise that I have been dealt a great hand. I realise now that I am one of the fortunate few. Most people in their lives go to work and struggle, and don't love what they do. They never have the luxury of being able to say the things I've just said. I go to bed at night knowing that there are people out there I have touched and inspired and reached. I have been blessed with many gifts that I am eternally grateful for. Not my talent, necessarily, but the love and support of many people, some of whom have never met me, but have cared enough about me to buy my records, watch my television shows, see my performances. And to those people, I will forever be indebted.

Over the past few years, I've realised that in my 20s and 30s I missed out on so much. I was unable to connect with most people and the various cultures throughout the world. I savour every moment now, every day is a gift. I've never enjoyed playing and performing as much as I do now. I guess the old adage is true: you never appreciate things in your 20s as much as you do in your 50s. Now I am in my 50s, when I strap my guitar around my neck and go out and sing the songs I sang when I was 20, in many ways I feel younger than I did then.

I have searched for and found happiness in so many ways,

in so many people, in so many places. But, most importantly, I found it within myself. I wake up with a smile on my face every day. I'm proud of the things that I've accomplished. I don't dwell on the mistakes I've made. I invest my time in people whom I know appreciate and reciprocate. And I have been able to pursue my other passion – breeding horses.

When I was a little boy, I used to read the sports pages every day and I was fascinated with horse racing. From as far back as I can remember I had photographs of horses on my bedroom walls. Why? I have no idea. No one in my family has any connection with horses. I used to love to ride. I can remember going riding every weekend with my buddies when I was a teenager in Los Angeles.

Shaun Cassidy: His real passion is horses and horse racing. That is indicative of his gambler's spirit, which applies to everything he does. He throws the dice a lot. He's done it in his work and his personal life. His heart and his soul are in horse racing. We own miniature donkeys and we live in an equestrian community. David came out here and was talking to the donkeys like a horse whisperer. He goes into a very calm, serene place when he's around horses or the track. He needs that. That is uniquely him. I don't know where that came from him in his life. I don't think our father ever took him to the race track. It may have come from his grandfather. David's had a love for horses his whole life.

Sue Shifrin Cassidy: The only thing that brings David true joy and happiness is his horses. You never hear about this. David's life is his horse business. He spends 90 per cent of his life working on his horses. It's all he thinks about, all he talks about, all he cares about (except, maybe, major league baseball). He has control in that world. Show business is something that you have very little control over. It kind of happens to you; it chews you up and spits you out. You're the flavour of the month, then you're out. It's horrible on the ego, especially if you're a sensitive person.

The first thing David ever responded to as a baby was a horse. He had horse pictures all around his room. And he had a horse. He loved them. As a kid, he and his mother used to go riding on weekends. David went to see the legendary racehorse Secretariat when he first began running and that was when David started to fall in love with horses as a business and bought his first horse. Today he does everything. He handicaps, he breeds, he races, he buys and sells. He is one of the world's experts on pedigrees. He can tell you anything about any horse's pedigree and about what their distances are, their times. He is an aficionado on the thoroughbred industry. He's very respected. He's had a lot of success, as well as some huge disappointments. But he calls the shots. That's what he loves about it. And the people in the horse business are his true friends. Those are the people he wants to be with, the people he wants to know.

Ryan Cassidy: Horses give David a freedom; he doesn't have to feel like he has to be 'on'. Horses are these beautiful, magnificent animals that he loves and they don't judge him. They don't tell him what to do. They don't want an autograph. They can be stars themselves and not care about what people think. I think, deep down inside, he wants to escape from his profession and not always be David Cassidy. He wants to enjoy his family and his homes and his horses.

I have devoted many years to educating myself about breeding thoroughbreds. I continue to run my thoroughbred business, with the hopes of some day breeding a classic winner. I have a small business, but it is a fairly successful one. I can afford to do it on my own terms. It has to make financial sense, as any business should, but, in a sense, for me, it fulfils a dream. I love to go to the farms. I buy and sell and breed and race in my home state of New York mostly. I'm extremely concerned about the future of thoroughbred racing in North America and around the world. For the racing in New York to be considered the best in the world, it needs to change. I'm an advocate for the State of New York and its thoroughbred breeding business. It needs to be run by people who appreciate the history, its legacy and its significance in our culture.

I plan on spending a good part of the next few years investing more of my time and energy towards securing New York as a leader in the breeding of thoroughbreds. I hope some day to assist the franchise, whatever that franchise is, in becoming the finest racing circuit in the world. I have no interest in financially benefiting from it. I do, however, have an interest in preserving its legacy and, in some ways, I suppose, my own.

With that thought in mind, I believe that if you dare to do something, do it well. Whatever you do. Never dream of mediocrity. Strive to be the best. I know now that I will never own the New York Yankees, which is what I used to dream about as a kid, so, by owning my own horses, I own my own sports franchise in New York. It's just not baseball. I draft my own players (the jockeys). I hire my own manager (or trainer). And we work together at being the best, in whatever capacity we are capable of, with whatever financial means we have.

I currently have a relationship with a trainer, Gary Contessa, who's become my friend. We have had quite a bit of success together. And over the past seven or eight years, we have flourished. As a breeder and owner, he has assisted me. We have bought some wonderful horses together. He has become the leading trainer in New York. I have made a small contribution to his success, and he has made a large contribution to mine. I'm eternally grateful for his friendship, his support and the dream that we have shared.

The thoroughbred business has afforded me an opportunity to meet people from so many different walks of life. It's a great melting pot, where kings and princes mix with riders, grooms, gamblers, businessmen, dreamers, schemers, winners and losers. It's a great equaliser and leveller. The little guy can still succeed, dream, even find the brass ring. I love that.

Keeping and racing my horses in New York has allowed me to meet and work with some of the finest people I've ever known. I have cultivated friendships in this business that have been very significant for me. I lost a dear friend of mine last year, Robert Scanlon. He lived in Florida with his family. I knew him for many years. We went to Ireland together; he took me to the Irish Derby. He became a kind of godfather to my son. I wept like a baby at his funeral. I gave the eulogy, then fell apart. I admired his courage, his instincts, his humour, his work ethic. His wife, Connie, and his son, David, are still dear friends of mine.

My friends Jerry and Darlene Bilinski and their daughter, Annie, have become very close with my family. We are partners in a few horses. I board my horses at their farm. We share the same dreams and passions, and much of the same philosophies. Jerry is a man of great integrity who appreciates his life as much as I appreciate mine.

Jerry Bilinski: David's got a love for horses and feels a deep connection with them. When he comes out and sees his horses on the farm, he's in a different world. I'm amazed at how much he knows about pedigrees, bloodlines and the race history of famous horses. We work well together because we both know the ups and downs of the horse business.

David has what he calls 'the golden chair'. When my horses do well he'll say, 'You're in the golden chair.' When his horses do well I'll jokingly say, 'We've got room on the golden chair for you.' We joke about that all the time.

David has a horse called Mayan King that was in a stakes race in Kentucky. Late in the afternoon on the day of one of David's shows at a casino in Connecticut, I watched the race and the horse didn't do well. A couple of hours later, David performed. Knowing how discouraging it is when your horse doesn't run well, I was impressed by how he was able to perform. I could feel his pain but he went up on that stage with a big smile and sang his heart out. I wouldn't have been able to do that.

I'm an equine veterinarian and I sent David a picture of me doing a rectal exam on a mare with a note saying, 'I've looked everywhere for the right Christmas gift and I think I may have found it.' He called me a month later and said, 'Whenever I get depressed over work, I look at your picture and say to myself, "I could be doing *that*."'

Besides his family, I think David's passion for horses is the most important thing in his life.

31 It's a Family Affair

Regrets, I have a few, but then again, a few I need to mention.

Recently there's been a lot written about my daughter, Katherine – or Katie, more accurately. In the past year or two, Katie and I have formed a deep, caring, loving, supportive relationship. She now lives on her own. She's doing what she loves to do, which is acting. She's realising her dream. She is working hard at developing her craft. She realises that doing what you love to do and being good at it and working at it is far more important than having a bit of fame. I have preached that to her for a number of years. She does not pursue the fame or the money as much as she pursues the love of the work. Now, as a young, self-supporting adult, she understands that. I'm very proud of her.

I have always been someone who has cared deeply about being a role model, about doing the right things in life, about understanding what is really important and that fame for the sake of fame is emptiness. It's just window dressing. It's just fluff.

I hope that Katie is able to enjoy some of the rewards that I have been able to reap. But the important things are to be able to wake up in the morning and feel good about yourself, feel good about your work, try every day to be better at what you do and be a better person. All we have is what we create. The love you make is the love you take. It took me a while to figure that out.

I hope that I have been able to inspire Katie, and Beau, who seems to be on the same path and also has an enormous amount of potential. My wish is that they find happiness in their lives, not just fame or money. That is what I pursue. That is what I believe in. I'm very proud of my son and daughter. I think they're both going to be very successful. I'll help them if I can, if I believe it's the right thing for them. Katie now understands, at the age of 19, that I couldn't support her wanting to become the next Britney Spears when she was 15. She's glad it didn't really happen for her then. She's discovered that she is a very good actress and is working every day to become better at her craft. She doesn't want to be famous because of me – she was driven towards that by another influence in her life – and now understands why I couldn't support her becoming a pop diva. I would not support that for any young person, let alone my own child. I wouldn't advise any parent to put their child in a situation where they're going to lose their teenage years. It's an unhealthy environment to be in.

Once that brief fame is over and you're only 17 or 18, what do you do with the rest of your life? My advice was falling on deaf ears for a while, but fortunately Katie's grown up and matured and she gets it now. Beau knows it too. He's going to college. He says, 'I'm going to school. I want to get as good as I can get before the world sees me, because you only have one chance.'

And that's what Katie's doing, and I'm very proud of her. She's really doing it by herself. I supported her financially until she was 19 and now she wants to be self-sufficient. She doesn't want Daddy to take care of her. She wants to make it her own way and that shows character.

I've tried to demystify David Cassidy, and to reach out and let people inside. I want to give people a real insight into the experience of being phenomenally famous and rich, and having all of the things many people dream about, now more than ever because of the whole *American Idol* phenomenon. Many people have said to me, 'You're the only living original American Idol now that Elvis and Ricky Nelson are dead.' But the odd thing is I never wanted it. Isn't that funny? I mean, millions of people all over the world are now trying to be an idol and I never wanted it. I wanted to be an actor and would never have pursued a career as a musician and singer. I just happened to be cast in the most unique role in television in *The Partridge Family.*

The things that I find so important in my life are the people who surround me and the experiences that we have shared together. My brothers and I love, assist and care for one another. That's not to say that we don't have issues with each other. I probably have the least because I didn't grow up in the same house. We're all committed to our families and to our loving relationships with our children and our wives and our partners in our life. My brother Patrick and his wife Melissa are fantastic friends to each other and to us. My brother Shaun and his wife and young son recently came to visit and spent a couple of wonderful days with us. Shaun was so giving to my son, realising how unique he is and knowing how important it is to be there for one another. Ryan and I are closer now than we've ever been. He comes down and spends time with us. I get on with him. We have a strong bond. I think he's one of the kindest, nicest, most genuinely caring human beings I've ever met.

Ryan Cassidy: There's a 17-year age difference between David and me. I didn't have much in common with him when I was a kid except that we had the same dad. But in the last few years I found that we both love houses and antique cars. We really connect and understand each other on a personal level. I can call David and talk to him about anything now. I don't look at him as just my half-brother; he's my good friend and someone I can rely on.

The people that David feels he's most comfortable with and trusts the most are Shaun, Patrick and myself. Because he's effectively an only child, he doesn't consider us to be half-brothers, he considers us to be full brothers. And when I hang out with him I forget that he has a different mother. My mom had a lot to do with his life too and I think he sort of looks at my mother as a mother, too, not just a stepmother. There have been times when Shaun, Patrick, David and I had issues that could have torn us apart as brothers. We're very alike, but very different too. I think the glue that kept us together was the fact that, without having our father around, we had to take care of each other. Our deep bond comes out of that.

2005 was a time in my life and Shaun's when we were both having some relationship problems. Shaun was in the middle of a separation from his second wife. He said, 'We need to go on a trip, just the four of us.' He planned it and got David involved. So all the brothers flew to Atlanta, Georgia, for our cousin Charlie Douglas's wedding. We rented a van and drove to Savannah and spent two nights there. Then we drove all over Florida – Miami, Orlando, Jacksonville, Key West. It was a week when we shared time and hung out together, just the four of us. We went swimming with dolphins together. We went to this tiny little island at the end of Key West. Shaun jokingly called it 'The Brotherly Love Tour'. We even had T-shirts made.

Shaun Cassidy: That trip brought us closer together, but it was a rollercoaster. I thought it would be fun to get in the car with my three brothers and drive some place. I didn't think it was so novel at the time, but I've subsequently heard so many people say that a lot of 45-year-old guys don't do things like that! After much haranguing – David didn't like the idea of being in a car for ten days – we finally all agreed to do it. You get four siblings in a car and you're alternating driving. Whoever was behind the wheel was basically at the end of a cattle prod. You were tortured beyond belief by the other three. You had three backseat drivers whenever you were driving. We alternated sharing rooms with each other and we had the most amazing time. But you definitely revert to when you were kids in the back of a station wagon. All the role-playing that exists in families comes out. We had some really good breakthroughs. We were all going through some transitional periods in our lives. We kind of counselled each other and stuff came out about all of us that I didn't know. That was great. It was very bonding.

Halfway through the trip, at Disney World, Patrick hit me. The happiest place on earth and he punched me out. But we recovered from that. We ended up in Miami Beach at the Delano Hotel, which was like walking into Studio 54 at one in the morning in the 70s. We swam with dolphins there. That trip was the most beautiful, healing experience. It sounds weird and Hunter Thompson-like, and maybe that's what it was. It was just great.

Patrick Cassidy: That was an amazing experience in so many ways. So much so that we're planning to do it again. We had such a fantastic time. It was cathartic. It was so insightful. The amazing thing from my perspective was how four people that share the same genetic makeup and life experiences can have such different opinions about what happened. I was so amazed at Shaun's viewpoint about my mother and David's viewpoint about our father versus mine and Ryan's. The first couple of days of the trek we laughed hysterically all the time. Then, by the third day, the little nuances in each of our personalities started to get the better of us, specifically between

Shaun and me, because we're the closest in age. The repartee between us can be very volatile at times. David's always been the sensible one, the peacemaker.

It all culminated on the fourth day, at Disney World. Shaun said something to me that really bothered me and I ended up slugging him. Ryan and I stayed at Disney World and Shaun and David went back to the hotel. David discussed the relationship between Shaun and me and how it needed to change. It was very therapeutic. By the end, when we got to Key West, which was such a beautiful place to end our time together, we'd all moved forwards. We understood things about each other that we hadn't before.

I find that David's own neuroses about life and about himself is what makes him so funny. When I'm with him, I laugh to the point where my ribs are hurting. He's also incredibly generous. He's been incredibly helpful and supportive in terms of advice.

All of our families have a commitment now to one another that we've never had before and I attribute some of that to the choices that we've made in our partners and our own personal evolution as people.

Later in her life, my mother married Al Williams, a distant cousin of hers. He was her companion for 30 years until he sadly passed away in 2005. I had encouraged them to get married. They had a great relationship; they really took care of one another, and it was a blessing for me. Finally my mother had a relationship that really worked and was the most fulfilling and successful one, although it was not a romantic relationship. But the right reason to get married is to find someone who loves you and cares for you and someone you feel the same way about and are willing to commit to, a great friend. That's far more important at the end of the day than looking at somebody across a room and getting hot.

*

There's a lot that's positive about fame. The money brought unique rewards. I was able to buy my mother a Mercedes Benz. While my dad lived with Shirley, he lived pretty high on the hog because of her fame and success. My mother, on the other hand, never had that kind of money and to be able to give things like that to her was a wonderful thing. And I feel the same way about being able to give my children great things. I show Beau my love by being tough and a disciplinarian. He knows he has to earn things he wants.

A lot of people are surprised that I am just a regular parent, like everyone else. I coached Little League. I showed up at all my son's games. I go to his performances at school. He's in the All-State Choir and I saw them perform at Carnegie Hall. He is tremendously gifted. I've talked with him a lot about a career in show business, about my father's struggle, my struggle, my brothers' struggles. He understands there's a work ethic involved and he knows what it takes.

So where am I today? I'm a wealthy man in many ways. I'm probably happier now than I've ever been before in my life. I've learned a lot about life and about myself and how to distance myself from the parasites of this world. I'm not unscathed. I have been hurt, I have been disappointed. I realised that I just had to let all that go. I have no fear of failure any longer.

My attitude used to be that we were all in a race and those of us who achieved the most success, the most fame, the most money, the most power were the winners. That isn't how I view life any more. That view is for fools.

There is no race. There are no trophies. The only people who really win are the people who get hugged by their loved ones every morning and can go to bed at night knowing they've done right by themselves and by the people they love. The quality of my life is great now because of the people I have cultivated relationships with and choose to spend time with.

I no longer have any time – not another minute, not another second – to waste with people who don't share that perspective and embrace it. I've had enough of twisted views of reality with my father and other bad relationships. My closest friends tend to be family. But that's OK. I spend a lot of time by myself. And that's OK, too. That time alone is precious to me.

After many long, difficult and sometimes painful years of analysis, it felt like I finally hit the home stretch. I experienced some real breakthroughs. I realised that I had to let the reins go and let my life take me down whatever path was intended. I have no great disappointments in my life any more. I'm just enjoying the ride. I simply embrace it all now.

Instead of griping and grumbling when things go wrong I tell myself, *OK, I've worked for three months on this project, put everything I could into it and it didn't happen. Well, it was not intended to happen.* There is something to be learned from the experience. Maybe it's worked out in a way that will ultimately be for my higher good.

How do I fill my time these days, when I'm not busy with work? I enjoy going to the theatre, to the movies and to sporting events. The Rangers or baseball games, preferably at Yankee Stadium, and thoroughbred racing would be my first choices. I mostly listen to old school music and some jazz. And, of course, I read everything I can find pertaining to horses.

Over ten years ago, I was asked if I'd be willing to speak to students at the high school in my old home-town, West Orange, New Jersey. Afterwards, my friend and I got in his big old Lincoln and drove around the town. Past Tony Corners, where my grandfather bought me a Slinky and a Mr Machine so many years ago. Past the homes of childhood friends. Past what used to be my school (it's now the Board of Education offices). We stopped at my old house, which hasn't changed much; there were still clothes lines round the back. I remembered those kids who'd taunted me as I played out front.

We headed back to New York, where I was then living. There are quicker ways to drive to New York from West Orange now than there were when I was a kid. But we drove there the old way. And as we drove we talked about Kevin Hunter and Ruth Aarons and the others from my past.

Then I realised where we were.

'This is Route 3, isn't it?' I asked.

My friend nodded. We were very near the spot where my father, in that shiny new Cadillac that was just *so Jack*, had casually shattered my world with the news that he and Mom were divorcing. I remembered. I remembered the exact spot.

And I realised that I'd made my peace with Jack Cassidy. I hadn't exactly forgiven him, but I'd made my peace with him. There were no ghosts I needed to do battle with here.

A car pulled up alongside ours. The driver honked and signalled for me to lower my window.

'We saw you in *Blood Brothers*,' said the guy, who looked around my age.

The woman sitting alongside him added cheerfully, 'We love your work.' And they drove off.

Afterword

For me, the important thing about this book is that people begin to understand who I really am, not just the events that took place in my life. I know who I am – I know I'm a human being who is genuinely caring about other people – and I would like people to know the real me. But I don't care what people think about me. I no longer worry about it.

I have gone through so many changes as a human being, but the one thing that's stayed with me is, I believe, my compassion; my ability to connect with others. My son has compassion. My daughter has it. My wife has it. And the people I like, the ones I'm attracted to, have it. If I have any gift, it's that I've been able to lift people up.

I am a non-violent guy. I abhor violence. I abhor people who propagate violence. And the world is filled with it. I believe part of my purpose now, especially since the traumatic wake-up call of 9/11, is to help people to celebrate life. I like to think that I am able to touch people through what I do, make them feel uplifted, even if it's just for a couple of hours when I perform.

The more I look at our society, the more I realise that most people don't make any contribution whatsoever. I applaud people who go out and do community work. Helping others is so important. It's why we're here. The more selfish we are, the more vulnerable and the weaker we are. The more we practise the things we preached in the 60s – 'Come on, people, now. Love one another' – the better off we will be. That's not just crap. We live in such a cynical world and I feel so saddened by the loss of many of the voices of my generation – the people I admired, like John Lennon. He stood by what he believed in.

My brother, Shaun, came over the other day and we played *Cream – Live at The Royal Albert Hall.* That's the only band other than The Police that I would care to go and see these days. If they ever come to any place near me, I'm going. Those three guys started 40 years ago and are still embracing their music, which is what the David Cassidy show is all about.

The Partridge Family music was great music for what it was. I love it, I embrace it, I'm not sick of it. People perceive that I hated *The Partridge Family* and the fame that went with it. I never did. I loved it. I just wanted people to see the real me. And I couldn't let them. There was no way to break through the machine that had created my persona. The little voice inside me was going, *But it's not me. It's not really me.* But the essence of me came through. I think I know that now.

What I've also learned is not to compare yourself to other people. Be the best you can be and don't try to be 19 again. Don't try to be a legend. Don't try to be James Dean or Elvis or John Lennon or Madonna, or anyone else. Be yourself. Embrace what you are. Only take baby steps, don't try to grab it all. And don't let money or fame seduce you down that road. The journey is the journey, it's not the result.

The Legacy: A Note from Beau

A friend of mine, who helped me edit this book, asked my son (without my knowledge) to write down what he would like people to know about me and this is what he said:

Beau Cassidy: Having a famous father has its ups and downs. The ups are that you get an opportunity to be around a guy who has experienced a lot of unusual things and has learned from his mistakes. The downs are that you don't get to see him enough and you are under much more of a microscope because of being the son of a famous person. But, I really don't want to talk about his fame. What I really want to do is talk about who he is as a person.

My dad is a really interesting guy. A lot of the things that have happened in his life, he tries to avoid talking about to me. He's complicated in the fact that he has such deep pain, so it's hard to get an idea of who he is. He's been so damaged by people deceiving him and his parents not being there to give him guidance when he was in need of it.

His father, being an alcoholic and an egomaniac, had a big impact on him. I know it's gotta be tough to live with that. There are a lot of things that he has never told me, and I don't think he will ever tell me.

Dad has a very sarcastic sense of humour and this has rubbed off on me because I want to connect with him. Sometimes it's funny and sometimes it's inappropriate, to say the least, but 95 per cent of the time it is all meant in good humour.

But, you know, we share a lot of things. We are both avid Yankee fans. This past July, we attended a Yankee/ Red Sox game and we sat right behind home plate. It was one of the greatest experiences of my life, partly because we were watching the greatest rivalry in sports, but mostly because I was spending it with my father, and I saw how much joy it brought to him seeing how happy I was being there with him. We also share a love for music. I remember him telling me that when he was my age he was in a band, and now I am in my own band called Cooper with my high-school friends. He loves to sing; I love to sing. He loves to act; I love to act.

Another memory that I have is getting a chance to sing with him in front of 15,000 people at Wembley Arena, where he met my Mom 30 years before. This marked the first time that I had ever sung publicly with my dad. The feeling of being in front of so many people with him and hitting that last harmonic note gave me an exhilaration that I have never felt before or since.

The second time that I sang publicly with him was this past summer when he and I got a chance to sing the *Star Spangled Banner* at Wrigley Field in Chicago at a Cubs game, this time in front of 35,000 people! To tell you the truth, all that I can really remember from that experience, because it was so amazing, was giving Dad the biggest hug I can remember giving him, at the very end. How many kids get to do what I did with my dad?

When all is said and done, he really is a wonderful father. I know without a doubt that he loves me more than anything on the planet and that he would jump into a pit of spikes for me. He wants what is best for me, but he's told me that I have to work to get it and it won't just be given to me. He wants me to earn what I get, and that's a wonderful quality.

As I get older, our relationship gets better because we are able to talk on almost the same level about things, communicate our feelings openly and share passions with one another. He pays more attention to me now than all of the other things in his life put together, and that's really hard to find in a dad.

He's my dad and I'm darn proud of it.

I was grateful for my life before I wrote this book, but how could any man be happier or prouder than I am after reading this? This is what it's all about, folks.

Index